Early praise for *Programming Clojure, Third Edition*

Programming Clojure is an inspiration of Clojure knowledge and has furthered my understanding of the nuances of Clojure. One of the new sections includes a step-by-step on building an application that made me want to drop everything and code along.

➤ **Nola Stowe**
CTO/Founder, Ruby Geek LLC

If you are interested in learning the ins and outs of the Clojure language, *Programming Clojure* will provide you with a valuable resource. The book not only covers the basics of the language, but also builds on the basics to allow readers to understand and apply more advanced concepts like spec and macros.

➤ **Joy Clark**
Consultant, innoQ Deutschland GmbH

This book is very effective at teaching Clojure's unique take on functional programming and data manipulation. It explains concepts clearly and covers the mechanics of nearly every part of the language, with helpful commentary that goes beyond the code.

➤ **Ghadi Shayban**
Engineer, healthfinch

The third edition of *Programming Clojure* is an excellent resource for new and old Clojure programmers. It provides a thorough account of the language's rationale and features, including approachable explanations of more recent features like transducers and spec.

➤ **Michael Fogleman**
Developer

T0256857

Programming Clojure, Third Edition

Alex Miller
with Stuart Halloway
and Aaron Bedra

The Pragmatic Bookshelf

Raleigh, North Carolina

Many of the designations used by manufacturers and sellers to distinguish their products are claimed as trademarks. Where those designations appear in this book, and The Pragmatic Programmers, LLC was aware of a trademark claim, the designations have been printed in initial capital letters or in all capitals. The Pragmatic Starter Kit, The Pragmatic Programmer, Pragmatic Programming, Pragmatic Bookshelf, PragProg and the linking *g* device are trademarks of The Pragmatic Programmers, LLC.

Every precaution was taken in the preparation of this book. However, the publisher assumes no responsibility for errors or omissions, or for damages that may result from the use of information (including program listings) contained herein.

Our Pragmatic books, screencasts, and audio books can help you and your team create better software and have more fun. Visit us at *https://pragprog.com*.

The team that produced this book includes:

Publisher: Andy Hunt
VP of Operations: Janet Furlow
Managing Editor: Brian MacDonald
Supervising Editor: Jacquelyn Carter
Copy Editor: Paula Robertson
Indexing: Potomac Indexing, LLC
Layout: Gilson Graphics

For sales, volume licensing, and support, please contact *support@pragprog.com*.

For international rights, please contact *rights@pragprog.com*.

Copyright © 2018 The Pragmatic Programmers, LLC.
All rights reserved.

No part of this publication may be reproduced, stored in a retrieval system, or transmitted, in any form, or by any means, electronic, mechanical, photocopying, recording, or otherwise, without the prior consent of the publisher.

ISBN-13: 978-1-68050-246-6

Book version: P1.0—February 2018

Contents

Acknowledgments

Many people have contributed to what is good in this book. The problems and errors that remain are ours alone.

Thanks to Rich Hickey for creating the excellent Clojure language and fostering a community around it. Thanks to the awesome team at Cognitect (formerly Relevance) for creating an atmosphere in which good ideas can grow and thrive. Thanks to the Clojure community for using Clojure and turning an idea into a working ecosystem.

Thanks to all the readers and technical reviewers who have suggested improvements across all three editions of the book. Jeff Brown suggested the coin toss problem in *Lazier Than Lazy*, on page 93. David Liebke wrote the original content for Chapter 7, *Protocols and Datatypes*, on page 167.

Thanks to everyone at Pragmatic Bookshelf. Thanks especially to our editor, Jacquelyn Carter, and former editors Michael Swaine and Susannah Pfalzer for focus and advice. Thanks also to Dave Thomas and Andy Hunt.

Thanks to my wife and family for their love, support, and the precious gift of time to create.—*Alex*

Thanks to my wife, Joey, and to my children, Hattie, Harper, Mabel Faire, and Truman. You all make the sun rise.—*Stuart*

Thanks to my wife, Erin, for endless love and encouragement.—*Aaron*

Introduction

Clojure is a dynamic programming language for the Java Virtual Machine (JVM) with a compelling combination of features:

- *Clojure is elegant.* Clojure's clean, careful design lets you write programs that get right to the essence of a problem, without a lot of clutter and ceremony.

- *Clojure is Lisp reloaded.* Clojure has the power inherent in Lisp but is not constrained by the history of Lisp.

- *Clojure is a functional language.* Data structures are immutable, and most functions are free from side effects. This makes it easier to write correct programs and to compose large programs from smaller ones.

- *Clojure simplifies concurrent programming.* Many languages build a concurrency model around locking, which is difficult to use correctly. Clojure provides several alternatives to locking: software transactional memory, agents, atoms, and dynamic variables.

- *Clojure embraces Java.* Calling from Clojure to Java is direct and fast, with no translation layer.

- *Unlike many popular dynamic languages, Clojure is fast.* Clojure is written to take advantage of the optimizations possible on modern JVMs.

Many other languages cover *some* of the features described in the previous list. Of all these languages, Clojure stands out. The individual features listed earlier are powerful and interesting. Their clean synergy in Clojure is compelling. We will cover all these features and more in Chapter 1, *Getting Started*, on page 1.

Who This Book Is For

Clojure is a powerful, general-purpose programming language. As such, this book is for programmers with experience in a programming language like

Java, C#, Python, or Ruby, but new to Clojure and looking for a powerful, elegant language.

Clojure is built on top of the Java Virtual Machine, and it is *fast*. This book will be of particular interest to Java programmers who want the expressiveness of a dynamic language without compromising on performance.

Clojure is helping to redefine what features belong in a general-purpose language. If you program in Lisp, use a functional language such as Haskell, or write explicitly concurrent programs, you'll enjoy Clojure. Clojure combines ideas from Lisp, functional programming, and concurrent programming and makes them more approachable to programmers seeing these ideas for the first time.

Clojure is part of a larger phenomenon. Languages such as Erlang, F#, Haskell, and Scala have garnered attention recently for their support of functional programming or their concurrency model. Enthusiasts of these languages will find much common ground with Clojure.

What's in This Book

Chapter 1, *Getting Started*, on page 1 demonstrates Clojure's elegance as a general-purpose language, plus the functional style and concurrency model that make Clojure unique. It also walks you through installing Clojure and developing code interactively at the REPL.

Chapter 2, *Exploring Clojure*, on page 19 is a breadth-first overview of all of Clojure's core constructs. After this chapter, you'll be able to read most day-to-day Clojure code.

The next two chapters cover functional programming. Chapter 3, *Unifying Data with Sequences*, on page 51 shows how all data can be unified under the powerful *sequence* metaphor.

Chapter 4, *Functional Programming*, on page 81 shows you how to write functional code in the same style used by the sequence library.

Chapter 5, *Specifications*, on page 113 demonstrates how to write specifications for your data structures and functions and use them to aid in development and testing.

Chapter 6, *State and Concurrency*, on page 137 delves into Clojure's concurrency model. Clojure provides four powerful models for dealing with concurrency, plus all of the goodness of Java's concurrency libraries.

Chapter 7, *Protocols and Datatypes*, on page 167 walks through records, types, and protocols in Clojure. These concepts were introduced in Clojure 1.2.0 and enhanced in 1.3.0.

Chapter 8, *Macros*, on page 187 shows off Lisp's signature feature. Macros take advantage of the fact that Clojure code is data to provide metaprogramming abilities that are difficult or impossible in anything but a Lisp.

Chapter 9, *Multimethods*, on page 209 covers one of Clojure's answers to polymorphism. Polymorphism usually means "take the *class* of the *first* argument and dispatch a method based on that." Clojure's multimethods let you choose *any function* of *all* the arguments and dispatch based on that.

Chapter 10, *Java Interop*, on page 225 shows you how to call Java from Clojure and call Clojure from Java. You'll see how to take Clojure straight to the metal and get Java-level performance.

Finally, Chapter 11, *Building an Application*, on page 249 provides a view into a complete Clojure workflow. You will build an application from scratch, working through solving the various parts to a problem and thinking about simplicity and quality.

How to Read This Book

All readers should begin by reading the first two chapters in order. Pay particular attention to *Simplicity and Power in Action*, on page 1, which provides an overview of Clojure's advantages.

Experiment continuously. Clojure provides an interactive environment where you can get immediate feedback; see *Using the REPL*, on page 10 for more information.

After you read the first two chapters, skip around as you like. But read Chapter 3, *Unifying Data with Sequences*, on page 51 before you read Chapter 6, *State and Concurrency*, on page 137. These chapters lead you from Clojure's immutable data structures to a powerful model for writing correct concurrency programs.

As you make the move to longer code examples in later chapters, make sure you use an editor that provides Clojure indentation for you. If you can, try to use an editor that supports parentheses balancing, such as Emacs' paredit mode or the Cursive plugin for IntelliJ. This feature will be a huge help as you're learning to program in Clojure.

For Functional Programmers

- Clojure's approach to FP strikes a balance between academic purity and the realities of execution on the current generation of JVMs. Read Chapter 4, *Functional Programming*, on page 81 carefully to understand how Clojure idioms differ from languages such as Haskell.

- The concurrency model of Clojure (Chapter 6, *State and Concurrency*, on page 137) provides several explicit ways to deal with side effects and state and will make FP appealing to a broader audience.

For Java/C# Programmers

- Read Chapter 2, *Exploring Clojure*, on page 19 carefully. Clojure has very little syntax (compared to Java or C#), and we cover the ground rules fairly quickly.

- Pay close attention to macros in Chapter 8, *Macros*, on page 187. These are the most alien part of Clojure when viewed from a Java or C# perspective.

For Lisp Programmers

- Some of Chapter 2, *Exploring Clojure*, on page 19 will be review, but read it anyway. Clojure preserves the key features of Lisp, but it breaks with Lisp tradition in several places, and they are covered here.

- Pay close attention to the lazy sequences in Chapter 4, *Functional Programming*, on page 81.

- If you like Emacs, get a mode for Clojure that makes you happy before working through the code examples in later chapters. There are many options, but consider inf-clojure for a minimalist setup and CIDER for a full-feature environment.

For Perl/Python/Ruby Programmers

- Read Chapter 6, *State and Concurrency*, on page 137 carefully. Intraprocess concurrency is very important in Clojure.

- Embrace macros (Chapter 8, *Macros*, on page 187). But do not expect to easily translate metaprogramming idioms from your language into macros. Remember always that macros execute at read time, not runtime.

Notation Conventions

The following notation conventions are used throughout the book.

Literal code examples use the following font:

```
(+ 2 2)
```

The result of executing a code example is preceded by ->.

```
(+ 2 2)
-> 4
```

Where console output cannot easily be distinguished from code and results, it's preceded by a pipe character (|).

```
(println "hello")
| hello
-> nil
```

When introducing a Clojure form for the first time, we'll show the grammar for the form like this:

```
(example-fn required-arg)
(example-fn optional-arg?)
(example-fn zero-or-more-arg*)
(example-fn one-or-more-arg+)
(example-fn & collection-of-variable-args)
```

The grammar is informal, using ?, *, +, and & to document different argument-passing styles, as shown previously.

Clojure code is organized into *libs* (libraries). Where examples in the book depend on a library that's not part of the Clojure core, we document that dependency with a require form:

```
(require '[lib-name :refer [var-names+] :as alias])
```

The require form has several options. The :refer option can be used to make either specific vars (or all vars with :all) available in the current namespace. The :alias option can be used to create an alias for references to the library. For example, a commonly used function is file, from the clojure.java.io library:

```
(require '[clojure.java.io :as io])
(io/file "hello.txt")
-> #<File hello.txt>
```

Clojure returns nil from a successful call to require. For brevity, this is omitted from the example listings.

While reading the book, you'll enter code in an interactive environment called the REPL. The REPL prompt looks like this:

```
user=>
```

The user in the prompt indicates the namespace you're currently working in. For most of the examples, the current namespace is irrelevant. Where the namespace is irrelevant, we use the following syntax for interaction with the REPL:

```
(+ 2 2)          ; input line without namespace prompt
-> 4             ; return value
```

In those instances where the current namespace is important, we use this:

```
user=> (+ 2 2)  ; input line with namespace prompt
-> 4             ; return value
```

Web Resources and Feedback

Programming Clojure's official home on the web is the *Programming Clojure* home page[1] at the Pragmatic Bookshelf website. From there, you can order electronic or paper copies of the book and download sample code. You can also offer feedback by submitting errata entries[2] or posting in the forum.[3]

Downloading Sample Code

The sample code for the book is available from the following location:

- The *Programming Clojure* home page[4] links to the official copy of the source code and is updated to match each release of the book.

Individual examples are in the examples directory, unless otherwise noted.

Throughout the book, listings begin with their filename, set apart from the actual code by a gray background. For example, the following listing comes from src/examples/preface.clj:

src/examples/preface.clj
```
(println "hello")
```

If you're reading the book in PDF form, you can click the little gray box preceding a code listing to download that listing directly. With the sample code in hand, you are ready to get started. We'll begin by meeting the combination of features that make Clojure unique.

---

1. https://www.pragprog.com/titles/shcloj3/programming-clojure
2. https://www.pragprog.com/titles/shcloj3/errata
3. http://forums.pragprog.com/forums/439
4. http://www.pragprog.com/titles/shcloj3

CHAPTER 1

Getting Started

Clojure is a functional programming language on the JVM with great support for managing state and concurrency. Two key concepts drive everything in Clojure: simplicity and power.

Simplicity has several meanings that are relevant in software, but the definition we care about is the original one: a thing is simple if it is not compound. Simple components allow systems to do what their designers intend, without also doing other things irrelevant to the task at hand.

Power also has many meanings. The one we care about is whether the capabilities are adequate for the tasks we want to undertake. To feel powerful as a programmer, you need to build on a platform that's itself capable and widely deployed, such as the JVM. Then, your tools must give you full, unrestricted access to that power. Power is often an essential requirement for projects that must get the most out of their platform.

As programmers, we've spent years choosing between power and simplicity in our tools. Some trade-offs are fundamental, but power vs. simplicity is not one of them. Clojure shows that they can instead go hand in hand.

We're going to start by diving into some examples to see how Clojure differentiates itself from other languages. Then, one of the ways Clojure puts simple and powerful tools in your hands is by encouraging interactive development with the REPL. We'll see how to work efficiently at the REPL and also how to use the REPL to explore the environment and other libraries.

Simplicity and Power in Action

All of the distinctive features in Clojure are there to provide simplicity, power, or both. Some of these features include concise and expressive programs, the power of Lisp updated with a modern syntax, an immutable-first approach to state and concurrency, and an embrace of the JVM host and its ecosystem. Let's look at a few examples that demonstrate these high-level features.

Clojure Is Elegant

Clojure is high signal, low noise. As a result, Clojure programs are short programs. Short programs are cheaper to build, cheaper to deploy, and cheaper to maintain. This is particularly true when the programs are concise rather than merely terse. As an example, consider the following Java code, from Apache Commons:[1]

```
data/snippets/isBlank.java
public class StringUtils {
    public static boolean isBlank(final CharSequence str) {
        int strLen;
        if (str == null || (strLen = str.length()) == 0) {
            return true;
        }
        for (int i = 0; i < strLen; i++) {
            if (Character.isWhitespace(str.charAt(i)) == false) {
                return false;
            }
        }
        return true;
    }
}
```

The isBlank() method checks to see whether a string is *blank*: either empty or consisting of only whitespace. Here is a similar implementation in Clojure:

```
src/examples/introduction.clj
(defn blank? [str]
  (every? #(Character/isWhitespace %) str))
```

The Clojure version is shorter. But even more important, it's *simpler*: it has no variables, no mutable state, and no branches. This is possible thanks to *higher-order functions*. A higher-order function is a function that takes functions as arguments and/or returns functions as results. The every? function takes a function and a collection as its arguments and returns true if that function returns true for every item in the collection. Note that this definition also works correctly for special cases like null and the empty string without requiring explicit checks.

Because the Clojure version has no branches, it's easier to read and test. These benefits are magnified in larger programs. Also, while the code is concise, it's

---

1. https://github.com/apache/commons-lang/blob/master/src/main/java/org/apache/commons/lang3/StringUtils.java

still readable. In fact, the Clojure program reads like a *definition* of blank: a string is blank if every character in it is whitespace. This is much better than the Commons method, which hides the definition of blank behind the implementation detail of loops and if statements.

As another example, consider defining a trivial Person class in Java:

```
data/snippets/Person.java
public class Person {
    private String firstName;
    private String lastName;

    public Person(String firstName, String lastName) {
        this.firstName = firstName;
        this.lastName = lastName;
    }

    public String getFirstName() {
        return firstName;
    }

    public void setFirstName(String firstName) {
        this.firstName = firstName;
    }

    public String getLastName() {
        return lastName;
    }

    public void setLastName(String lastName) {
        this.lastName = lastName;
    }
}
```

In Clojure, you'd define Person with a single line:

```
(defrecord Person [first-name last-name])
```

and work with the record like so:

```
(def foo (->Person "Aaron" "Bedra"))
-> #'user/foo
(:first-name foo)
-> Aaron
```

defrecord and related functions are covered in *Protocols*, on page 171.

Other than being an order of magnitude shorter, the Clojure approach differs in that a Clojure Person is *immutable*. Immutable data structures are inherently thread safe, and update capabilities can be layered when using Clojure's references, agents, and atoms, which are covered in Chapter 6, *State and Concurrency*, on page 137. Because records are immutable, Clojure also provides correct implementations of hashCode() and equals() automatically.

Clojure has a lot of elegance baked in, but if you find something missing, you can add it yourself, thanks to the power of Lisp.

Clojure Is Lisp Reloaded

Clojure is a Lisp. Lisps have a tiny language core, almost no syntax, and a powerful macro facility. With these features, you can bend Lisp to meet your design, instead of the other way around. Clojure takes a new approach to Lisp by keeping the essential ideas while embracing a set of syntax enhancements that make Clojure friendlier to non-Lisp programmers.

Consider the following snippet of Java code:

```
public class Person {
  private String firstName;
  public String getFirstName() {
  // continues
```

In this code, getFirstName() is a method. Methods are polymorphic and give the programmer control over meaning, but the interpretation of *every other word* in the example is *fixed by the language*. Sometimes you really need to change what these words mean. So, for example, you might do the following:

- Redefine private to mean "private for production code but public for serialization and unit tests."

- Redefine class to automatically generate getters and setters for private fields, unless otherwise directed.

- Create a subclass of class that provides callback hooks for life-cycle events. For example, a life-cycle–aware class could fire an event whenever an instance of the class is created.

These kinds of needs are commonplace. In most languages, you would have to petition the language implementer to add the kinds of features mentioned here. In Clojure, you can add your own language features with *macros* (Chapter 8, *Macros*, on page 187). Clojure itself is built out of macros such as defrecord:

```
(defrecord name [arg1 arg2 arg3])
```

If you need different semantics, write your own macro. If you want a variant of records with strong typing and configurable nil-checking for all fields, you can create your own defrecord macro, to be used like this:

```
(defrecord name [Type :arg1 Type :arg2 Type :arg3]
  :allow-nils false)
```

This ability to reprogram the language from within the language is the unique advantage of Lisp. You will see facets of this idea described in various ways:

- Lisp is homoiconic.[2] That is, Lisp code is just Lisp data. This makes it easy for programs to write other programs.

- The whole language is there, all the time. Paul Graham's essay "Revenge of the Nerds"[3] explains why this is so powerful.

The downside of Lisp's simple, regular syntax, at least for beginners, is the prevalence of parentheses and lists as the core datatype. Clojure offers a combination of features that make Lisp more approachable:

- Clojure generalizes Lisp's physical list into an abstraction called a *sequence*. This preserves the power of lists, while extending that power to a variety of other data structures, including ones you make yourself.

- Clojure's reliance on the JVM provides a standard library and a deployment platform with great reach.

- Clojure's approach to symbol resolution and syntax quoting makes it easier to write many common macros.

Many Clojure programmers will be new to Lisp, and they've probably heard bad things about all those parentheses. Clojure keeps the parentheses (and the power of Lisp!) but improves on traditional Lisp syntax in several ways:

- Clojure provides a convenient literal syntax for a wide variety of data structures besides just lists: regular expressions, maps, sets, vectors, and metadata. These features make Clojure code less "listy" than most Lisps. For example, function parameters are specified in a vector [] instead of a list ().

src/examples/introduction.clj
```
(defn hello-world [username]
  (println (format "Hello, %s" username)))
```

The vector makes the argument list jump out visually and makes Clojure function definitions easy to read.

- In Clojure, unlike most Lisps, commas to separate elements are optional —this provides concise literal collections. In fact, Clojure treats commas as whitespace and ignores them completely.

---

2. http://en.wikipedia.org/wiki/Homoiconicity
3. http://www.paulgraham.com/icad.html

```
; make vectors look like arrays in other languages
[1, 2, 3, 4]
-> [1 2 3 4]
```

- Idiomatic Clojure does not nest parentheses more than necessary. Consider the cond macro, present in both Common Lisp and Clojure. cond evaluates a set of test/result pairs, returning the first result for which a test form yields true. Each test/result pair is grouped with parentheses:

```
; Common Lisp cond
(cond ((= x 10) "equal")
      ((> x 10) "more"))
```

Clojure avoids the extra parentheses:

```
; Clojure cond
(cond (= x 10) "equal"
      (> x 10) "more")
```

This is an aesthetic decision, and both approaches have their supporters. The important thing is that Clojure takes the opportunity to improve on Lisp traditions when it can do so without compromising Lisp's power.

Clojure is an excellent Lisp, for both Lisp experts and Lisp beginners.

Clojure Is a Functional Language

Clojure is a functional language but not a pure functional language like Haskell. Functional languages have the following properties:

- Functions are *first-class objects*. That is, functions can be created at runtime, passed around, returned, and in general, used like any other datatype.

- Data is immutable.

- Functions are *pure*; that is, they have no side effects.

For many tasks, functional programs are easier to understand, less error prone, and *much* easier to reuse. For example, the following short program searches a database of compositions for every composer who has written a composition named "Requiem":

```
(for [c compositions :when (= (:name c) "Requiem")] (:composer c))
-> ("W. A. Mozart" "Giuseppe Verdi")
```

The name for does not introduce a loop but a *list comprehension*. Read the earlier code as, "For each c in compositions, where the name of c is "Requiem", yield the composer of c." List comprehension is covered more fully in *Transforming Sequences*, on page 62.

This example has four desirable properties:

- It is *simple*; it has no loops, variables, or mutable state.
- It is *thread safe*; no locking is needed.
- It is *parallelizable*; you could farm out individual steps to multiple threads without changing the code for each step.
- It is *generic*; compositions could be a plain set, XML or a database result set.

Contrast functional programs with *imperative* programs, where explicit statements alter program state. Most object-oriented programs are written in an imperative style and have *none* of the advantages listed here; they are unnecessarily complex, not thread safe, not parallelizable, and difficult to generalize. (For a head-to-head comparison of functional and imperative styles, skip forward to *Where's My for Loop?*, on page 45.)

People have known about the advantages of functional languages for a while now. And yet, pure functional languages like Haskell have not taken over the world, because developers find that not everything fits easily into the pure functional view.

There are four reasons that Clojure can attract more interest now than functional languages have in the past:

- Functional programming is more urgent today than ever before. Massively multicore hardware is here, and functional languages provide a clear approach for taking advantage of it. Functional programming is covered in Chapter 4, *Functional Programming*, on page 81.
- Purely functional languages can make it awkward to model state that really needs to change. Clojure provides a structured mechanism for working with changeable state via software transactional memory and refs (on page 139), agents (on page 147), atoms (on page 146), and dynamic binding (on page 152).
- Many functional languages are statically typed. Clojure's dynamic typing makes it more accessible for programmers learning FP. However, Clojure provides specs to describe your data and functions, for use as you need it, with greater expressivity than most static type systems.

- Clojure's Java invocation approach is *not* functional. When you call Java, you enter the familiar, mutable world. This offers a comfortable haven for beginners learning functional programming and a pragmatic alternative to functional style when you need it. Java invocation is covered in Chapter 10, *Java Interop*, on page 225.

Clojure's approach to changing state enables concurrency without explicit locking and complements Clojure's functional core.

Clojure Simplifies Concurrent Programming

Clojure's support for functional programming makes it easy to write thread-safe code. Since immutable data structures cannot *ever* change, there's no danger of data corruption based on another thread's activity.

However, Clojure's support for concurrency goes beyond just functional programming. When you need references to mutable data, Clojure protects them via software transactional memory (STM). STM is a higher-level approach to thread safety than the locking mechanisms that Java provides. Rather than create fragile, error-prone locking strategies, you can protect shared state with transactions. This is much more productive, because many programmers have a good understanding of transactions based on experience with databases.

For example, the following code creates a working, thread-safe, in-memory database of accounts:

```
(def accounts (ref #{}))
(defrecord Account [id balance])
```

The ref function creates a transactionally protected reference to the current state of the database. Updating is trivial. This code adds a new account to the database:

```
(dosync
  (alter accounts conj (->Account "CLJ" 1000.00)))
```

The dosync causes the update to accounts to execute inside a transaction. This guarantees thread safety, and it's easier to use than locking. With transactions, you never have to worry about which objects to lock or in what order. The transactional approach will also perform better under some common usage scenarios, because readers will never block, for example.

Although the example here is trivial, the technique is general, and it works on real-world problems. See Chapter 6, *State and Concurrency*, on page 137 for more on concurrency and STM in Clojure.

Clojure Embraces the Java Virtual Machine

Clojure gives you clean, simple, direct access to Java. You can call any Java API directly:

```
(System/getProperties)
-> {java.runtime.name=Java(TM) SE Runtime Environment
... many more ...
```

Clojure adds a lot of syntactic sugar for calling Java. We won't get into the details here (see *Calling Java*, on page 39), but notice that in the following code, the Clojure version has *fewer parentheses* than the Java version:

```
// Java
"hello".getClass().getProtectionDomain()

; Clojure
(.. "hello" getClass getProtectionDomain)
```

Clojure provides simple functions for implementing Java interfaces and subclassing Java classes. Also, all Clojure functions implement Callable and Runnable. This makes it trivial to pass the following anonymous function to the constructor for a Java Thread.

```
(.start (new Thread (fn [] (println "Hello" (Thread/currentThread)))))
-> Hello #object[java.lang.Thread 0x2057ff1f Thread[Thread-0,5,main]]
```

The funny output here is Clojure's way of printing a Java instance. java.lang.Thread is the class name of the instance, 0x2057ff1f is the hash code of the instance, and Thread[Thread-0,5,main] is the instance's toString representation.

(Note that in the preceding example, the new thread will run to completion, but its output may interleave in some strange way with the REPL prompt. This is not a problem with Clojure but simply the result of having more than one thread writing to an output stream.)

Because the Java invocation syntax in Clojure is clean and simple, it's idiomatic to use Java directly, rather than to hide Java behind Lispy wrappers.

Now that you've seen a few of the reasons to use Clojure, it's time to start writing some code.

Clojure Coding Quick Start

Clojure is built and distributed in a Java archive (a jar file) that can be run on the Java Virtual Machine (JVM). Running programs on the Java Virtual Machine requires assembling a *classpath* that contains all of the code required to run your program, which includes Clojure itself, your code, and any Java or Clojure dependencies needed by your code.

To run Clojure and the code in this book, you need two things:

- *A Java runtime.* Download[4] and install Java version 6 or higher (however, using at least version 8 is recommended for improved performance).

- *Clojure command line tools.* The Clojure "Getting Started" page[5] contains the latest instructions on installing the Clojure command line tools. These tools have support for managing library dependencies and running programs with the appropriate classpath.

You will use the command line tools (specifically clj) to install Clojure and all of the dependencies for the sample code in this book. For more details on basic usage of clj, see the guide[6] and reference[7] pages. Don't worry about learning everything now, though, because this book will guide you through the commands necessary to follow along.

While you're working through the book, use the version of Clojure tied to the book's sample code. See *Downloading Sample Code*, on page xvi for instructions on downloading the sample code.

You can test your install by navigating to the directory where you placed the sample code and running a Clojure *read-eval-print loop* (REPL) using the clj tool:

```
clj
```

The clj tool uses an optional configuration file, deps.edn, to declare dependencies. When clj starts, it will download any necessary dependencies (and their transitive dependencies). If you have just installed the clj tool, you may see statements about Clojure and other dependencies being downloaded. Once the REPL starts, it prints some helpful version information, then prompts you with:

```
user=>
```

Now you are ready for "Hello World."

Using the REPL

To see how to use the REPL, let's create a few variants of "Hello World." First, type (println "hello world") at the REPL prompt:

---

4. http://www.oracle.com/technetwork/java/javase/downloads/index.html
5. https://clojure.org/guides/getting_started
6. https://clojure.org/guides/deps_and_cli
7. https://clojure.org/reference/deps_and_cli

```
user=> (println "hello world")
-> hello world
-> nil
```

The second line, hello world, is the console output you requested. The third line is the return value from the println expression.

Next, encapsulate your "Hello World" into a function that can address a person by name:

```
(defn hello [name] (str "Hello, " name))
-> #'user/hello
```

Let's break this down:

- defn defines a function.

- hello is the function name.

- hello takes one argument, name.

- str is a function call that concatenates an arbitrary list of arguments into a string.

- defn, hello, name, and str are all *symbols*, which are names that refer to things. Legal symbols are defined in *Symbols*, on page 21.

Look at the return value, #'user/hello. The prefix #' indicates that the function was stored in a Clojure *var*, and user is the *namespace* of the function. (The user namespace is the REPL default, like the default package in Java.) You don't need to worry about vars and namespaces yet; they're covered in *Vars, Bindings, and Namespaces*, on page 31.

Now you can call hello, passing in your name:

```
user=> (hello "Stu")
-> "Hello, Stu"
```

If you get your REPL into a state that confuses you, the simplest fix is to kill the REPL with Ctrl+C on Windows or Ctrl+D on *nix and then start another one.

Special Variables

The REPL includes several useful, special variables. When you're working in the REPL, the results of evaluating the three most recent expressions are stored in the special variables *1, *2, and *3, respectively. This makes it easy to work iteratively. Say hello to a few different names:

```
user=> (hello "Stu")
-> "Hello, Stu"
```

```
user=> (hello "Clojure")
-> "Hello, Clojure"
```

You can use the special variables to combine the results of your recent work:

```
(str *1 " and " *2)
-> "Hello, Clojure and Hello, Stu"
```

If you make a mistake in the REPL, you'll see a Java exception. The details are often omitted for brevity. For example, dividing by zero is a no-no:

```
user=> (/ 1 0)
-> ArithmeticException Divide by zero  clojure.lang.Numbers.divide (Numbers.java:158)
```

Here the problem is obvious, but sometimes the problem is more subtle and you want the detailed stack trace. The *e special variable holds the last exception. Because Clojure exceptions are Java exceptions, you can ask for the stack trace by calling pst (print stack trace).

```
user=> (pst)
-> ArithmeticException Divide by zero
|   clojure.lang.Numbers.divide (Numbers.java:158)
|   clojure.lang.Numbers.divide (Numbers.java:3808)
|   user/eval1247 (form-init5722005119880062985.clj:1)
|   user/eval1247 (form-init5722005119880062985.clj:1)
|   clojure.lang.Compiler.eval (Compiler.java:6927)
|   clojure.lang.Compiler.eval (Compiler.java:6890)
|   clojure.core/eval (core.clj:3105)
|   clojure.core/eval (core.clj:3101)
|   clojure.main/repl/read-eval-print--7408/fn--7411 (main.clj:240)
|   clojure.main/repl/read-eval-print--7408 (main.clj:240)
|   clojure.main/repl/fn--7417 (main.clj:258)
|   clojure.main/repl (main.clj:258)
```

Java interop is covered in Chapter 10, *Java Interop*, on page 225.

If you have a block of code that's too large to conveniently type at the REPL, save the code into a file, and then load that file from the REPL. You can use an absolute path or a path relative to where you launched the REPL:

```
; save some work in temp.clj, and then ...
user=> (load-file "temp.clj")
```

The REPL is a terrific environment for trying ideas and getting immediate feedback. Keep a REPL open at all times while you read this book.

Adding Shared State

The hello function of the previous section is *pure*; that is, it has no side effects. Pure functions are easy to develop, test, and understand, and you should prefer them for many tasks.

That said, most programs have some shared state and will use impure functions to manage that shared state. Let's extend hello to keep track of past visitors. First, you need a data structure to track the visitors. A set will do the trick:

```
#{}
-> #{}
```

The #{} is a literal for an empty set. Next, you need conj:

```
(conj coll item)
```

conj is short for conjoin, and it builds a new collection with an item added. conj an element onto a set to see that a new set is created:

```
(conj #{} "Stu")
-> #{"Stu"}
```

Now that you can build new sets, you need some way to keep track of the *current* set of visitors. Clojure provides several *reference types* (refs) for this purpose. The most basic reference type is the atom:

```
(atom initial-state)
```

To name your atom, you can use def:

```
(def symbol initial-value?)
```

def is like defn but more general. A def can define functions *or* data. Use atom to create an atom, and use def to bind the atom to the name visitors:

```
(def visitors (atom #{}))
-> #'user/visitors
```

To update a reference, you must use a function, such as swap!:

```
(swap! r update-fn & args)
```

swap! applies an update-fn to reference r, with optional args if necessary. Try to swap! a visitor into visitors, using conj as the update function:

```
(swap! visitors conj "Stu")
-> #{"Stu"}
```

atom is one of several reference types in Clojure. Choosing the appropriate reference type requires care (discussed in Chapter 6, *State and Concurrency*, on page 137).

At any time, you can peek inside the ref with deref or with the shorter @:

```
(deref visitors)
-> #{"Stu"}

@visitors
-> #{"Stu"}
```

Now you're ready to build the new, more elaborate version of hello:

```
src/examples/introduction.clj
(defn hello
  "Writes hello message to *out*. Calls you by username.
  Knows if you have been here before."
  [username]
  (swap! visitors conj username)
  (str "Hello, " username))
```

Next, check that visitors are correctly tracked in memory:

```
(hello "Rich")
-> "Hello, Rich"

@visitors
-> #{"Aaron" "Stu" "Rich"}
```

In all probability, your visitors list is different from the one shown here. That's the problem with state! Your results will vary, depending on when things happened. You can reason about a function with direct local knowledge. Reasoning about state requires a full understanding of history.

Avoid state where possible. But when you need it, make it sane and manageable by using refs such as atoms. Atoms (and all other Clojure reference types) are safe for multiple threads and processors. Better yet, this safety comes without any need for locks, which are notoriously tricky to use.

At this point, you should feel comfortable entering small bits of code at the REPL. Larger units of code aren't that different; you can load and run Clojure libraries from the REPL as well. Let's explore that next.

Navigating Clojure Libraries

Clojure code is packaged in *libraries*. Each Clojure library belongs to a *namespace*, which is analogous to a Java package. You can load a Clojure library with require:

```
(require quoted-namespace-symbol)
```

When you require a library named clojure.java.io, Clojure looks for a file named clojure/java/io.clj on the CLASSPATH. Try it:

```
user=> (require 'clojure.java.io)
-> nil
```

The leading single quote (') is required, and it *quotes* the library name. The nil returned indicates success. While you're at it, test that you can load the sample code for this chapter, examples.introduction:

```
user=> (require 'examples.introduction)
-> nil
```

The examples.introduction library includes an implementation of the Fibonacci numbers, which is the traditional "Hello World" program for functional languages. We'll explore the Fibonacci numbers in more detail in *How to Be Lazy*, on page 85. For now, just make sure you can execute the sample function fibs. Enter the following line of code at the REPL to take the first 10 Fibonacci numbers:

```
(take 10 examples.introduction/fibs)
-> (0 1 1 2 3 5 8 13 21 34)
```

If you see the first 10 Fibonacci numbers as listed here, you have successfully installed the book samples.

The book samples are all unit tested, with tests located in the examples/test directory. The tests for the samples themselves are not explicitly covered in the book, but you may find them useful for reference.

Often you can find the documentation you need right at the REPL. The most basic helper function (a macro) is doc:

```
(doc name)
```

Use doc to print the documentation for str:

```
user=> (doc str)
-------------------------
clojure.core/str
([] [x] [x & ys])
With no args, returns the empty string. With one arg x, returns
x.toString().  (str nil) returns the empty string. With more than
one arg, returns the concatenation of the str values of the args.
```

The first line of doc's output contains the fully qualified name of the function. The next line contains the possible argument lists, generated directly from the code. (Some common argument names and their uses are explained in *Conventions for Parameter Names*, on page 17.) Finally, the remaining lines contain the function's *doc string*, if the function definition included one.

You can add a doc string to your own functions by placing it immediately after the function name:

```
src/examples/introduction.clj
(defn hello
  "Writes hello message to *out*. Calls you by username"
  [username]
  (println (str "Hello, " username)))
```

Sometimes you won't know the exact name you want documentation for. The find-doc function will search for anything whose doc output matches a regular expression or string you pass in:

```
(find-doc s)
```

Use find-doc to explore how Clojure does reduce:

```
user=> (find-doc "reduce")
-----------------------
clojure.core/areduce
([a idx ret init expr])
Macro
... details elided ...
-----------------------
clojure.core/reduce
([f coll] [f val coll])
... details elided ...
```

reduce reduces Clojure collections and is covered in *Transforming Sequences*, on page 62. areduce is for interoperation with Java arrays and is covered in *Using Java Arrays*, on page 241.

Much of Clojure is written in Clojure, and it is instructive to read the source code. You can view the source of a Clojure function using the repl library.

```
(clojure.repl/source a-symbol)
```

Try viewing the source of the simple identity function:

```
(require '[clojure.repl :refer [source]])
(source identity)

-> (defn identity
```

```
"Returns its argument."
{:added "1.0"
 :static true}
[x] x)
```

Of course, you can also use Java's Reflection API. You can use methods, such as class, ancestors, and instance?, to reflect against the underlying Java object model and tell, for example, that Clojure's collections are also Java collections:

```
(instance? java.util.Collection [1 2 3])
-> true
```

Clojure's complete API is documented at https://clojure.github.io/clojure. The right sidebar links to all functions and macros by name, and you can find a helpful grouping of functions in the Clojure Cheatsheet.[8]

Conventions for Parameter Names

The documentation strings for reduce and areduce show several terse parameter names. Here are some parameter names and how they are normally used:

Parameter	Usage	Parameter	Usage	Parameter	Usage
a	A Java array	agt	An agent	coll	A collection
expr	An expression	f	A function	idx	An index
r	A ref	v	A vector	val	A value

These names may seem a little terse, but there's a good reason for them: the "good names" are often taken by Clojure functions! Naming a parameter that collides with a function name is legal but considered bad style: the parameter will shadow the function, which will be unavailable while the parameter is in scope. So, don't call your refs ref, your agents agent, or your counts count. Those names refer to functions.

Wrapping Up

You have just experienced the whirlwind tour of Clojure. You've seen Clojure's expressive syntax, learned about Clojure's approach to Lisp, and seen how easy it is to call Java code from Clojure.

You have Clojure running in your own environment, and you've written short programs at the REPL to demonstrate functional programming and the reference model for dealing with state. Now it's time to explore the entire language.

---

8. https://clojure.org/api/cheatsheet

CHAPTER 2

Exploring Clojure

Clojure offers great power through functional style, concurrency support, and clean Java interop. But before you can appreciate all these features, you have to start with the language basics. Clojure is very expressive, and this chapter covers many concepts quite quickly. Don't worry if you don't understand every detail; we'll revisit these topics in more detail in later chapters. If possible, bring up a REPL and follow along with the examples as you read.

We'll start by looking at how to read and understand Clojure code, introducing the key parts of Clojure syntax. If your background is primarily in imperative languages, this tour may seem to be missing key language constructs, such as variables and for loops. Don't worry, you'll soon learn how to work in new ways that don't require them.

Reading Clojure

In this section, we'll cover many of the key parts of Clojure syntax and how they're used to form Clojure programs. In Clojure, there are no statements, only expressions that can be nested in mostly arbitrary ways. When evaluated, every expression returns a value that's used in the parent expression. This is a simple model, yet sufficient to cover everything in Clojure.

Numbers

To begin our exploration, let's consider a simple arithmetic expression as expressed in Clojure:

```
(+ 2 3)
-> 5
```

All Clojure code is made up of expressions, and every expression, when evaluated, returns a value. In Clojure, parentheses are used to indicate a list, in this example, a list containing the symbol + and the numbers 2 and 3.

Clojure's runtime evaluates lists as function calls. The first element (+ in this example) is always treated as the operation with the remaining elements treated as arguments. The style of placing the function first is called *prefix notation*, as opposed to the more familiar *infix notation*, 2 + 3.

A practical advantage of prefix notation is that you can easily extend it for arbitrary numbers of arguments:

```
(+ 1 2 3 4)
-> 10
```

Even the degenerate case of no arguments works as you'd expect, returning zero. This helps to eliminate special-case logic for boundary conditions:

```
(+)
-> 0
```

Many mathematical and comparison operators have the names and semantics that you'd expect from other programming languages. Addition, subtraction, multiplication, comparison, and equality all work as you would expect:

```
(- 10 5)
-> 5
(* 3 10 10)
-> 300
(> 5 2)
-> true
(>= 5 5)
-> true
(< 5 2)
-> false
(= 5 2)
-> false
```

Division may surprise you:

```
(/ 22 7)
-> 22/7
```

As you can see, Clojure has a built-in ratio type.

If what you actually want is decimal division, use a floating-point literal for the dividend:

```
(/ 22.0 7)
-> 3.142857142857143
```

If you want to stick to integers, you can get the integer quotient and remainder with quot and rem:

```
(quot 22 7)
-> 3

(rem 22 7)
-> 1
```

If you need to do arbitrary-precision, floating-point math, append M to a number to create a BigDecimal literal:

```
(+ 1 (/ 0.00001 100000000000000000000))
-> 1.0

(+ 1 (/ 0.00001M 100000000000000000000))
-> 1.0000000000000000000000001M
```

For arbitrary-precision integers, you can append N to create a BigInt literal:

```
(* 1000N 1000 1000 1000 1000 1000 1000)
-> 1000000000000000000000N
```

Notice that only one BigInt literal is needed and is contagious to the entire calculation.

Next, let's see how we can group values using Clojure collections.

Symbols

Forms such as +, concat, and java.lang.String are called *symbols* and are used to name things. For example, + names the function that adds things together. Symbols name all sorts of things in Clojure:

- Functions like str and concat
- "Operators" like + and -, which are, after all, just functions
- Java classes like java.lang.String and java.util.Random
- Namespaces like clojure.core and Java packages like java.lang

Symbols cannot start with a number but can consist of alphanumeric characters, as well as +, -, *, /, !, ?, ., _, and '. The list of legal symbol characters is a minimum set that Clojure promises to support. You should stick to these characters in your own code, but do not assume the list is exhaustive. Clojure can use other, undocumented characters in symbols that it employs internally and may add more legal symbol characters in the future. See Clojure's online documentation[1] for updates to the list of legal symbol characters.

---

1. https://clojure.org/reference/reader

Clojure treats / and . specially in order to support namespaces; see *Namespaces*, on page 34 for details.

Collections

Clojure provides four primary collection types—lists, vectors, sets, and maps. All Clojure collections are heterogeneous (can hold any type of data) and are compared for equality based on their contents. The four Clojure collection types are used in combination to create larger composite data structures.

First let's consider vectors, which are sequential, indexed collections. We can create a vector of the numbers 1, 2, and 3 using the following:

```
[1 2 3]
-> [1 2 3]
```

Lists are sequential collections stored as a linked list. A list is printed as (1 2 3), but we can't create a literal list at the REPL like we can with vectors. As we discussed in the previous section, Clojure function calls are represented as lists and evaluated by invoking the first element as the function. Thus (1 2 3) would be interpreted as invoking the function 1 with the arguments 2 and 3.

If we want a list to be read and interpreted as data (not evaluated like a function call), we can use the quote special form:

```
(quote (1 2 3))
-> (1 2 3)
```

Quoting also has a *reader macro* form (') understood by the reader. Reader macros are abbreviations of longer list forms and are used as shortcuts to improve readability. We'll see more of these as we explore. Here's how the quote looks in the shorter form:

```
'(1 2 3)
-> (1 2 3)
```

Sets are unordered collections that do not contain duplicates:

```
#{1 2 3 5}
-> #{1 3 2 5}
```

Because sets are unordered, you may see the elements printed in a different order than the original literal, and you should not expect any particular order. Sets are a good choice when you want fast addition and removal of elements and the ability to quickly check for whether a set contains a value.

Finally, Clojure maps are collections of key/value pairs. You can use a map literal to create a lookup table for the inventors of programming languages:

```
{"Lisp" "McCarthy" "Clojure" "Hickey"}
-> {"Lisp" "McCarthy", "Clojure" "Hickey"}
```

The key "Lisp" is associated with the value "McCarthy" and the key "Clojure" is associated with the value "Hickey". Like sets, maps are unordered, and the key/value pairs may be printed in an order different than the original map literal.

You may have noticed that the printed version lists a comma between the two key/value pairs. In Clojure, commas are whitespace and you're free to use them as an optional delimiter if you find it improves readability:

```
{"Lisp" "McCarthy", "Clojure" "Hickey"}
-> {"Lisp" "McCarthy", "Clojure" "Hickey"}
```

Any Clojure data structure can be a key in a map. However, the most common key type is the Clojure keyword.

A *keyword* is like a symbol, except that keywords begin with a colon (:). Keywords resolve to themselves:

```
:foo
-> :foo
```

The fact that keywords resolve to themselves makes keywords useful as keys. You could redefine the inventors map using keywords as keys: {:Lisp "McCarthy" :Clojure "Hickey"}

If several maps have keys in common, you can leverage this by creating a record with defrecord:

```
(defrecord name [arguments])
```

For example, consider using the defrecord to create a Book record:

```
(defrecord Book [title author])
-> user.Book
```

Then, you can instantiate that record with the ->Book constructor function:

```
(->Book "title" "author")
```

Once you instantiate a Book, it behaves almost like any other map. We will learn more about when and how to use records in Chapter 7, *Protocols and Datatypes*, on page 167.

Strings and Characters

Strings are another kind of form. They are delimited by double quotes and are allowed to span multiple lines. Clojure strings reuse the Java String implementation.

```
"This is a\nmultiline string"
-> "This is a\nmultiline string"
```

```
"This is also
a multiline string"
-> "This is also\na multiline string"
```

As you can see, the REPL always shows string literals with escaped newlines. If you actually print a multiline string, it will print on multiple lines:

```
(println "another\nmultiline\nstring")
| another
| multiline
| string
-> nil
```

Perhaps the most common string function you'll use is str, which takes any number of objects, converts them to strings, and concatenates the results into a single string. Any nils passed to str are ignored:

```
(str 1 2 nil 3)
-> "123"
```

Clojure characters are also Java characters. Their literal syntax is \{letter}, where letter can be a letter, or in a few special cases, the name of a character: backspace, formfeed, newline, return, space, or tab:

```
(str \h \e \y \space \y \o \u)
-> "hey you"
```

Booleans and nil

Clojure's rules for Booleans are easy to understand:

- true is true, and false is false.
- In addition to false, nil evaluates to false when used in a Boolean context.
- Other than false and nil, *everything else* evaluates to true in a Boolean context.

Note that true, false, and nil follow the rules for symbols but are read as other special values (either a Boolean or nil). These are the only special-case tokens like this in Clojure—anything else symbol-like is read as a symbol.

The empty list is not false in Clojure:

```
;      (if part)    (else part)
(if () "() is true" "() is false")
-> "() is true"
```

Zero is not false in Clojure, either:

```
;      (if part)        (else part)
(if 0 "Zero is true" "Zero is false")
-> "Zero is true"
```

A *predicate* is a function that returns either true or false. In Clojure, it's common to name predicates with a trailing question mark, for example, true?, false?, nil?, and zero?:

```
(true?  expr)
(false? expr)
(nil?   expr)
(zero?  expr)
```

true? tests whether a value is exactly the true value, *not* whether the value evaluates to true in a Boolean context. The only thing that's true? is true itself:

```
(true? true)
-> true

(true? "foo")
-> false
```

nil? and false? work the same way. Only nil is nil?, and only false is false?.

zero? works with any numeric type, returning true if it's zero:

```
(zero? 0.0)
-> true

(zero? (/ 22 7))
-> false
```

There are many more predicates in Clojure—go to the REPL and type:

```
(find-doc #"\?$")
```

The find-doc function is a REPL facility (included in the clojure.repl namespace) that searches all docstrings matching either a string or a regular expression. The syntax used here #"\?$" is a literal regular expression. Clojure uses Java's built-in regular expression library and is equivalent to a compiled Java Pattern. Clojure provides a set of functions designed for using regular expressions to find and/or replace matches in a string.

Functions

In Clojure, a function call is simply a list whose first element resolves to a function. For example, this call to str concatenates its arguments to create a string:

```
(str "hello" " " "world")
-> "hello world"
```

Function names are typically hyphenated, as in clear-agent-errors. If a function is a predicate, then by convention, its name should end with a question mark. As an example, the following predicates test the type of their argument, and all end with a question mark:

```
(string? "hello")
-> true

(keyword? :hello)
-> true

(symbol? 'hello)
-> true
```

To define your own functions, use defn:

```
(defn name doc-string? attr-map? [params*] prepost-map? body)
```

The name is a symbol naming the function (implicitly defined within the current namespace). The doc-string is an optional string describing the function. The attr-map associates metadata with the function's var. It's covered separately in *Metadata*, on page 37. The prepost-map? can be used to define preconditions and postconditions that are automatically checked on invocation, and the body contains any number of expressions. The result of the final expression is the return value of the function.

Let's create a greeting function that takes a name and returns a greeting preceded by "Hello":

```
src/examples/exploring.clj
(defn greeting
  "Returns a greeting of the form 'Hello, username.'"
  [username]
  (str "Hello, " username))
```

You can call greeting:

```
(greeting "world")
-> "Hello, world"
```

You can also consult the documentation for greeting:

```
user=> (doc greeting)
-------------------------
exploring/greeting
([username])
Returns a greeting of the form 'Hello, username.'
```

What does greeting do if the caller omits username?

```
(greeting)
-> ArityException Wrong number of args (0) passed to: user/greeting
clojure.lang.AFn.throwArity (AFn.java:429)
```

Clojure functions enforce their *arity*, that is, their expected number of arguments. If you call a function with an incorrect number of arguments, Clojure throws an ArityException. If you want to make greeting issue a generic greeting when the caller omits username, you can use this alternate form of defn, which takes multiple argument lists and method bodies:

```
(defn name doc-string? attr-map?
  ([params*] body)+)
```

Different arities of the same function can call one another, so you can easily create a zero-argument greeting that delegates to the one-argument greeting, passing in a default username:

```
src/examples/exploring.clj
(defn greeting
  "Returns a greeting of the form 'Hello, username.'
   Default username is 'world'."
  ([] (greeting "world"))
  ([username] (str "Hello, " username)))
```

You can verify that the new greeting works as expected:

```
(greeting)
-> "Hello, world"
```

You can create a function with variable arity by including an ampersand in the parameter list. Clojure binds the name after the ampersand to a sequence of all the remaining parameters. There may be only one variable arity parameter, and it must be last in the parameter list.

The following function allows two people to go on a date with a variable number of chaperones:

```
src/examples/exploring.clj
(defn date [person-1 person-2 & chaperones]
  (println person-1 "and" person-2
           "went out with" (count chaperones) "chaperones."))

(date "Romeo" "Juliet" "Friar Lawrence" "Nurse")
| Romeo and Juliet went out with 2 chaperones.
```

Writing function implementations differing by arity is useful. But if you come from an object-oriented background, you'll want *polymorphism*, that is, different implementations that are selected by *type*. Clojure can do this and a whole lot more. See Chapter 9, *Multimethods*, on page 209 and Chapter 7, *Protocols and Datatypes*, on page 167 for details.

defn is intended for defining functions at the top level. If you want to create a function from within another function, you should use an anonymous function form instead.

Anonymous Functions

In addition to named functions with defn, you can also create anonymous functions with fn. At least three reasons exist to create an anonymous function:

- The function is so brief and self-explanatory that giving it a name makes the code harder to read, not easier.

- The function is being used only from inside another function and needs a local name, not a top-level binding.

- The function is created inside another function for the purpose of capturing the values of parameters or local bindings.

Functions used as predicates when filtering data are often brief and self-explanatory. For example, imagine that you want to create an index for a sequence of words, and you don't care about words shorter than three characters. You can write an indexable-word? function like this:

```
src/examples/exploring.clj
(defn indexable-word? [word]
  (> (count word) 2))
```

Then, you can use indexable-word? to extract indexable words from a sentence:

```
(require '[clojure.string :as str])
(filter indexable-word? (str/split "A fine day it is" #"\W+"))
-> ("fine" "day")
```

The call to split breaks the sentence into words, and then filter calls indexable-word? once for each word, returning those for which indexable-word? returns true.

Anonymous functions let you do the same thing in a single line. The simplest anonymous fn form is the following:

```
(fn [params*] body)
```

With this form, you can plug the implementation of indexable-word? directly into the call to filter:

```
(filter (fn [w] (> (count w) 2)) (str/split "A fine day" #"\W+"))
-> ("fine" "day")
```

There's an even shorter reader macro syntax for anonymous functions, using implicit parameter names. The parameters are named %1, %2, and optionally, a final %& to collect the rest of a variable number of arguments. You can also use just % for the first parameter, preferred for single-argument functions. This syntax looks like this:

```
#(body)
```

You can rewrite the call to filter with the shorter anonymous form:

```
(filter #(> (count %) 2) (str/split "A fine day it is" #"\W+"))
-> ("fine" "day")
```

A second motivation for anonymous functions is when you want to use a named function but only inside the scope of another function. Continuing with the indexable-word? example, you could write this:

```
src/examples/exploring.clj
(defn indexable-words [text]
  (let [indexable-word? (fn [w] (> (count w) 2))]
    (filter indexable-word? (str/split text #"\W+"))))
```

The let binds the name indexable-word? to the same anonymous function you wrote earlier, this time inside the lexical scope of indexable-words. (let is covered in more detail under *Vars, Bindings, and Namespaces*, on page 31.) You can verify that indexable-words works as expected:

```
(indexable-words "a fine day it is")
-> ("fine" "day")
```

The combination of let and an anonymous function says the following to readers of your code: "The function indexable-word? is interesting enough to have a name but is relevant only inside indexable-words."

A third reason to use anonymous functions is when you create a function dynamically at runtime. Earlier, you implemented a simple greeting function. Extending this idea, you can create a make-greeter function that creates greeting functions. make-greeter will take a greeting-prefix and return a new function that composes greetings from the greeting-prefix and a name.

src/examples/exploring.clj
```
(defn make-greeter [greeting-prefix]
  (fn [username] (str greeting-prefix ", " username)))
```

It makes no sense to name the fn, because it's creating a *different* function each time make-greeter is called. However, you may want to name the results of specific calls to make-greeter. You can use def to name functions created by make-greeter:

```
(def hello-greeting (make-greeter "Hello"))
-> #'user/hello-greeting
```

```
(def aloha-greeting (make-greeter "Aloha"))
-> #'user/aloha-greeting
```

Now, you can call these functions, just like any other functions:

```
(hello-greeting "world")
-> "Hello, world"
```

```
(aloha-greeting "world")
-> "Aloha, world"
```

Moreover, there's no need to give each greeter a name. You can simply create a greeter and place it in the first (function) slot of a form:

```
((make-greeter "Howdy") "pardner")
-> "Howdy, pardner"
```

As you can see, the different greeter functions remember the value of greeting-prefix at the time they were created. More formally, the greeter functions are *closures* over the value of greeting-prefix.

When to Use Anonymous Functions

Anonymous functions have a terse syntax—sometimes too terse. You may actually prefer to be explicit, creating named functions such as indexable-word?. That's perfectly fine and will certainly be the right choice if indexable-word? needs to be called from more than one place.

Anonymous functions are an option, not a requirement. Use the anonymous forms only when you find that they make your code more readable. They take a little getting used to, so don't be surprised if you gradually use them more and more.

Vars, Bindings, and Namespaces

One of the most important tools in a programming language is the ability to name and remember values or functions for later use. In Clojure, a *namespace* is a collection of names (symbols) that refer to *vars*. Each var is bound to a value. Let's consider vars more closely.

Vars

When you define an object with def or defn, that object is stored in a Clojure *var*. For example, the following def creates a var named user/foo:

```
(def foo 10)
-> #'user/foo
```

The symbol user/foo refers to a var that is *bound* to the value 10. If you ask Clojure to evaluate the symbol foo, it will return the value of the associated var:

```
foo
-> 10
```

The initial value of a var is called its *root binding*. Sometimes it's useful to have thread-local bindings for a var; this is covered in *Managing Per-Thread State with Vars*, on page 152.

You can refer to a var directly. The var special form returns a var itself, not the var's value:

```
(var a-symbol)
```

You can use var to return the var bound to user/foo:

```
(var foo)
-> #'user/foo
```

You will almost never see the var form directly in Clojure code. Instead, you'll see the equivalent reader macro #', which also returns the var for a symbol:

```
#'foo
-> #'user/foo
```

Why would you want to refer to a var directly? Most of the time, you won't, and you can often simply ignore the distinction between symbols and vars.

But keep in the back of your mind that vars have many abilities other than just storing a value:

- The same var can be aliased into more than one namespace (*Namespaces*, on page 34). This allows you to use convenient short names.

- Vars can have metadata (*Metadata*, on page 37). Var metadata includes documentation (*Navigating Clojure Libraries*, on page 14), type hints for optimization, and unit tests.

- Vars can be dynamically rebound on a per-thread basis (*Managing Per-Thread State with Vars*, on page 152).

Bindings

Vars are bound to names, but there are other kinds of bindings as well. For example, in a function call, argument values bind to parameter names. In the following call, the name number is locally bound to the value 10 inside the triple function:

```
(defn triple [number] (* 3 number))
-> #'user/triple

(triple 10)
-> 30
```

A function's parameter bindings have a *lexical* scope: they're visible only inside the text of the function body. Functions are not the only way to create a lexical binding. The special form let does nothing other than create a set of lexical bindings:

```
(let [bindings*] exprs*)
```

The bindings are then in effect for exprs, and the value of the let is the value of the last expression in exprs.

Imagine that you want coordinates for the four corners of a square, given the bottom, left, and size. You can let the top and right coordinates, based on the values given:

src/examples/exploring.clj
```
(defn square-corners [bottom left size]
  (let [top (+ bottom size)
        right (+ left size)]
    [[bottom left] [top left] [top right] [bottom right]]))
```

The let binds top and right. This saves you the trouble of calculating top and right more than once. (Both are needed twice to generate the return value.) The let then returns its last form, which in this example becomes the return value of square-corners.

Destructuring

In many programming languages, you bind a variable to an *entire* collection when you need to access only *part* of the collection.

Imagine that you're working with a database of book authors. You track both first and last names, but some functions need to use only the first name:

src/examples/exploring.clj
```
(defn greet-author-1 [author]
  (println "Hello," (:first-name author)))
```

The greet-author-1 function works fine:

```
(greet-author-1 {:last-name "Vinge" :first-name "Vernor"})
| Hello, Vernor
```

Having to bind author is unsatisfying. You don't need the author; all you need is the first-name. Clojure solves this with *destructuring*. Any place that you bind names, you can nest a vector or a map in the binding to reach into a collection and bind only the part you want. Here is a variant of greet-author that binds only the first name:

src/examples/exploring.clj
```
(defn greet-author-2 [{fname :first-name}]
  (println "Hello," fname))
```

The binding form {fname :first-name} tells Clojure to bind fname to the :first-name of the function argument. greet-author-2 behaves just like greet-author-1:

```
(greet-author-2 {:last-name "Vinge" :first-name "Vernor"})
| Hello, Vernor
```

Just as you can use a map to destructure any associative collection, you can use a vector to destructure any sequential collection. For example, you could bind only the first two coordinates in a three-dimensional coordinate space:

```
(let [[x y] [1 2 3]]
[x y])
-> [1 2]
```

The expression [x y] destructures the vector [1 2 3], binding x to 1 and y to 2. Since no symbol lines up with the final element 3, it's not bound to anything.

Sometimes you want to skip elements at the start of a collection. Here's how you could bind only the z coordinate:

```
(let [[_ _ z] [1 2 3]]
z)
-> 3
```

The underscore (_) is a legal symbol and is often used to indicate, "I don't care about this binding." Binding proceeds from left to right, so the _ is actually bound twice:

```
; *not* idiomatic!
(let [[_ _ z] [1 2 3]]
  _)
-> 2
```

It's also possible to simultaneously bind both a collection and elements within the collection. Inside a destructuring expression, an :as clause gives you a binding for the entire enclosing structure. For example, you could capture the x and y coordinates individually, plus the entire collection as coords, to report the total number of dimensions:

```
(let [[x y :as coords] [1 2 3 4 5 6]]
(str "x: " x ", y: " y ", total dimensions " (count coords)))
-> "x: 1, y: 2, total dimensions 6"
```

Try using destructuring to create an ellipsize function. ellipsize should take a string and return the first three words followed by an ellipsis (...).

```
src/examples/exploring.clj
(require '[clojure.string :as str])
(defn ellipsize [words]
  (let [[w1 w2 w3] (str/split words #"\s+")]
    (str/join " " [w1 w2 w3 "..."]))))

(ellipsize "The quick brown fox jumps over the lazy dog.")
-> "The quick brown ..."
```

split splits the string around whitespace, and then the destructuring form [w1 w2 w3] grabs the first three words. The destructuring ignores any extra items, which is exactly what we want. Finally, join reassembles the three words, adding the ellipsis at the end.

Destructuring has several other features not shown here and is a mini-language in itself. The Snake game in *A Clojure Snake*, on page 157 makes heavy use of destructuring. For a complete list of destructuring options, see the online documentation for binding forms[2] and the destructuring guide.[3]

Namespaces

Root bindings live in a namespace. You can see evidence of this when you start the Clojure REPL and create a binding:

---

2.   https://clojure.org/reference/special_forms#binding-forms
3.   https://clojure.org/guides/destructuring

```
user=> (def foo 10)
-> #'user/foo
```

The user=> prompt tells you that you're currently working in the user namespace. Most of the REPL session listings in this book omit the REPL prompt for brevity. In this section, the REPL prompt will be included whenever the current namespace is important. You should treat user as a scratch namespace for exploratory development.

When Clojure resolves the name foo, it namespace-qualifies foo in the current namespace user. You can verify this by calling resolve:

```
(resolve sym)
```

resolve returns the var or class that a symbol will resolve to in the current namespace. Use resolve to explicitly resolve the symbol foo:

```
(resolve 'foo)
-> #'user/foo
```

You can switch namespaces, creating a new one if needed, with in-ns:

```
(in-ns name)
```

Try creating a myapp namespace:

```
user=> (in-ns 'myapp)
-> #object[clojure.lang.Namespace 0x5b025dc7 "myapp"]
myapp=>
```

Now you're in the myapp namespace, and anything you def or defn will belong to myapp.

When you create a new namespace with in-ns, the java.lang package is automatically available to you:

```
myapp=> String
-> java.lang.String
```

While you're learning Clojure, you should use the clojure.core namespace whenever you move to a new namespace, making Clojure's core functions available in the new namespace as well:

```
myapp=> (clojure.core/use 'clojure.core)
-> nil
```

By default, the class names outside java.lang must be fully qualified. You can't just say File:

```
myapp=> File/separator
-> java.lang.Exception: No such namespace: File
```

Instead, you must specify the fully qualified java.io.File. Note that your file separator character may be different from that shown here:

```
myapp=> java.io.File/separator
-> "/"
```

If you want to use a short name, rather than a fully qualified class name, you can import classes from a Java package into the current namespace using import.

```
(import '(package Class+))
```

Once you import a class, you can use its short name:

```
(import '(java.io InputStream File))
-> java.io.File

(.exists (File. "/tmp"))
-> true
```

import is only for Java classes. To use a Clojure var from another namespace without the namespace qualified, you must refer the external vars into the current namespace. For example, take Clojure's split function that resides in clojure.string:

```
(require 'clojure.string)
(clojure.string/split "Something,separated,by,commas" #",")
-> ["Something" "separated" "by" "commas"]

(split "Something,separated,by,commas" #",")
-> Unable to resolve symbol: split in this context
```

If you wish to refer to split with a namespace alias, call require on split's namespace and give it the alias str:

```
(require '[clojure.string :as str])
(str/split "Something,separated,by,commas" #",")
                -> ["Something" "separated" "by" "commas"]
```

This simple form of require causes the current namespace to reference *all* public vars in clojure.string via the alias str.

It's common to import Java classes and require namespaces at the top of a source file, using the ns macro:

```
(ns name & references)
```

The ns macro sets the current namespace (available as *ns*) to name, creating the namespace if necessary. The references can include :import, :require, and :use, which work like the similarly named functions to set up the namespace mappings in a single form at the top of a source file. For example, the following call to ns appears at the top of the sample code for this chapter:

src/examples/exploring.clj
```
(ns examples.exploring
  (:require [clojure.string :as str])
  (:import (java.io File)))
```

The namespace functions can do quite a bit more than we've shown here.

You can examine namespaces and add or remove mappings at any time. To find out more, issue this command at the REPL. Since we've moved around a bit in the REPL, we'll also ensure that we're in the user namespace so that our REPL utilities are available to us:

```
(in-ns 'user)
(find-doc "ns-")
```

Alternately, browse the reference documentation.[4]

Metadata

The Wikipedia entry on metadata[5] begins by saying that metadata is "data about data." That is true but not usably specific. In Clojure, metadata is data that is *orthogonal to the logical value of an object*. For example, a person's first and last names are plain old data. The fact that a person object can be serialized to XML has nothing to do with the person and is therefore metadata. Likewise, the fact that a person object is dirty and needs to be flushed to the database is metadata.

The Clojure language itself uses metadata in several places. For example, vars have a metadata map containing documentation, type information, and source information. Here is the metadata for the str var:

---

4.   https://clojure.org/reference/namespaces
5.   http://en.wikipedia.org/wiki/Metadata

```
(meta #'str)
{:ns #object[clojure.lang.Namespace 0x62ccf439 "clojure.core"],
 :name str,
 :added "1.0",
 :file "clojure/core.clj",
 :line 544,
 :column 1,
 :tag java.lang.String,
 :arglists ([] [x] [x & ys]),
 :doc
"With no args, ...[etc]"}
```

Some common metadata keys and their uses are shown in the following table.

Key	Used For	Key	Used For
:ns	Namespace	:column	Source column number
:name	Local name	:tag	Expected argument or return type
:added	Version this function was added	:arglists	Parameter info used by doc
:file	Source file	:doc	Documentation used by doc
:line	Source line number	:macro	True for macros

Much of the metadata on a var is added automatically by the Clojure compiler. To add your own key/value pairs to a var, use the metadata reader macro:

```
^metadata form
```

For example, you could create a simple shout function that upcases a string and then document that shout both expects and returns a string, using the :tag key:

```
; see also shorter form below
(defn ^{:tag String} shout [^{:tag String} s] (clojure.string/upper-case s))
-> #'user/shout
```

You can inspect shout's metadata to see that Clojure added the :tag:

```
(meta #'shout)
-> {:arglists ([s]),
:ns #object[clojure.lang.Namespace 0x284c1da6 "user"],
:name shout,
:line 32,
:column 1,
:file "NO_SOURCE_PATH",
:tag java.lang.String}
```

You provided the :tag, and Clojure provided the other keys. The :file value NO_SOURCE_PATH indicates that the code was entered at the REPL.

Because :tag metadata is so common, you can also use the short-form ^Classname, which expands to ^{:tag Classname}. Using the shorter form, you can rewrite shout as follows:

```
(defn ^String shout [^String s] (clojure.string/upper-case s))
-> #'user/shout
```

If you find the metadata disruptive when you're reading the definition of a function, you can place the metadata last. Use a variant of defn that wraps one or more body forms in parentheses, followed by a metadata map:

```
(defn shout
([s] (clojure.string/upper-case s))
{:tag String})
```

Calling Java

Clojure provides simple, direct syntax for calling Java code: creating objects, invoking methods, and accessing static methods and fields. In addition, Clojure provides syntactic sugar that makes calling Java from Clojure more concise than calling Java from Java!

Not all types in Java are created equal: the primitives and arrays work differently. Where Java has special cases, Clojure gives you direct access to these as well. Finally, Clojure provides a set of convenience functions for common tasks that would be unwieldy in Java.

The first step in many Java interop scenarios is creating a Java object. Clojure provides the new special form for this purpose:

```
(new classname)
```

Try creating a new Random:

```
(new java.util.Random)
-> #object[java.util.Random 0x30dae81 "java.util.Random@30dae81"]
```

Another more frequently used shortcut for creating a new instance of a class is to append a trailing . to the class name:

```
(java.util.Random.)
-> #object[java.util.Random 0x133314b "java.util.Random@133314b"]
```

The REPL simply prints out the new Random instance indicating its class, hash code, and the result of calling its toString() method. To use a Random instance, you need to save it away somewhere. For now, simply use def to save the Random into a Clojure Var:

```
(def rnd (new java.util.Random))
-> #'user/rnd
```

Now you can call methods on rnd using Clojure's dot (.) special form:

```
(. class-or-instance member-symbol & args)
(. class-or-instance (member-symbol & args))
```

The . can call methods. For example, the following code calls the no-argument version of nextInt():

```
(. rnd nextInt)
-> -791474443
```

Random also has a nextInt() that takes an argument. You can call that version by adding the argument to the list:

```
(. rnd nextInt 10)
-> 8
```

The . syntax can also be used to access instance fields, static methods, and static fields:

```
;; Instance field
(def p (java.awt.Point. 10 20))
(. p x)
-> 10

;; Static method
(. System lineSeparator)
-> "\n"

;; Static field
(. Math PI)
-> 3.141592653589793
```

In cases where there are both a method and a field of the same name, the method will be preferred. The member name can be prefixed with a - to apply only to fields:

```
;; Instance field
(def p (java.awt.Point. 10 20))
(. p -x)
-> 10

;; Static field
(. Math -PI)
-> 3.141592653589793
```

However, Clojure also provides a more concise syntax for both instance and static access that is preferred:

```
(.method instance & args)
(.field instance)
(.-field instance)
(Class/method & args)
Class/field
```

Rewriting the examples above with the more concise style looks like this:

```
(.nextInt rnd 10)
-> 0

(.x p)    ;; or (.-x p)
-> 10

(System/lineSeparator)
-> "\n"
```

```
Math/PI
-> 3.141592653589793
```

Notice in the previous examples that Math is not fully qualified, because Clojure imports java.lang classes automatically. To avoid typing java.util.Random everywhere, you can import it:

```
(import (package-symbol & class-name-symbols)*)
```

import takes a variable number of lists, with the first part of each list being a package name and the rest being names to import from that package. The following import allows unqualified access to Random, Locale, and MessageFormat:

```
(import '(java.util Random Locale)
        '(java.text MessageFormat))
-> java.text.MessageFormat

Random
-> java.util.Random

Locale
-> java.util.Locale

MessageFormat
-> java.text.MessageFormat
```

At this point, you have almost everything you need to call Java from Clojure. You can do the following:

- Import class names
- Create instances
- Access fields
- Invoke methods

However, there isn't anything particularly exciting about the syntax. It's just "Java with different parentheses."

Although reaching into Java from Clojure is easy, remembering how all of the Java bits underneath work can be daunting. Clojure provides a javadoc function that will make your life much easier. This provides a pleasant experience from the REPL when exploring.

```
(javadoc java.net.URL)
```

Comments

There are several ways to create comments in Clojure. The most common is to use ;, which creates a comment to the end of the line. While everything after the first ; is ignored, you'll often see multiple semicolons to make a greater visual impact:

```
;; this is a comment
```

Clojure also contains a comment macro that ignores its body and returns nil. This is useful to wrap around a block of existing code. However, because it's still read by the Clojure reader, it must be valid code.

```
(comment
  (defn ignore-me []
    ;; not done yet
    ))
```

One common use of the comment macro is to save a chunk of utility or test code in a comment block at the end of the file, which is useful in combination with REPL-based development.

Clojure also contains a reader macro #_ to tell the reader to read the next form but ignore it.

```
(defn triple [number]
  #_(println "debug triple" number)
  (* 3 number))
```

In this example, the println expression is being read but ignored due to the #_ reader macro.

At this point, we've seen a broad overview of the basics of Clojure syntax. In the next section, we'll dive into the constructs that Clojure provides for flow control.

Flow Control

Clojure has very few flow control forms. In this section, you'll meet if, do, and loop/recur. As it turns out, this is almost all you'll ever need. Clojure provides a library of additional forms, but they're largely built from these primitives.

Branch with if

Clojure's if evaluates its first argument. If the argument is logically true, it returns the result of evaluating its second argument:

```
src/examples/exploring.clj
(defn is-small? [number]
  (if (< number 100) "yes"))

(is-small? 50)
-> "yes"
```

If the first argument to if is logically false, it returns nil:

```
(is-small? 50000)
-> nil
```

If you want to define a result for the "else" part of if, add it as a third argument:

```
src/examples/exploring.clj
(defn is-small? [number]
  (if (< number 100) "yes" "no"))

(is-small? 50000)
-> "no"
```

The when and when-not control flow macros are built on top of if and are described in *when and when-not*, on page 193.

Introduce Side Effects with do

Clojure's if allows only one form for each branch. What if you want to do more than one thing on a branch? For example, you might want to log that a certain branch was chosen. do takes any number of forms, evaluates them all, and returns the last.

You can use a do to print a logging statement from within an if:

```
src/examples/exploring.clj
(defn is-small? [number]
  (if (< number 100)
    "yes"
    (do
      (println "Saw a big number" number)
      "no")))
```

which results in:

```
(is-small? 200)
| Saw a big number 200
-> "no"
```

This is an example of a *side effect*. The println doesn't contribute to the return value of is-small? at all. Instead, it reaches into the world outside the function and actually *does something*.

Many programming languages mix pure functions and side effects in a completely ad hoc fashion. Not Clojure. In Clojure, side effects are explicit and unusual. do is one way to say "side effects to follow." Since do ignores the return values of all its forms except the last, those forms must have side effects to be of any use at all.

Recur with loop/recur

The Swiss Army knife of flow control in Clojure is loop:

```
(loop [bindings*] exprs*)
```

The loop special form works like let, establishing bindings and then evaluating exprs. The difference is that loop sets a *recursion point*, which can then be targeted by the recur special form:

```
(recur exprs*)
```

recur binds new values for loop's bindings and returns control to the top of the loop. For example, the following loop/recur returns a countdown:

```
src/examples/exploring.clj
(loop [result [] x 5]
  (if (zero? x)
    result
    (recur (conj result x) (dec x))))

-> [5 4 3 2 1]
```

The first time through, loop binds result to an empty vector and binds x to 5. Since x is not zero, recur then rebinds the names x and result:

- result binds to the previous result conjoined with the previous x.
- x binds to the decrement of the previous x.

Control then returns to the top of the loop. Since x is again not zero, the loop continues, accumulating the result and decrementing x. Eventually, x reaches zero, and the if terminates the recurrence, returning result.

Instead of using a loop, you can recur back to the top of a function. This makes it simple to write a function whose entire body acts as an implicit loop:

```
src/examples/exploring.clj
(defn countdown [result x]
  (if (zero? x)
    result
    (recur (conj result x) (dec x))))

(countdown [] 5)
-> [5 4 3 2 1]
```

recur is a powerful building block. But you may not use it very often, because many common recursions are provided by Clojure's sequence library.

For example, countdown could also be expressed as any of these:

```
(into [] (take 5 (iterate dec 5)))
-> [5 4 3 2 1]

(into [] (drop-last (reverse (range 6))))
-> [5 4 3 2 1]

(vec (reverse (rest (range 6))))
-> [5 4 3 2 1]
```

Don't expect these forms to make sense yet—just be aware that there are often alternatives to using recur directly. The sequence library functions used here are described in *Using the Sequence Library*, on page 56. Clojure *will not* perform automatic tail-call optimization (TCO). However, it will optimize calls to recur. Chapter 4, *Functional Programming*, on page 81 defines TCO and explores recursion and TCO in detail.

At this point, you've seen quite a few language features but still no variables. Some things really do vary, and Chapter 6, *State and Concurrency*, on page 137 will show you how Clojure deals with changeable *references*. But most variables in traditional languages are unnecessary and downright dangerous. Let's see how Clojure gets rid of them.

Where's My for Loop?

Clojure has no for loop and no direct mutable variables. Clojure provides *indirect* mutable references, but these must be explicitly called out in your code. See Chapter 6, *State and Concurrency*, on page 137 for details. So how do you write all that code you're accustomed to writing with for loops?

Rather than create a hypothetical example, we decided to grab a piece of open source Java code (sort of) randomly, find a method with some for loops and variables, and port it to Clojure. We opened the Apache Commons project, which is very widely used. We selected the StringUtils class in Commons Lang, assuming that such a class would require little domain knowledge to understand. We then browsed for a method that had multiple for loops and local variables and found indexOfAny:

data/snippets/StringUtils.java
```java
// From Apache Commons Lang, http://commons.apache.org/lang/
public static int indexOfAny(String str, char[] searchChars) {
    if (isEmpty(str) || ArrayUtils.isEmpty(searchChars)) {
        return -1;
    }
    for (int i = 0; i < str.length(); i++) {
        char ch = str.charAt(i);
        for (int j = 0; j < searchChars.length; j++) {
            if (searchChars[j] == ch) {
                return i;
            }
        }
    }
    return -1;
}
```

indexOfAny walks str and reports the index of the first char that matches any char in searchChars, returning -1 if no match is found.

Here are some example results from the documentation for indexOfAny:

```
StringUtils.indexOfAny(null, *)                    = -1
StringUtils.indexOfAny("", *)                      = -1
StringUtils.indexOfAny(*, null)                    = -1
StringUtils.indexOfAny(*, [])                      = -1
StringUtils.indexOfAny("zzabyycdxx",['z','a']) =  0
StringUtils.indexOfAny("zzabyycdxx",['b','y']) =  3
StringUtils.indexOfAny("aba", ['z'])           = -1
```

Two ifs, two fors, three possible points of return, and three mutable local variables are in indexOfAny, and the method is 14 lines long, as counted by David A. Wheeler's SLOCCount.[6]

Now let's build a Clojure index-of-any, step by step. If we just wanted to find the matches, we could use a Clojure filter. But we want to find the *index* of a match. So we create indexed, a function that takes a collection and returns an indexed collection:

src/examples/exploring.clj
```clojure
(defn indexed [coll] (map-indexed vector coll))
```

---

6. http://www.dwheeler.com/sloccount/

indexed returns a sequence of pairs of the form [idx elt]. Try indexing a string:

```
(indexed "abcde")
-> ([0 \a] [1 \b] [2 \c] [3 \d] [4 \e])
```

Next, we want to find the indices of all the characters in the string that match the search set.

Create an index-filter function that is similar to Clojure's filter but that returns the indices instead of the matches themselves:

```
src/examples/exploring.clj
(defn index-filter [pred coll]
  (when pred
    (for [[idx elt] (indexed coll) :when (pred elt)] idx)))
```

Clojure's for is *not* a loop but a sequence comprehension (see *Transforming Sequences*, on page 62). The index/element pairs of (indexed coll) are bound to the names idx and elt. The comprehension yields the value of idx for each matching pair, for only those pairs where (pred elt) is true.

Clojure sets are functions that test membership in the set. So you can pass a set of characters and a string to index-filter and get back the indices of all characters in the string that belong to the set. Try it with a few different strings and character sets:

```
(index-filter #{\a \b} "abcdbbb")
-> (0 1 4 5 6)

(index-filter #{\a \b} "xyz")
-> ()
```

At this point, we've accomplished *more* than the stated objective. index-filter returns the indices of all the matches, and we need only the first index. So, index-of-any simply takes the first result from index-filter:

```
src/examples/exploring.clj
(defn index-of-any [pred coll]
  (first (index-filter pred coll)))
```

Test that index-of-any works correctly with a few different inputs:

```
(index-of-any #{\z \a} "zzabyycdxx")
-> 0
(index-of-any #{\b \y} "zzabyycdxx")
-> 3
```

As the following table shows, the Clojure version is simpler than the imperative version by every metric.

Metric	LOC	Branches	Exits/Method	Variables
Imperative version	14	4	3	3
Functional version	6	1	1	0

What accounts for the difference?

- The imperative indexOfAny must deal with several special cases: null or empty strings, a null or empty set of search characters, and the absence of a match. These special cases add branches and exits to the method. With a functional approach, most of these kinds of special cases just work without any explicit code.

- The imperative indexOfAny introduces local variables to traverse collections (both the string and the character set). By using higher-order functions such as map and sequence comprehensions such as for, the functional index-of-any avoids all need for variables.

Unnecessary complexity tends to snowball. For example, the special case branches in the imperative indexOfAny use the magic number -1 to indicate a nonmatch. Should the magic number be a symbolic constant? Whatever you think the right answer is, *the question itself disappears* in the functional version. While shorter and simpler, the functional index-of-any is also *vastly more general*:

- indexOfAny searches a string, while index-of-any can search any sequence.

- indexOfAny matches against a set of characters, while index-of-any can match against any predicate.

- indexOfAny returns the first match, while index-filter returns all the matches and can be further composed with other filters.

As an example of how much more general the functional index-of-any is, you could use code like we just wrote to find the third occurrence of "heads" in a series of coin flips:

```
(nth
(index-filter #{:h} [:t :t :h :t :h :t :t :t :h :h])
2)
-> 8
```

So, writing index-of-any in a functional style, without loops or variables, is simpler, less error prone, and more general than the imperative indexOfAny. On larger units of code, these advantages become even more telling.

Wrapping Up

This has been a long chapter. But think about how much ground you've covered: you can work with basic Clojure data and collections, define and call functions, work with Java APIs, manage namespaces, and read and write metadata. You can write purely functional code, and yet you can easily introduce side effects when you need to. You've also met Lisp concepts including reader macros, special forms, and destructuring.

While we'll still introduce many features of Clojure in the remainder of the book, virtually all of it (macros are a notable counter-example) is built upon the syntax and structures introduced so far.

Next, we'll dive into sequences, a grand unifying abstraction over how we traverse and transform data in Clojure.

CHAPTER 3

Unifying Data with Sequences

Programs manipulate data. At the lowest level, programs work with structures such as strings, lists, vectors, maps, sets, and trees. At a higher level, these same data structure abstractions crop up again and again. For example:

- XML data is a tree.
- Database result sets can be viewed as lists or vectors.
- Directory hierarchies are trees.
- Files are often viewed as one big string or as a vector of lines.

In Clojure, all these data structures can be accessed through a single abstraction: the sequence (or *seq*).

A seq (pronounced "seek") is a *logical* list. It's logical because Clojure does not tie sequences to the concrete implementation details of the list data structure. Instead, the seq is an abstraction that can be used everywhere.

Collections that can be viewed as seqs are called *seq-able* (pronounced "SEEK-a-bull"). In this chapter, you'll meet a variety of seq-able collections:

- All Clojure collections
- All Java collections
- Java arrays and strings
- Regular expression matches
- Directory structures
- I/O streams
- XML trees

You'll also meet the sequence library, a set of functions that can work with any seq-able. Because so many things are sequences, the sequence library is much more powerful and general than the collection API in most languages. The sequence library includes functions to create, filter, and transform data.

These functions act as the collection API for Clojure, and they also replace many of the loops you would write in an imperative language.

In this chapter, you will become a power user of Clojure sequences. You'll see how to use a common set of very expressive functions with a wide range of datatypes. Then, in the next chapter (Chapter 4, *Functional Programming*, on page 81), you'll learn the functional style in which the sequence library is written.

Everything Is a Sequence

Every aggregate data structure in Clojure can be viewed as a sequence. A sequence has three core capabilities:

- You can get the first item in a sequence:

```
(first aseq)
```

first returns nil if its argument is empty or nil.

- You can get everything after the first item—the rest of a sequence:

```
(rest aseq)
```

rest returns an empty seq (not nil) if there are no more items.

- You can construct a new sequence by adding an item to the front of an existing sequence. This is called consing:

```
(cons elem aseq)
```

Under the hood, these three capabilities are declared in the Java interface clojure.lang.ISeq. (Keep this in mind when reading about Clojure, because the name ISeq is often used interchangeably with seq.)

The seq function will return a seq on any seq-able collection:

```
(seq coll)
```

seq will return nil if its coll is empty or nil. The next function will return the seq of items after the first:

```
(next aseq)
```

(next aseq) is equivalent to (seq (rest aseq)).

The seq functions work on lists:

```
(first '(1 2 3))
-> 1

(rest '(1 2 3))
-> (2 3)

(cons 0 '(1 2 3))
-> (0 1 2 3)
```

The seq functions work on all other Clojure data structures as well. For example, you can use the seq functions on vectors:

```
(first [1 2 3])
-> 1

(rest [1 2 3])
-> (2 3)

(cons 0 [1 2 3])
-> (0 1 2 3)
```

The Origin of Cons

Clojure's sequence is an abstraction based on Lisp's concrete lists. In the original implementation of Lisp, the three fundamental list operations were named car, cdr, and cons. car and cdr are acronyms that refer to implementation details of Lisp on the original IBM 704 platform. Many Lisps, including Clojure, replace these esoteric names with the more meaningful names first and rest.

The third function, cons, is short for construct. Lisp programmers use cons as a noun, verb, and adjective. You use cons to create a data structure called a *cons cell*, or just a *cons* for short.

Most Lisps, including Clojure, retain the original cons name, since "construct" is a pretty good mnemonic for what cons does. It also helps remind you that sequences are immutable. For convenience, you might say that cons adds an element to a sequence, but it's more accurate to say that cons *constructs* a new sequence, which is like the original sequence but with one element added.

When you apply rest or cons to a vector, the result is a seq, not a vector. In the REPL, seqs print just like lists, as you can see in the earlier output. You can check the actual returned type by using the seq? predicate:

```
(seq? (rest [1 2 3]))
-> true
```

The generality of seqs is very powerful, but sometimes you want to produce a specific implementation type. This is covered in *Calling Structure-Specific Functions*, on page 72.

You can treat maps as seqs, if you think of a map as a sequence of map entries (where each entry is a key/value pair):

```
(first {:fname "Aaron" :lname "Bedra"})
-> [:lname "Bedra"]

(rest {:fname "Aaron" :lname "Bedra"})
-> ([:fname "Aaron"])

(cons [:mname "James"] {:fname "Aaron" :lname "Bedra"})
-> ([:mname "James"] [:lname "Bedra"] [:fname "Aaron"])
```

You can also treat sets as seqs:

```
(first #{:the :quick :brown :fox})
-> :brown

(rest #{:the :quick :brown :fox})
-> (:quick :fox :the)

(cons :jumped #{:the :quick :brown :fox})
-> (:jumped :brown :quick :fox :the)
```

Maps and sets have a stable traversal order, but that order depends on implementation details, and you shouldn't rely on it. Elements of a set will not necessarily come back in the order that you put them in:

```
#{:the :quick :brown :fox}
-> #{:fox :the :quick :brown}
```

If you want a reliable order, you can use this:

```
(sorted-set & elements)
```

sorted-set will sort the values by their natural sort order:

```
(sorted-set :the :quick :brown :fox)
-> #{:brown :fox :quick :the}
```

Likewise, key/value pairs in maps won't necessarily come back in the order you put them in:

```
{:a 1 :b 2 :c 3}
-> {:a 1, :c 3, :b 2}
```

You can create a sorted map with sorted-map:

```
(sorted-map & elements)
```

sorted-maps won't come back in the order you put them in either, but they *will* come back sorted by key:

```
(sorted-map :c 3 :b 2 :a 1)
-> {:a 1, :b 2, :c 3}
```

In addition to the core capabilities of seq, two other capabilities are worth meeting immediately: conj and into.

```
(conj coll element & elements)
(into to-coll from-coll)
```

conj adds one or more elements to a collection, and into adds all the items in one collection to another. Both conj and into add items at an efficient insertion spot for the underlying data structure. For lists, conj and into add to the front:

```
(conj '(1 2 3) :a)
-> (:a 1 2 3)
(into '(1 2 3) '(:a :b :c))
-> (:c :b :a 1 2 3)
```

For vectors, conj and into add elements to the back:

```
(conj [1 2 3] :a)
-> [1 2 3 :a]
(into [1 2 3] [:a :b :c])
-> [1 2 3 :a :b :c]
```

Because conj (and related functions) do the efficient thing for the underlying data structure, you can often write code that is both efficient and completely decoupled from a specific underlying implementation.

The Clojure sequence library is particularly suited for large (or even infinite) sequences. Most Clojure sequences are *lazy*: they generate elements only when they are actually needed. Thus, Clojure's sequence functions can process sequences too large to fit in memory.

Clojure sequences are *immutable*: they never change. This makes it easier to reason about programs and means that Clojure sequences are safe for concurrent access. It does, however, create a small problem for human language. English-language descriptions flow much more smoothly when describing mutable things. Consider the following two descriptions for a hypothetical sequence function triple:

- triple triples each element of a sequence.
- triple takes a sequence and returns a new sequence with each element of the original sequence tripled.

> ## Why Do Functions on Vectors Return Lists?
>
> When you try examples at the REPL, the results of rest and cons appear to be lists, even when the inputs are vectors, maps, or sets. Does this mean that Clojure is converting everything to a list internally? No! The sequence functions always return a seq regardless of their inputs. You can verify this by using the seq? predicate:
>
> ```
> (list? (rest [1 2 3])
> -> false
>
> (seq? (rest [1 2 3]))
> -> true
> ```
>
> As you can see, the result of (rest [1 2 3]) is not a list but a sequence. Sequences are logical lists (but not concrete lists). Both lists and sequences print in the same way.

The latter version is specific and accurate. The former is much easier to read, but it might lead to the mistaken impression that a sequence is actually changing. Don't be fooled: *sequences never change.* If you see the phrase "foo changes x," mentally substitute "foo returns a changed copy of x."

Using the Sequence Library

The Clojure sequence library provides a rich set of functionality that can work with any sequence. If you come from an object-oriented background where nouns rule, the sequence library is truly "Revenge of the Verbs." The functions provide a rich backbone of functionality that can take advantage of any data structure that obeys the basic first/rest/cons contract.

The following functions are grouped into four broad categories:

- Functions that create sequences
- Functions that filter sequences
- Sequence predicates
- Functions that transform sequences

These divisions are somewhat arbitrary. Since sequences are immutable, *most* of the sequence functions create new sequences. Some of the sequence functions both filter and transform. Nevertheless, these divisions provide a rough road map through a large library.

Creating Sequences

Clojure provides a number of functions that create sequences. range produces a sequence from a start to an end, incrementing by step each time.

```
(range start? end? step?)
```

Ranges include their start but not their end. If you do not specify them, start defaults to zero, end defaults to positive infinity, and step defaults to 1. Try creating some ranges at the REPL:

```
(range 10)          ;; end only
-> (0 1 2 3 4 5 6 7 8 9)

(range 10 20)         ;; start + end
-> (10 11 12 13 14 15 16 17 18 19)

(range 1 25 2)         ;; step by 2
-> (1 3 5 7 9 11 13 15 17 19 21 23)

(range 0 -1 -0.25)  ;; negative step
-> (0 -0.25 -0.5 -0.75)

(range 1/2 4 1)       ;; ratios
-> (1/2 3/2 5/2 7/2)
```

The repeat function repeats an element x n times:

```
(repeat n x)
```

Try to repeat some items from the REPL:

```
(repeat 5 1)
-> (1 1 1 1 1)

(repeat 10 "x")
-> ("x" "x" "x" "x" "x" "x" "x" "x" "x" "x")
```

Both range and repeat represent ideas that can be extended infinitely.

iterate begins with a value x and continues forever, applying a function f to each value to calculate the next.

```
(iterate f x)
```

If you begin with 1 and iterate with inc, you can generate the whole numbers:

```
(take 10 (iterate inc 1))
-> (1 2 3 4 5 6 7 8 9 10)
```

Since the sequence is infinite, you need another new function to help you view the sequence from the REPL.

```
(take n sequence)
```

take returns a lazy sequence of the first n items from a collection and provides one way to create a finite view onto an infinite collection.

The whole numbers are a pretty useful sequence to have around, so let's def them for future use:

```
(def whole-numbers (iterate inc 1))
-> #'user/whole-numbers
```

When called with a single argument, repeat returns a lazy, infinite sequence:

```
(repeat x)
```

Try repeating at the REPL. Don't forget to wrap the result in a take:

```
(take 20 (repeat 1))
-> (1 1 1 1 1 1 1 1 1 1 1 1 1 1 1 1 1 1 1 1)
```

The cycle function takes a collection and cycles it infinitely:

```
(cycle coll)
```

Try cycling some collections at the REPL:

```
(take 10 (cycle (range 3)))
-> (0 1 2 0 1 2 0 1 2 0)
```

The interleave function takes multiple collections and produces a new collection that interleaves values from each collection until one of the collections is exhausted.

```
(interleave & colls)
```

When one of the collections is exhausted, the interleave stops. So, you can mix finite and infinite collections:

```
(interleave whole-numbers ["A" "B" "C" "D" "E"])
-> (1 "A" 2 "B" 3 "C" 4 "D" 5 "E")
```

Closely related to interleave is interpose, which returns a sequence with each of the elements of the input collection segregated by a separator:

```
(interpose separator coll)
```

You can use interpose to build delimited strings:

```
(interpose "," ["apples" "bananas" "grapes"])
-> ("apples" "," "bananas" "," "grapes")
```

interpose works nicely with (apply str ...) to produce output strings:

```
(apply str (interpose "," ["apples" "bananas" "grapes"]))
-> "apples,bananas,grapes"
```

The (apply str (interpose separator sequence)) idiom is common enough that Clojure provides a performance-optimized version as clojure.string/join:

```
(join separator sequence)
```

Use clojure.string/join to comma-delimit a list of words:

```
(require '[clojure.string :refer [join]])
(join \, ["apples" "bananas" "grapes"])
-> "apples,bananas,grapes"
```

For each collection type in Clojure, there is a function that takes an arbitrary number of arguments and creates a collection of that type:

```
(list & elements)
(vector & elements)
(hash-set & elements)
(hash-map key-1 val-1 ...)
```

hash-set has a cousin set that works a little differently: set expects a collection as its first argument:

```
(set [1 2 3])
-> #{1 2 3}
```

hash-set takes a variable list of arguments:

```
(hash-set 1 2 3)
-> #{1 2 3}
```

vector also has a cousin, vec, which takes a single collection argument instead of a variable argument list:

```
(vec (range 3))
-> [0 1 2]
```

Now that you have the basics of creating sequences, you can use other Clojure functions to filter and transform them.

Filtering Sequences

Clojure provides a number of functions that filter a sequence, returning a subsequence of the original sequence. The most basic of these is filter:

```
(filter pred coll)
```

filter takes a predicate and a collection and returns a sequence of objects for which the filter returns true (when interpreted in a Boolean context). You can filter the whole-numbers from the previous section to get the odd numbers or the even numbers:

```
(take 10 (filter even? whole-numbers))
-> (2 4 6 8 10 12 14 16 18 20)

(take 10 (filter odd? whole-numbers))
-> (1 3 5 7 9 11 13 15 17 19)
```

You can take from a sequence while a predicate remains true with take-while:

```
(take-while pred coll)
```

For example, to take all the characters in a string up to the first vowel, we can define some useful helper functions:

```
(def vowel? #{\a\e\i\o\u})
(def consonant? (complement vowel?))
```

Then use those predicates to take the characters from the string up to the first vowel:

```
(take-while consonant? "the-quick-brown-fox")
-> (\t \h)
```

A couple of interesting things are happening here:

- Sets act as functions that look up a value in the set and return either the value or nil if not found. So, you can read #{\a\e\i\o\u} as "the function that tests to see whether its argument is a vowel."

- complement reverses the behavior of another function. Here we create consonant? by defining it as the function that is the complement of vowel?.

The opposite of take-while is drop-while:

```
(drop-while pred coll)
```

drop-while drops elements from the beginning of a sequence while a predicate is true and then returns the rest. You could use drop-while to drop all leading non-vowels from a string:

```
(drop-while consonant? "the-quick-brown-fox")
-> (\e \- \q \u \i \c \k \- \b \r \o \w \n \- \f \o \x)
```

split-at and split-with will split a collection into two collections:

```
(split-at index coll)
(split-with pred coll)
```

split-at takes an index, and split-with takes a predicate:

```
(split-at 5 (range 10))
->[(0 1 2 3 4) (5 6 7 8 9)]
(split-with #(<= % 10) (range 0 20 2))
->[(0 2 4 6 8 10) (12 14 16 18)]
```

All the take-, split-, and drop- functions return lazy sequences, of course.

Sequence Predicates

Filter functions take a predicate and return a sequence. Closely related are the sequence predicates. A sequence predicate asks how some other predicate applies to every item in a sequence. For example, the every? predicate asks whether some other predicate is true for every element of a sequence.

```
(every? pred coll)
```

```
(every? odd? [1 3 5])
-> true
(every? odd? [1 3 5 8])
-> false
```

A lower bar is set by some:

```
(some pred coll)
```

some returns the first non-false value for its predicate or returns nil if no element matched:

```
(some even? [1 2 3])
-> true
(some even? [1 3 5])
-> nil
```

Notice that some does not end with a question mark. some is not a predicate, although it's often used like one. some returns the *actual value* of the first match instead of true. The distinction is invisible when you pair some with even?, since even? is itself a predicate. To see a non-true match, try using some with identity to find the first logically true value in a sequence:

```
(some identity [nil false 1 nil 2])
-> 1
```

A common use of some is to perform a linear search to see if a sequence contains a matching element, which is typically written as a set of a single element. For example to see if a sequence contains the value 3:

```
(some #{3} (range 20))
-> 3
```

Note that the value returned is the value in the sequence, which would act as a truthy value if this was used as a conditional test.

The behavior of the other predicates is obvious from their names:

```
(not-every? pred coll)
(not-any? pred coll)
```

Not every whole number is even:

```
(not-every? even? whole-numbers)
-> true
```

But it would be a lie to claim that not any whole number is even:

```
(not-any? even? whole-numbers)
-> false
```

Note that we picked questions to which we already knew the answer. In general, you have to be careful when applying predicates to infinite collections. They might run forever.

Transforming Sequences

Transformation functions transform the values in the sequence. The simplest transformation is map:

```
(map f coll)
```

map takes a source collection coll and a function f, and it returns a new sequence by invoking f on each element in the coll. You could use map to wrap every element in a collection with an HTML tag.

```
(map #(format "<p>%s</p>" %) ["the" "quick" "brown" "fox"])
-> ("<p>the</p>" "<p>quick</p>" "<p>brown</p>" "<p>fox</p>")
```

map can also take more than one collection argument. f must then be a function of multiple arguments. map will call f with one argument from each collection, stopping whenever the smallest collection is exhausted:

```
(map #(format "<%s>%s</%s>" %1 %2 %1)
["h1" "h2" "h3" "h1"] ["the" "quick" "brown" "fox"])
-> ("<h1>the</h1>" "<h2>quick</h2>" "<h3>brown</h3>"
"<h1>fox</h1>")
```

Another common transformation is reduce:

```
(reduce f coll)
```

f is a function of two arguments. reduce applies f on the first two elements in coll and then applies f to the result and the third element, and so on. reduce is useful for functions that "total up" a sequence in some way. You can use reduce to add items:

```
(reduce + (range 1 11))
-> 55
```

or to multiply them:

```
(reduce * (range 1 11))
-> 3628800
```

You can sort a collection with sort or sort-by:

```
(sort comp? coll)
(sort-by a-fn comp? coll)
```

sort sorts a collection by the natural order of its elements, where sort-by sorts a sequence by the result of calling a-fn on each element:

```
(sort [42 1 7 11])
 > (1 7 11 42)

(sort-by #(.toString %) [42 1 7 11])
-> (1 11 42 7)
```

If you don't want to sort by natural order, you can specify an optional comparison function comp for either sort or sort-by:

```
(sort > [42 1 7 11])
-> (42 11 7 1)

(sort-by :grade > [{:grade 83} {:grade 90} {:grade 77}])
-> ({:grade 90} {:grade 83} {:grade 77})
```

The granddaddy of all filters and transformations is the *list comprehension*. A list comprehension creates a list based on an existing list, using set notation. In other words, a comprehension states the properties that the result list must satisfy. In general, a list comprehension will consist of the following:

- Input list(s)
- Placeholder bindings for elements in the input lists
- Predicates on the elements
- An output form that produces output from the elements of the input lists that satisfy the predicates

Of course, Clojure generalizes the notion of list comprehension to *sequence* comprehension. Clojure comprehensions use the for macro. Note that the list comprehension for has nothing to do with the for loop found in imperative languages.

```
(for [binding-form coll-expr filter-expr? ...] expr)
```

for takes a vector of binding-form/coll-exprs, plus optional filter-exprs, and then yields a sequence of exprs.

List comprehension is more general than functions such as map and filter and can in fact emulate most of the filtering and transformation functions described earlier.

You can rewrite the previous map example as a list comprehension:

```
(for [word ["the" "quick" "brown" "fox"]]
  (format "<p>%s</p>" word))
-> ("<p>the</p>" "<p>quick</p>" "<p>brown</p>" "<p>fox</p>")
```

This reads almost like English: "For [each] word in [a sequence of words], format [according to format instructions]."

Comprehensions can emulate filter using a :when clause. You can pass even? to :when to filter the even numbers:

```
(take 10 (for [n whole-numbers :when (even? n)] n))
-> (2 4 6 8 10 12 14 16 18 20)
```

A :while clause continues the evaluation only while its expression holds true:

```
(for [n whole-numbers :while (even? n)] n)
-> ()
```

The real power of for comes when you work with more than one binding expression. For example, you can express all possible positions on a chessboard in algebraic notation by binding both rank and file:

```
(for [file "ABCDEFGH"
      rank (range 1 9)]
  (format "%c%d" file rank))
-> ("A1" "A2" ... elided ... "H7" ""H8")
```

Clojure iterates over the rightmost binding expression in a sequence comprehension first and then works its way left. Because rank is listed to the right of file in the binding form, rank iterates faster. If you want files to iterate faster, you can reverse the binding order and list rank first:

```
(for [rank (range 1 9)
      file "ABCDEFGH"]
  (format "%c%d" file rank))
-> ("A1" "B1" ... elided ... "G8" "H8")
```

In many languages, transformations, filters, and comprehensions do their work immediately. Do not assume this in Clojure. Most sequence functions do not traverse elements until you actually try to use them.

Lazy and Infinite Sequences

Most Clojure sequences are *lazy*; in other words, elements are not calculated until they're needed. Using lazy sequences has many benefits:

- You can postpone expensive computations that may not in fact be needed.
- You can work with huge data sets that don't fit into memory.
- You can delay I/O until it's absolutely needed.

Consider the code and following expression that produces (mostly) prime numbers using wheel factorization:[1]

```
src/examples/primes.clj
(ns examples.primes)
;; Taken from clojure.contrib.lazy-seqs
; primes cannot be written efficiently as a function, because
; it needs to look back on the whole sequence. contrast with
; fibs and powers-of-2 which only need a fixed buffer of 1 or 2
; previous values.
(def primes
  (concat
   [2 3 5 7]
   (lazy-seq
    (let [primes-from
          (fn primes-from [n [f & r]]
            (if (some #(zero? (rem n %))
                      (take-while #(<= (* % %) n) primes))
              (recur (+ n f) r)
              (lazy-seq (cons n (primes-from (+ n f) r)))))
          wheel (cycle [2 4 2 4 6 2 6 4 2 4 6 6 2 6  4  2
                        6 4 6 8 4 2 4 2 4 8 6 4 6 2  4  6
                        2 6 6 4 2 4 6 2 6 4 2 4 2 10 2 10])]
      (primes-from 11 wheel)))))

(require '[examples.primes :refer :all])
(def ordinals-and-primes (map vector (iterate inc 1) primes))
-> #'user/ordinals-and-primes
```

---

1. https://en.wikipedia.org/wiki/Wheel_factorization

ordinals-and-primes includes pairs like [5, 11] (11 is the fifth prime number). Both ordinals and primes are infinite, but ordinals-and-primes fits into memory just fine, because it's lazy. Just take what you need from it:

```
(take 5 (drop 1000 ordinals-and-primes))
-> ([1001 7927] [1002 7933] [1003 7937] [1004 7949] [1005 7951])
```

When should you prefer lazy sequences? Most of the time. Most sequence functions return lazy sequences, so you "pay" only for what you use. More important, lazy sequences do not require any special effort on your part. In the previous example, iterate, primes, and map return lazy sequences, so ordinals-and-primes gets laziness "for free."

Lazy sequences are critical to functional programming in Clojure. *How to Be Lazy*, on page 85 explores creating and using lazy sequences in much greater detail. Additionally, *Eager Transformations*, on page 107 talks about those cases when you should prefer non-lazy approaches.

When you're viewing a large sequence from the REPL, you may want to use take to prevent the REPL from evaluating the entire sequence. In other contexts, you may have the opposite problem. You've created a lazy sequence, and you want to force the sequence to evaluate fully. The problem usually arises when the code generating the sequence has side effects. Consider the following sequence, which embeds side effects via println:

```
(def x (for [i (range 1 3)] (do (println i) i)))
-> #'user/x
```

Newcomers to Clojure are surprised that the previous code prints nothing. Since the definition of x doesn't actually use the elements, Clojure does not evaluate the comprehension to get them. You can force evaluation with doall:

```
(doall coll)
```

doall forces Clojure to walk the elements of a sequence and returns the elements as a result:

```
(doall x)
| 1
| 2
-> (1 2)
```

You can also use dorun:

```
(dorun coll)
```

dorun walks the elements of a sequence without keeping past elements in memory. As a result, dorun can walk collections too large to fit in memory.

```
(def x (for [i (range 1 3)] (do (println i) i)))
-> #'user/x

(dorun x)
| 1
| 2
-> nil
```

The nil return value is a telltale reminder that dorun does not hold a reference to the entire sequence. The dorun and doall functions help you deal with side effects, while most of the rest of Clojure discourages side effects, so you'll usually not need these functions.

Clojure Makes Java Seq-able

The seq abstraction of first/rest applies to anything that there can be more than one of. In the Java world, that includes the following:

* The Collections API
* Regular expressions
* File system traversal
* XML processing
* Relational database results

Clojure wraps these Java APIs, making the sequence library available for almost everything you do.

Seq-ing Java Collections

If you try to apply the sequence functions to Java collections, you'll find that they behave as sequences. Collections that can act as sequences are called *seq-able*. For example, arrays are seq-able:

```
; String.getBytes returns a byte array
(first (.getBytes "hello"))
-> 104

(rest (.getBytes "hello"))
-> (101 108 108 111)

(cons (int \h) (.getBytes "ello"))
-> (104 101 108 108 111)
```

Hashtables and Maps are also seq-able:

```
; System.getProperties returns a Hashtable
(first (System/getProperties))
-> #object[java.util.Hashtable$Entry 0x12468a38
    "java.runtime.name=Java(TM) SE Runtime Environment"]

(rest (System/getProperties))
-> (#object[java.util.Hashtable$Entry 0x5b239d7d
    "sun.boot.library.path=/Library/... etc. ...
```

Remember that sequences are immutable, even when the underlying Java collection is mutable. So, you can't update the system properties by consing a new item onto (System/getProperties). cons will return a new sequence; the existing properties are unchanged.

Since strings are sequences of characters, they also are seq-able:

```
(first "Hello")
-> \H

(rest "Hello")
-> (\e \l \l \o)

(cons \H "ello")
-> (\H \e \l \l \o)
```

Clojure will automatically obtain a sequence from a collection, but it won't automatically convert a sequence back to the original collection type. With most collection types this behavior is intuitive, but with strings you'll often want to convert the result to a string. Consider reversing a string. Clojure provides reverse:

```
; probably not what you want
(reverse "hello")
-> (\o \l \l \e \h)
```

To convert a sequence back to a string, use (apply str seq):

```
(apply str (reverse "hello"))
-> "olleh"
```

The Java collections are seq-able, but for most scenarios, they don't offer advantages over Clojure's built-in collections. Prefer the Java collections only in interop scenarios where you're working with legacy Java APIs.

Seq-ing Regular Expressions

Clojure's regular expressions use the java.util.regex library under the hood. At the lowest level, this exposes the mutable nature of Java's Matcher. You can use re-matcher to create a Matcher for a regular expression and a string and then loop on re-find to iterate over the matches.

```
(re-matcher regexp string)
```

src/examples/sequences.clj
```
; don't do this!
(let [m (re-matcher #"\w+" "the quick brown fox")]
  (loop [match (re-find m)]
    (when match
      (println match)
      (recur (re-find m)))))
```
```
| the
| quick
| brown
| fox
-> nil
```

Much better is to use the higher-level re-seq.

```
(re-seq regexp string)
```

re-seq exposes an immutable seq over the matches. This gives you the power of all of Clojure's sequence functions. Try these expressions at the REPL:

```
(re-seq #"\w+" "the quick brown fox")
-> ("the" "quick" "brown" "fox")

(sort (re-seq #"\w+" "the quick brown fox"))
-> ("brown" "fox" "quick" "the")

(drop 2 (re-seq #"\w+" "the quick brown fox"))
-> ("brown" "fox")

(map clojure.string/upper-case (re-seq #"\w+" "the quick brown fox"))
-> ("THE" "QUICK" "BROWN" "FOX")
```

re-seq is an example of how good abstractions reduce code bloat. Regular expression matches are not a special thing, requiring special methods to deal with them. They are sequences, just like everything else. Thanks to the number of sequence functions, you get more functionality "for free" than you would likely end up with after a misguided foray into writing regexp-specific functions.

Seq-ing the File System

You can seq over the file system. For starters, you can call java.io.File directly:

```
(import 'java.io.File)
(.listFiles (File. "."))
-> [Ljava.io.File;@1f70f15e
```

The [Ljava.io.File… is Java's toString() representation for an array of Files. Sequence functions would call seq on this automatically, but the REPL doesn't.

So, seq it yourself:

```
(seq (.listFiles (File. ".")))
-> (#object[java.io.File 0x44fe9319 "./clojurebreaker"] ...)
```

If the default print format for files doesn't suit you, you could map them to a string form with getName:

```
; overkill
(map #(.getName %) (seq (.listFiles (File. "."))))
-> ("clojurebreaker" "data" ...)
```

Once you decide to use a function like map, calling seq is redundant. Sequence library functions call seq for you, so you don't have to. The previous code simplifies to this:

```
(map #(.getName %) (.listFiles (File. ".")))
-> ("clojurebreaker" "data" ...)
```

Often, you want to recursively traverse the entire directory tree. Clojure provides a depth-first walk via file-seq. If you file-seq from the sample code directory for this book, you will see a lot of files:

```
(count (file-seq (File. ".")))
-> 169
```

What if you want to see only the files that have been changed recently? Write a predicate recently-modified? that checks to see whether a file was touched in the last half hour:

src/examples/sequences.clj
```
(defn minutes-to-millis [mins] (* mins 1000 60))

(defn recently-modified? [file]
  (> (.lastModified file)
     (- (System/currentTimeMillis) (minutes-to-millis 30))))
```

Give it a try:

```
(filter recently-modified? (file-seq (File. ".")))
-> (./sequences ./sequences/sequences.clj)
```

Note that your results will vary from those shown here.

Seq-ing a Stream

In Java, a Reader provides a stream of characters. You can seq over the lines of any Java Reader using line-seq. To get a Reader, you can always use Clojure's clojure.java.io library. The clojure.java.io library provides a reader function that returns a reader on a stream, file, URL, or URI.

```
(require '[clojure.java.io :refer [reader]])
; leaves reader open...
(take 2 (line-seq (reader "src/examples/utils.clj")))
-> ("(ns examples.utils" "  (:import [java.io BufferedReader InputStreamReader]))")
```

Since readers can represent non-memory resources that need to be closed, you should wrap reader creation in a with-open. Create an expression that uses the sequence function count, to count the number of lines in a file, and uses with-open to correctly close the reader when the body is complete:

```
(with-open [rdr (reader "src/examples/utils.clj")]
  (count (line-seq rdr)))
-> 64
```

To make the example more useful, add a filter to count only non-blank lines:

```
(with-open [rdr (reader "src/examples/utils.clj")]
  (count (filter #(re-find #"\S" %) (line-seq rdr))))
-> 53
```

Using seqs both on the file system and on the contents of individual files, you can quickly create interesting utilities. Create a program that defines these three predicates:

- non-blank? detects non-blank lines.
- non-svn? detects files that are not Subversion metadata.
- clojure-source? detects Clojure source code files.

Then, create a clojure-loc function that counts the lines of Clojure code in a directory tree, using a combination of sequence functions along the way: reduce, for, count, and filter.

src/examples/sequences.clj
```
(use '[clojure.java.io :only (reader)])
(use '[clojure.string :only (blank?)])
(defn non-blank? [line] (not (blank? line)))

(defn non-svn? [file] (not (.contains (.toString file) ".svn")))

(defn clojure-source? [file] (.endsWith (.toString file) ".clj"))

(defn clojure-loc [base-file]
  (reduce
   +
   (for [file (file-seq base-file)
         :when (and (clojure-source? file) (non-svn? file))]
     (with-open [rdr (reader file)]
       (count (filter non-blank? (line-seq rdr)))))))
```

Now let's use clojure-loc to find out how much Clojure code is in Clojure itself:

```
(clojure-loc (java.io.File. "/home/abedra/src/opensource/clojure/clojure"))
-> 38716
```

The clojure-loc function is very task specific, but because it's built out of sequence functions and simple predicates, you can easily tweak it to very different tasks.

Calling Structure-Specific Functions

Clojure's sequence functions allow you to write very general code. Sometimes you'll want to be more specific and take advantage of the characteristics of a specific data structure. Clojure includes functions that specifically target lists, vectors, maps, structs, and sets.

We'll take a quick tour of some of these structure-specific functions next. For a complete list of structure-specific functions in Clojure, see the Data Structures section of the Clojure website.[2]

Functions on Lists

Clojure supports the traditional names peek and pop for retrieving the first element of a list and the remainder, respectively:

```
(peek coll)
(pop coll)
```

Give a simple list a peek and pop:

```
(peek '(1 2 3))
-> 1

(pop '(1 2 3))
-> (2 3)
```

peek is the same as first, but pop is *not* the same as rest. pop will throw an exception if the sequence is empty:

```
(rest ())
-> ()

(pop ())
-> java.lang.IllegalStateException: Can't pop empty list
```

---

2. https://clojure.org/reference/data_structures

Functions on Vectors

Vectors also support peek and pop, but they deal with the element at the end of the vector:

```
(peek [1 2 3])
-> 3

(pop [1 2 3])
-> [1 2]
```

get returns the value at an index or returns nil if the index is outside the vector:

```
(get [:a :b :c] 1)
-> :b

(get [:a :b :c] 5)
-> nil
```

Vectors are themselves functions. They take an index argument and return a value, or they throw an exception if the index is out of bounds:

```
([:a :b :c] 1)
-> :b

([:a :b :c] 5)
-> java.lang.IndexOutOfBoundsException
```

assoc associates a new value with a particular index:

```
(assoc [0 1 2 3 4] 2 :two)
-> [0 1 :two 3 4]
```

subvec returns a subvector of a vector:

```
(subvec avec start end?)
```

If end is not specified, it defaults to the end of the vector:

```
(subvec [1 2 3 4 5] 3)
-> [4 5]

(subvec [1 2 3 4 5] 1 3)
-> [2 3]
```

Of course, you could simulate subvec with a combination of drop and take:

```
(take 2 (drop 1 [1 2 3 4 5]))
-> (2 3)
```

The difference is that take and drop are general and can work with any sequence. On the other hand, subvec is *much* faster for vectors. Whenever a structure-specific function like subvec duplicates functionality already available in the sequence library, it's probably there for performance. The documentation string for functions like subvec includes performance characteristics.

Functions on Maps

Clojure provides several functions for reading the keys and values in a map. keys returns a sequence of the keys, and vals returns a sequence of the values:

```
(keys map)
(vals map)
```

Try taking keys and values from a simple map:

```
(keys {:sundance "spaniel", :darwin "beagle"})
-> (:sundance :darwin)

(vals {:sundance "spaniel", :darwin "beagle"})
-> ("spaniel" "beagle")
```

Note that while maps are unordered, both keys and vals are guaranteed to return the keys and values in the same order as a seq on the map.

get returns the value for a key or returns nil.

```
(get map key value-if-not-found?)
```

Use your REPL to test that get behaves as expected for keys both present and missing:

```
(get {:sundance "spaniel", :darwin "beagle"} :darwin)
-> "beagle"
(get {:sundance "spaniel", :darwin "beagle"} :snoopy)
-> nil
```

There's an approach that's even simpler than get. Maps are functions of their keys. So you can leave out the get entirely, putting the map in function position at the beginning of a form:

```
({:sundance "spaniel", :darwin "beagle"} :darwin)
-> "beagle"

({:sundance "spaniel", :darwin "beagle"} :snoopy)
-> nil
```

Keywords are also functions. They take a collection as an argument and look themselves up in the collection. Since :darwin and :sundance are keywords, the earlier forms can be written with their elements in reverse order.

```
(:darwin {:sundance "spaniel", :darwin "beagle"} )
-> "beagle"
```

```
(:snoopy {:sundance "spaniel", :darwin "beagle"} )
-> nil
```

If you look up a key in a map and get nil back, you can't tell whether the key was missing from the map or present with a value of nil. The contains? function solves this problem by testing for the mere presence of a key.

```
(contains? map key)
```

Create a map where nil is a legal value:

```
(def score {:stu nil :joey 100})
```

:stu is present, but if you see the nil value, you might not think so:

```
(:stu score)
-> nil
```

If you use contains?, you can verify that :stu is in the game, although presumably not doing very well:

```
(contains? score :stu)
-> true
```

Another approach is to call get, passing in an optional third argument that will be returned if the key is not found:

```
(get score :stu :score-not-found)
-> nil
```

```
(get score :aaron :score-not-found)
-> :score-not-found
```

The default return value of :score-not-found makes it possible to distinguish that :aaron is not in the map, while :stu is present with a value of nil.

If nil is a legal value in map, use contains? or the three-argument form of get to test the presence of a key.

Clojure also provides several functions for building new maps:

- assoc returns a map with a key/value pair added.
- dissoc returns a map with a key removed.
- select-keys returns a map, keeping only a specified set of keys.
- merge combines maps. If multiple maps contain a key, the rightmost wins.

To test these functions, create some song data:

src/examples/sequences.clj

```
(def song {:name "Agnus Dei"
           :artist "Krzysztof Penderecki"
           :album "Polish Requiem"
           :genre "Classical"})
```

Next, create various modified versions of the song collection:

```
(assoc song :kind "MPEG Audio File")
-> {:name "Agnus Dei", :album "Polish Requiem",
:kind "MPEG Audio File", :genre "Classical",
:artist "Krzysztof Penderecki"}

(dissoc song :genre)
-> {:name "Agnus Dei", :album "Polish Requiem",
:artist "Krzysztof Penderecki"}

(select-keys song [:name :artist])
-> {:name "Agnus Dei", :artist "Krzysztof Penderecki"}

(merge song {:size 8118166, :time 507245})
-> {:name "Agnus Dei", :album "Polish Requiem",
:genre "Classical", :size 8118166,
:artist "Krzysztof Penderecki", :time 507245}
```

Remember that song itself never changes. Each of these functions returns a new collection.

The most interesting map construction function is merge-with.

```
(merge-with merge-fn & maps)
```

merge-with is like merge, except that when two or more maps have the same key, you can specify your own function for combining the values under the key. Use merge-with and concat to build a sequence of values under each key:

```
(merge-with
  concat
  {:rubble ["Barney"], :flintstone ["Fred"]}
  {:rubble ["Betty"], :flintstone ["Wilma"]}
  {:rubble ["Bam-Bam"], :flintstone ["Pebbles"]})
  -> {:rubble ("Barney" "Betty" "Bam-Bam"),
      :flintstone ("Fred" "Wilma" "Pebbles")}
```

Starting with three distinct collections of family members keyed by last name, the previous code combines them into one collection keyed by last name.

Functions on Sets

In addition to the set functions in the clojure.core namespace, Clojure provides a group of functions in the clojure.set namespace. To use these functions with unqualified names, call (require '[clojure.set :refer :all]) from the REPL. For the following examples, you'll also need the following vars:

src/examples/sequences.clj
```
(def languages #{"java" "c" "d" "clojure"})
(def beverages #{"java" "chai" "pop"})
```

The first group of clojure.set functions performs operations from set theory:

- union returns the set of all elements present in either input set.

- intersection returns the set of all elements present in *both* input sets.

- difference returns the set of all elements present in the first input set, minus those in the second.

- select returns the set of all elements matching a predicate.

Write an expression that finds the union of all languages and beverages:

```
(union languages beverages)
-> #{"java" "c" "d" "clojure" "chai" "pop"}
```

Next, try the languages that are not also beverages:

```
(difference languages beverages)
-> #{"c" "d" "clojure"}
```

If you enjoy terrible puns, you'll like the fact that some things are both languages *and* beverages:

```
(intersection languages beverages)
-> #{"java"}
```

A number of languages can't afford a name larger than a single character:

```
(select #(= 1 (count %)) languages)
-> #{"c" "d"}
```

Set union and set difference are part of set theory, but they're also part of *relational algebra*, which is the basis for query languages such as SQL. Relational algebra consists of six primitive operators: set union and set difference (described earlier), plus rename, selection, projection, and cross product.

Clojure sets (and maps) have everything we need to implement a basic relational algebra system. We'll use maps to describe each tuple (like a row in a relational database) and a set to contain all of the tuples in a relation (like a table in a relational database).

The following examples work against an in-memory database of musical compositions. First, we'll define the data in our "database", which are just sets of maps:

src/examples/sequences.clj

```
(def compositions
  #{{:name "The Art of the Fugue" :composer "J. S. Bach"}
    {:name "Musical Offering" :composer "J. S. Bach"}
    {:name "Requiem" :composer "Giuseppe Verdi"}
    {:name "Requiem" :composer "W. A. Mozart"}})
(def composers
  #{{:composer "J. S. Bach" :country "Germany"}
    {:composer "W. A. Mozart" :country "Austria"}
    {:composer "Giuseppe Verdi" :country "Italy"}})
(def nations
  #{{:nation "Germany" :language "German"}
    {:nation "Austria" :language "German"}
    {:nation "Italy" :language "Italian"}})
```

The rename function renames keys (*database columns*) based on a map from original names to new names.

```
(rename relation rename-map)
```

Rename the compositions to use a title key instead of name:

```
(rename compositions {:name :title})
-> #{{:title "Requiem", :composer "Giuseppe Verdi"}
     {:title "Musical Offering", :composer "J.S. Bach"}
     {:title "Requiem", :composer "W. A. Mozart"}
     {:title "The Art of the Fugue", :composer "J.S. Bach"}}
```

The select function returns maps, for which a predicate is true, and is analogous to the WHERE portion of a SQL SELECT:

```
(select pred relation)
```

Write a select expression that finds all the compositions whose title is "Requiem":

```
(select #(= (:name %) "Requiem") compositions)
-> #{{:name "Requiem", :composer "W. A. Mozart"}
     {:name "Requiem", :composer "Giuseppe Verdi"}}
```

The project function returns only the parts of maps that match a set of keys.

```
(project relation keys)
```

project is similar to a SQL SELECT that specifies a subset of columns. Write a projection that returns only the name of the compositions:

```
(project compositions [:name])
-> #{{:name "Musical Offering"}
    {:name "Requiem"}
    {:name "The Art of the Fugue"}}
```

The final relational primitive, which is a cross product, is the foundation for the various kinds of joins in relational databases. The cross product returns every possible combination of rows in the different tables. You can do this easily enough in Clojure with a list comprehension:

```
(for [m compositions c composers] (concat m c))
-> ... 4 x 3 = 12 rows ...
```

Although the cross product is theoretically interesting, you'll typically want some subset of the full cross product. For example, you might want to join sets based on shared keys:

```
(join relation-1 relation-2 keymap?)
```

You can join the composition names and composers on the shared key :composer:

```
(join compositions composers)
-> #{{:name "Requiem", :country "Austria",
      :composer "W. A. Mozart"}
    {:name "Musical Offering", :country "Germany",
     :composer "J. S. Bach"}
    {:name "Requiem", :country "Italy",
     :composer "Giuseppe Verdi"}
    {:name "The Art of the Fugue", :country "Germany",
     :composer "J. S. Bach"}}
```

If the key names in the two relations don't match, you can pass a keymap that maps the key names in relation-1 to their corresponding keys in relation-2. For example, you can join composers, which uses :country, to nations, which uses :nation. For example:

```
(join composers nations {:country :nation})
-> #{{:language "German", :nation "Austria",
      :composer "W. A. Mozart", :country "Austria"}
    {:language "German", :nation "Germany",
     :composer "J. S. Bach", :country "Germany"}
    {:language "Italian", :nation "Italy",
     :composer "Giuseppe Verdi", :country "Italy"}}
```

You can combine the relational primitives. Perhaps you want to know the set of all countries that are home to the composer of a requiem. You can use select to find all the requiems, join them with their composers, and project to narrow the results to just the country names:

```
(project
  (join
    (select #(= (:name %) "Requiem") compositions)
            composers)
    [:country])
-> #{{:country "Italy"} {:country "Austria"}}
```

The analogy between Clojure's relational algebra and a relational database is instructive. Remember, though, that Clojure's relational algebra is a general-purpose tool. You can use it on any kind of set-relational data. And while you're using it, you have the entire power of Clojure and Java at your disposal.

Wrapping Up

Clojure unifies all kinds of collections under a single abstraction, the sequence. Clojure also provides a comprehensive library for working with data in the form of sequences. In combination, they provide a great deal of reuse across every Clojure application and library.

Clojure's sequences are implemented using functional programming techniques: immutable data, recursive definition, and lazy realization. In the next chapter, you'll see how to use these techniques directly, further expanding the power of Clojure.

CHAPTER 4

Functional Programming

Functional programming (FP) is a big topic, not to be learned in 21 days[1] or in a single chapter of a book. Nevertheless, you can reach a first level of effectiveness using lazy and recursive techniques in Clojure fairly quickly, and that is what we'll accomplish this chapter.

We'll start with a quick overview of FP terms and concepts and an introduction to the guidelines of Clojure FP that we'll refer to throughout the chapter. Next we'll experience the power of lazy sequences by working through a series of implementations of the Fibonacci numbers. As cool as lazy sequences are, you rarely need to construct them yourself, and we'll see better ways to recast problems to solve them directly with the sequence library.

We'll close with some advanced techniques and see some scenarios where eager transformations have advantages over lazy sequences.

Functional Programming Concepts

Functional programming leads to code that is easier to write, read, test, and reuse. Here's how it works.

Pure Functions

Programs are built out of *pure functions*. A pure function has no *side effects*; that is, it doesn't depend on anything but its arguments, and its only influence on the outside world is through its return value.

Mathematical functions are pure functions. Two plus two is four, no matter where or when you ask. Also, asking doesn't *do* anything other than return the answer.

---

1. http://norvig.com/21-days.html

Program output is decidedly *impure*. For example, when you println, you change the outside world by pushing data onto an output stream. Also, the results of println depend on state outside the function: the standard output stream might be redirected, closed, or broken.

If you start writing pure functions, you'll quickly realize that pure functions and *immutable* data go hand in hand. Consider the following mystery function:

```
(defn mystery [input]
  (if input data-1 data-2))
```

If mystery is a pure function, then regardless of what it does, data-1 and data-2 have to be immutable! Otherwise, changes to the data would cause the function to return different values for the same input.

A single piece of mutable data can ruin the game, rendering an entire call chain of functions impure. So, once you make a commitment to writing pure functions, you end up using immutable data in large sections of your application.

Persistent Data Structures

Immutable data is critical to Clojure's approach to both FP and state. On the FP side, pure functions cannot have side effects, such as updating the state of a mutable object. On the state side, Clojure's reference types require immutable data structures to implement their concurrency guarantees.

The fly in the ointment is performance. When all data is immutable, "update" translates into "create a copy of the original data, plus my changes." This will use up memory quickly! Imagine that you have an address book that takes up 5 MB of memory. Then, you make five small updates. With a mutable address book, you are still consuming about 5 MB of memory. But if you have to copy the whole address book for each update, then an immutable version would balloon to 25 MB!

Clojure's data structures don't take this naive "copy everything" approach. Instead, all Clojure data structures are *persistent*. In this context, persistent means that the data structures preserve old copies of themselves by efficiently *sharing structure* between older and newer versions.

Structural sharing is easiest to visualize with a list. Consider list a with two elements:

```
(def a '(1 2))
-> #'user/a
```

Then from a, you can create a b with an additional element added:

```
(def b (cons 0 a))
-> #'user/b
```

b can reuse all of a's structure, rather than have its own private copy:

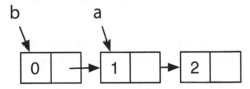

All of Clojure's data structures share structure where possible. For structures other than simple lists, the mechanics are more complex, of course. If you're interested in the details, check out the following articles:

- "Ideal Hash Trees"[2] by Phil Bagwell
- "Understanding Clojure's PersistentVector Implementation"[3] by Karl Krukow

Laziness and Recursion

Functional programs make heavy use of *recursion* and *laziness*. A recursion occurs when a function calls itself, either directly or indirectly. With laziness, an expression's evaluation is postponed until it's actually needed. Evaluating a lazy expression is called *realizing* the expression.

In Clojure, functions and expressions are not lazy. However, sequences *are* generally lazy. Because so much Clojure programming is sequence manipulation, you get many of the benefits of a fully lazy language. In particular, you can build complex expressions using lazy sequences and then "pay" only for the elements you actually need.

Lazy techniques imply pure functions. You never have to worry about when to call a pure function, since it always returns the same thing. Impure functions, on the other hand, do not play well with lazy techniques. As a programmer, you must explicitly control when an impure function is called, because if you call it at some other time, it may behave differently!

Referential Transparency

Laziness depends on the ability to replace a function call with its result at any time. Functions that have this ability are called *referentially transparent*,

---

2. http://lampwww.epfl.ch/papers/idealhashtrees.pdf
3. http://tinyurl.com/clojure-persistent-vector

because calls to such functions can be replaced without affecting the behavior of the program. In addition to laziness, referentially transparent functions can also benefit from the following:

- *Memoization*, automatic caching of results
- Automatic *parallelization*, moving function evaluation to another processor or machine

Pure functions are referentially transparent *by definition*. Most other functions are *not* referentially transparent, and those that are must be proven safe by code review.

Benefits of FP

Well, that is a lot of terminology, and we promised it would make your code easier to write, read, test, and compose. Here's how.

You'll find functional code easier to *write* because the relevant information is right in front of you, in a function's argument list. You don't have to worry about global scope, session scope, application scope, or thread scope. Functional code is easier to *read* for exactly the same reason.

Code that is easier to read and write is going to be easier to test, but functional code brings an additional benefit for testing. As projects get large, it often takes a lot of effort to set up the right environment to execute a test. This is much less of a problem with functional code, because there *is no relevant environment* beyond the function's arguments.

Functional code improves *reuse*. To reuse code, you must be able to do the following:

- Find and understand a piece of useful code.
- Compose the reusable code with other code.

The readability of functional code helps you find and understand the functions you need, but the benefit for *composing* code is even more compelling.

Composability is a hard problem. For years, programmers have used *encapsulation* to try to create composable code. Encapsulation creates a firewall, providing access to data only through a public API.

Encapsulation helps, but it's nowhere near enough. Even with encapsulated objects, there are far too many surprising interactions when you try to compose entire systems. The problem is those darn side effects. *Impure functions* violate encapsulation, because they let the outside world reach in (invisibly!) and change the behavior of your code. Pure functions, on the other hand, are truly encapsulated and composable. Put them anywhere you want in a system, and they will always behave in the same way.

Guidelines for Use

Clojure takes a unique approach to FP that strikes a balance between academic purity and the reality of running well on the JVM. That means there's a lot to learn all at once. But fear not. If you're new to FP, the following guidelines will help on your initial steps toward FP mastery, Clojure-style:

1. Avoid direct recursion. The JVM can't optimize recursive calls, and Clojure programs that recurse will blow their stack.

2. Use recur when you're producing scalar values or small, fixed sequences. Clojure *will* optimize calls that use an explicit recur.

3. When producing large or variable-sized sequences, always be lazy. (Do *not* recur.) Then, your callers can consume just the part of the sequence they actually need.

4. Be careful not to realize more of a lazy sequence than you need.

5. Know the sequence library. You can often write code without using recur or the lazy APIs at all.

6. Subdivide. Divide even simple-seeming problems into smaller pieces, and you'll often find solutions in the sequence library that lead to more general, reusable code.

The last two guidelines are particularly important. If you're new to FP, you can translate those to: "Ignore this chapter and just use the techniques in Chapter 3, *Unifying Data with Sequences*, on page 51 until you hit a wall."

Now, let's get started writing functional code.

How to Be Lazy

Before we get to laziness, we first need to delve into recursion as an approach to enumerating sequences of values.

Functional programs make great use of *recursive definitions*. A recursive definition consists of two parts:

- A *basis*, which explicitly enumerates some members of the sequence
- An *induction*, which provides rules for combining members of the sequence to produce additional members

Our challenge in this section is converting a recursive definition into working code. You might do this in several ways:

- A simple recursion, using a function that calls itself in some way to implement the induction step.

- A tail recursion, using a function calling itself only at the tail end of its execution. Tail recursion enables an important optimization.

- A lazy sequence that eliminates actual recursion and calculates a value later, when it's needed.

Choosing the right approach is important. Implementing a recursive definition poorly can lead to code that performs terribly, consumes all available stack and fails, consumes all available heap and fails, or does all of these. In Clojure, being lazy is often the right approach.

We'll explore all of these approaches by applying them to the Fibonacci numbers. Named for the Italian mathematician Leonardo (Fibonacci) of Pisa (c.1170–c.1250), the Fibonacci numbers were actually known to Indian mathematicians as far back as 200 BC. The Fibonacci numbers have many interesting properties, and they crop up again and again in algorithms, data structures, and even biology.[4] The Fibonaccis have a very simple recursive definition:

- Basis: F_0, the zeroth Fibonacci number, is zero. F_1, the first Fibonacci number, is one.

- Induction: For $n > 1$, F_n equals $F_{n-1} + F_{n-2}$.

Using this definition, the first 10 Fibonacci numbers are as follows:

(0 1 1 2 3 5 8 13 21 34)

Let's begin by implementing the Fibonaccis using a simple recursion. The following Clojure function will return the *nth* Fibonacci number:

src/examples/functional.clj
```
; bad idea
(defn stack-consuming-fibo [n]
  (cond
   (= n 0) 0
   (= n 1) 1
   :else (+ (stack-consuming-fibo (- n 1))
            (stack-consuming-fibo (- n 2))))))
```

---

4. http://en.wikipedia.org/wiki/Fibonacci_number

Lines 4 and 5 define the basis, and line 6 defines the induction. The implementation is recursive because stack-consuming-fibo calls itself on lines 6 and 7.

Test that stack-consuming-fibo works correctly for small values of n:

```
(stack-consuming-fibo 9)
-> 34
```

Good so far, but there's a problem calculating larger Fibonacci numbers such as $F_{1000000}$:

```
(stack-consuming-fibo 1000000)
-> StackOverflowError clojure.lang.Numbers.minus (Numbers.java:1837)
```

Because of the recursion, each call to stack-consuming-fibo for $n > 1$ begets two more calls to stack-consuming-fibo. At the JVM level, these calls are translated into method calls, each of which allocates a data structure called a *stack frame*.[5]

The stack-consuming-fibo creates a depth of stack frames proportional to n, which quickly exhausts the JVM stack and causes the StackOverflowError shown earlier. (It also creates a total number of stack frames that's exponential in n, so its performance is terrible even when the stack does not overflow.)

Clojure function calls are designated as *stack-consuming* because they allocate stack frames that use up stack space. In Clojure, you should almost always avoid stack-consuming recursion as shown in stack-consuming-fibo.

Tail Recursion

Functional programs can solve the stack-usage problem with *tail recursion*. A tail-recursive function is still defined recursively, but the recursion must come at the tail, that is, at an expression that's a return value of the function. Languages can then perform *tail-call optimization* (TCO), converting tail recursions into iterations that don't consume the stack.

The stack-consuming-fibo definition of Fibonacci is not tail recursive, because it calls add (+) *after* both calls to stack-consuming-fibo. To make fibo tail recursive, you must create a function whose arguments carry enough information to move the induction forward, without any extra "after" work (like an addition) that would push the recursion out of the tail position. For fibo, such a function needs to know two Fibonacci numbers, plus an ordinal n that can count down to zero as new Fibonaccis are calculated. You can write tail-fibo as follows:

---

5. http://tinyurl.com/jvm-spec-toc

```
                 src/examples/functional.clj
Line 1  (defn tail-fibo [n]
     2    (letfn [(fib
     3             [current next n]
     4             (if (zero? n)
     5               current
     6               (fib next (+ current next) (dec n))))]
     7      (fib 0N 1N n)))
```

Line 2 introduces the letfn macro:

```
(letfn fnspecs & body) ; fnspecs ==> [(fname [params*] exprs)+]
```

letfn is like let but is dedicated to creating local functions. Each function declared in a letfn can call itself or any other function in the same letfn block. Line 3 declares that fib has three arguments: the current Fibonacci, the next Fibonacci, and the number n of steps remaining.

Line 5 returns current when there are no steps remaining, and line 6 continues the calculation, decrementing the remaining steps by one. Finally, line 7 kicks off the recursion with the basis values 0 and 1, plus the ordinal n of the Fibonacci we're looking for.

tail-fibo works for small values of n:

```
(tail-fibo 9)
-> 34N
```

But although it's tail recursive, it still fails for large n:

```
(tail-fibo 1000000)
-> StackOverflowError java.lang.Integer.numberOfLeadingZeros (Integer.java:1054)
```

The problem here is the JVM. While functional languages such as Scheme or Haskell perform TCO, the JVM doesn't perform this optimization. The absence of TCO is unfortunate but not a showstopper for functional programs.

Clojure provides several pragmatic workarounds: explicit self-recursion with recur, lazy sequences, and explicit mutual recursion with trampoline. We'll discuss the first two here and defer the discussion of trampoline, which is a more advanced feature, until later in the chapter.

Self-recursion with recur

One special (and common) case of recursion that *can* be optimized away on the JVM is self-recursion. Fortunately, the tail-fibo is an example: it calls itself directly, not through some series of intermediate functions.

In Clojure, you can convert a function that tail-calls itself into an explicit self-recursion with recur. Using this approach, convert tail-fibo into recur-fibo:

```
src/examples/functional.clj
Line 1  ; better but not great
     2  (defn recur-fibo [n]
     3    (letfn [(fib
     4               [current next n]
     5               (if (zero? n)
     6                 current
     7                 (recur next (+ current next) (dec n))))]
     8      (fib 0N 1N n)))
```

The critical difference between tail-fibo and recur-fibo is on line 7, where recur replaces the call to fib.

The recur-fibo won't consume stack as it calculates Fibonacci numbers and can calculate F_n for large n if you have the patience:

```
(recur-fibo 9)
-> 34N

(recur-fibo 1000000)
-> 195 ... 208,982 other digits ... 875N
```

The complete value of $F_{1000000}$ is included in the sample code at output/f-1000000.

The recur-fibo calculates one Fibonacci number. But what if you want several? Calling recur-fibo multiple times would be wasteful, since none of the work from any call to recur-fibo is cached for the next call. But how many values should be cached? Which ones? These choices should be made by the *caller* of the function, not the implementer.

Ideally, you'd define sequences with an API that makes *no reference* to the specific range that a particular client cares about and then let clients pull the range they want with take and drop. This is exactly what lazy sequences provide.

Lazy Sequences

Lazy sequences are constructed using the macro lazy-seq:

```
(lazy-seq & body)
```

A lazy-seq invokes its body only when needed, that is, when seq is called directly or indirectly. lazy-seq then caches the result for subsequent calls. You can use lazy-seq to define a lazy Fibonacci series as follows:

```
src/examples/functional.clj
Line 1  (defn lazy-seq-fibo
     2    ([]
     3      (concat [0 1] (lazy-seq-fibo 0N 1N)))
     4    ([a b]
     5      (let [n (+ a b)]
     6        (lazy-seq
     7          (cons n (lazy-seq-fibo b n)))))))
```

On line 3, the zero-argument body returns the concatenation of the basis values [0 1] and then calls the two-argument body to calculate the rest of the values. On line 5, the two-argument body calculates the next value n in the series, and on line 7 it conses n onto the rest of the values.

The key is line 6, which makes its body lazy. Without this, the recursive call to lazy-seq-fibo on line 7 would happen immediately, and lazy-seq-fibo would recurse until it blew the stack. This illustrates the general pattern: wrap the recursive part of a function body with lazy-seq to replace recursion with laziness.

lazy-seq-fibo works for small values:

```
(take 10 (lazy-seq-fibo))
-> (0 1 1N 2N 3N 5N 8N 13N 21N 34N)
```

lazy-seq-fibo also works for large values. Use (rem ... 1000) to print only the last three digits of the one millionth Fibonacci number:

```
(rem (nth (lazy-seq-fibo) 1000000) 1000)
-> 875N
```

The lazy-seq-fibo approach follows guideline #3 on page 85, using laziness to implement an infinite sequence. But as is often the case, you don't need to explicitly call lazy-seq yourself. By guideline #5, you can reuse existing sequence library functions that return lazy sequences. Consider this use of iterate:

```
(take 5 (iterate (fn [[a b]] [b (+ a b)]) [0 1]))
-> ([0 1] [1 1] [1 2] [2 3] [3 5])
```

The iterate begins with the first pair of Fibonacci numbers: [0 1]. Working by pairs, it then calculates the Fibonaccis by carrying along just enough information (two values) to calculate the next value.

The Fibonaccis are simply the first value of each pair. They can be extracted by calling map first over the entire sequence, leading to the following definition of fibo suggested by Christophe Grand:

```
src/examples/functional.clj
(defn fibo []
  (map first (iterate (fn [[a b]] [b (+ a b)]) [0N 1N])))
```

fibo returns a lazy sequence because it builds on map and iterate, which also return lazy sequences. fibo is also *simple*. fibo is the shortest implementation we've seen so far. But if you're accustomed to writing imperative, looping code, correctly *choosing* fibo over other approaches may not seem simple at all! Learning to think recursively, lazily, and within the JVM's limitations on recursion—all at the same time—can be intimidating. Let the guidelines on page 85 help you. The Fibonacci numbers are infinite: guideline #3 correctly predicts that the right approach in Clojure will be a lazy sequence, and guideline #5 lets the existing sequence functions do most of the work.

Lazy definitions consume *some* stack and heap. But they don't consume resources proportional to the size of an entire (possibly infinite!) sequence. Instead, *you choose* how many resources to consume when you traverse the sequence. If you want the one millionth Fibonacci number, you can get it from fibo, without having to consume stack or heap space for all the previous values.

There's no such thing as a free lunch. But with lazy sequences, you can have an infinite menu and pay only for the menu items you're eating at a given moment. When writing Clojure programs, you should prefer lazy sequences over loop/recur for any sequence that varies in size and for any large sequence.

Coming to Realization

Lazy sequences consume significant resources only as they are *realized*, that is, when a portion of the sequence is actually instantiated in memory. Clojure works hard to be lazy and avoid realizing sequences until it's absolutely necessary. For example, take returns a lazy sequence and does no realization at all. You can see this by creating a var to hold, say, the first billion Fibonacci numbers:

```
(def lots-o-fibs (take 1000000000 (fibo)))
-> #'user/lots-o-fibs
```

The creation of lots-o-fibs returns almost immediately, because it does *almost nothing*. If you ever call a function that needs to *actually use* some values in lots-o-fibs, Clojure will calculate them. Even then, it'll do only what's necessary. For example, the following will return the 100th Fibonacci number from lots-o-fibs, without calculating the millions of other numbers that lots-o-fibs promises to provide:

```
(nth lots-o-fibs 100)
-> 354224848179261915075N
```

Most sequence functions return lazy sequences. If you aren't sure whether a function returns a lazy sequence, the function's documentation string typically will tell you the answer:

```
(doc take)
-------------------------
clojure.core/take
([n coll])
Returns a lazy seq of the first n items in coll, or all items if
there are fewer than n.
```

The REPL, however, is *not lazy*. The printer used by the REPL will, by default, print the entirety of a collection. That's why we stuffed the first billion Fibonaccis into lots-o-fibs, instead of evaluating them at the REPL. Don't enter the following at the REPL:

```
; don't do this
(take 1000000000 (fibo))
```

If you enter the previous expression, the printer will attempt to print a billion Fibonacci numbers, realizing the entire collection as it goes. You'll probably get bored and exit the REPL before Clojure runs out of memory.

As a convenience for working with lazy sequences, you can configure how many items the printer will print by setting the value of *print-length*:

```
(set! *print-length* 10)
-> 10
```

For collections with more than 10 items, the printer will now print only the first 10 followed by an ellipsis. So, you can safely print a billion fibos:

```
(take 1000000000 (fibo))
-> (0N 1N 1N 2N 3N 5N 8N 13N 21N 34N ...)
```

Or even all the fibos:

```
(fibo)
-> (0N 1N 1N 2N 3N 5N 8N 13N 21N 34N ...)
```

Lazy sequences are wonderful. They do only what's needed, and for the most part, you don't have to worry about them. If you ever want to force a sequence to be fully realized, you can use either doall or dorun, discussed in *Lazy and Infinite Sequences*, on page 65.

Losing Your Head

There's one last thing to consider when working with lazy sequences. Lazy sequences let you define a large (possibly infinite) sequence and then work with a small part of that sequence in memory at a given moment. This clever ploy will fail if you (or some API) unintentionally hold a reference to the part of the sequence you no longer care about.

The most common way this can happen is if you accidentally hold the head (first item) of a sequence. In the examples in previous sections, each variant of the Fibonacci numbers was defined as a function returning a sequence, not the sequence itself.

You could define the sequence directly as a top-level var:

```
src/examples/functional.clj
; holds the head (avoid!)
(def head-fibo (lazy-cat [0N 1N] (map + head-fibo (rest head-fibo))))
```

This definition uses lazy-cat, which is like concat except that the arguments are evaluated only when needed. This is a very pretty definition, in that it defines the recursion by mapping a sum over (each element of the Fibonaccis) and (each element of the *rest* of the Fibonaccis).

head-fibo works great for small Fibonacci numbers:

```
(take 10 head-fibo)
-> (0N 1N 1N 2N 3N 5N 8N 13N 21N 34N)
```

but not so well for huge ones:

```
(nth head-fibo 1000000)
-> java.lang.OutOfMemoryError: GC overhead limit exceeded
```

The problem is that the top-level var head-fibo *holds the head* of the collection. This prevents the garbage collector from reclaiming elements of the sequence after you've moved past those elements. So, any part of the Fibonacci sequence that you actually use gets cached for the life of the value referenced by head-fibo, which is likely to be the life of the program.

Unless you want to cache a sequence as you traverse it, you must be careful not to keep a reference to the head of the sequence. As the head-fibo example demonstrates, you should normally expose lazy sequences as a function that *returns* the sequence, not as a var that *contains* the sequence. If a caller of your function wants an explicit cache, the caller can always create its own var. With lazy sequences, losing your head is often a good idea.

Lazier Than Lazy

Clojure's lazy sequences are a great form of laziness at the language level. As a programmer, you can be *even lazier* by finding solutions that don't require explicit sequence manipulation at all. You can often combine existing sequence functions to solve a problem, without having to get your hands dirty at the level of recur or lazy sequences.

As an example of this, let's implement several solutions to the following problem. You are given a sequence of coin-toss results, where heads is :h and tails is :t:

```
[:h :t :t :h :h :h]
```

How many times in the sequence does heads come up twice in a row? In the previous example, the answer is two. Toss 3 and toss 4 are both heads, and toss 4 and toss 5 are both heads.

The sequence of coin tosses might be very large, but it'll be finite. Since you're looking for a scalar answer (a count), by rule 2, it's acceptable to use recur:

src/examples/functional.clj
```
Line 1  (defn count-heads-pairs [coll]
     2    (loop [cnt 0 coll coll]
     3      (if (empty? coll)
     4        cnt
     5        (recur (if (= :h (first coll) (second coll))
     6                 (inc cnt)
     7                 cnt)
     8               (rest coll)))))
```

Since the purpose of the function is to count something, the loop introduces a cnt binding, initially zero on line 2. The loop also introduces its own binding for the coll, so that we can shrink the coll each time through the recur. Line 3 provides the basis for the recurrence. If a sequence of coin tosses is empty, it certainly has zero runs of two heads in a row.

Line 5 is the meat of the function, incrementing the cnt by one if the first and second items of coll are both heads (:h).

Try a few inputs to see that count-heads-pairs works as advertised:

```
(count-heads-pairs [:h :h :h :t :h])
-> 2

(count-heads-pairs [:h :t :h :t :h])
-> 0
```

Although count-heads-pairs works, it fails as code prose. The key notion of "two in a rowness" is obscured by the boilerplate for loop/recur. To fix this, you need to use guidelines 5 and 6, subdividing the problem to take advantage of Clojure's sequence library.

Transforming the Input Sequence

The first problem you encounter is that almost all the sequence functions do something to each element in a sequence in turn. This doesn't help us at all, since we want to look at each element in the context of its immediate neighbors. So, let's transform the sequence. When you see this:

```
[:h :t :t :h :h :h]
```

you should mentally translate that into a sequence of every adjacent pair:

```
[[:h :t] [:t :t] [:t :h] [:h :h] [:h :h]]
```

Write a function named by-pairs that performs this transformation. Because the output of by-pairs varies based on the size of its input, according to rule 3, you should build this sequence lazily:

src/examples/functional.clj
```
Line 1  ; overly complex, better approaches follow...
     2  (defn by-pairs [coll]
     3    (let [take-pair (fn [c]
     4                      (when (next c) (take 2 c)))]
     5      (lazy-seq
     6        (when-let [pair (seq (take-pair coll))]
     7          (cons pair (by-pairs (rest coll)))))))
```

Line 3 defines a function that takes the first pair of elements from the collection. Line 5 ensures that the recursion is evaluated lazily.

Line 6 is a conditional: if the next pair doesn't contain two elements, we must be (almost) at the end of the list, and we implicitly terminate. If we do get two elements, then on line 7, we continue building the sequence by consing our pair onto the pairs to be had from the rest of the collection.

Check that by-pairs works:

```
(by-pairs [:h :t  :t :h :h :h])
-> ((:h :t) (:t :t) (:t :h) (:h :h) (:h :h))
```

Now that we can think of the coin tosses as a sequence *of pairs* of results, it's easy to describe count-heads-pairs in English:

"Count the pairs of results that are all heads."

This English description translates directly into existing sequence library functions: "Count" is count, of course, and "that are all heads" suggests a filter:

src/examples/functional.clj
```
(defn count-heads-pairs [coll]
  (count (filter (fn [pair] (every? #(= :h %) pair))
                 (by-pairs coll))))
```

This is much more expressive than the recur-based implementation, and it makes clear that we're counting all the adjacent pairs of heads. But we can make things even simpler. Clojure already has a more general version of by-pairs named partition:

```
(partition size step? coll)
```

partition breaks a collection into chunks of size size. So, you could break a heads/tails vector into a sequence of pairs:

```
(partition 2 [:h :t  :t :h :h :h])
-> ((:h :t) (:t :h) (:h :h))
```

This isn't quite the same as by-pairs, which yields overlapping pairs. But partition can do overlaps, too. The optional step argument determines how far partition moves down the collection before starting its next chunk. If not specified, step is the same as size. To make partition work like by-pairs, set size to 2 and set step to 1:

```
(partition 2 1 [:h :t  :t :h :h :h])
-> ((:h :t) (:t :t) (:t :h) (:h :h) (:h :h))

(by-pairs [:h :t  :t :h :h :h])
-> ((:h :t) (:t :t) (:t :h) (:h :h) (:h :h))
```

Another possible area of improvement is the count/filter idiom used to count the pairs that are both heads. This combination comes up often enough that it's worth encapsulating in a count-if function:

```
src/examples/functional.clj
(def ^{:doc "Count items matching a filter"}
  count-if (comp count filter))
```

comp is used to *compose* two or more functions:

```
(comp f & fs)
```

The composed function is a new function that applies the rightmost function to its arguments, the next-rightmost function to that result, and so on. So, count-if will first filter and then count the results of the filter:

```
(count-if odd? [1 2 3 4 5])
-> 3
```

Finally, you can use count-if and partition to create a count-runs function that's more general than count-heads-pairs:

```
src/examples/functional.clj
(defn count-runs
  "Count runs of length n where pred is true in coll."
  [n pred coll]
  (count-if #(every? pred %) (partition n 1 coll)))
```

count-runs is a winning combination: both simpler and more general than the previous versions of count-heads-pairs. You can use it to count pairs of heads:

```
(count-runs 2 #(= % :h) [:h :t :t :h :h :h])
-> 2
```

But you can just as easily use it to count pairs of tails:

```
(count-runs 2 #(= % :t) [:h :t :t :h :h :h])
-> 1
```

Or, instead of pairs, how about runs of three heads in a row?

```
(count-runs 3 #(= % :h) [:h :t :t :h :h :h])
-> 1
```

Currying and Partial Application

If you still want to have a function named count-heads-pairs, you can implement it in terms of count-runs:

```
src/examples/functional.clj
(def ^{:doc "Count runs of length two that are both heads"}
  count-heads-pairs (partial count-runs 2 #(= % :h)))
```

This version of count-heads-pairs builds a new function using partial:

```
(partial f & partial-args)
```

partial performs a *partial application* of a function. You specify a function f and part of the argument list when you perform the partial. You specify the remainder of the argument list later, when you call the function created by partial. So, the following:

```
(partial count-runs 1 #(= % :h))
```

is a more expressive way of saying this:

```
(fn [coll] (count-runs 1 #(= % :h) coll))
```

Partial application is similar but not identical to *currying*.

When you *curry* a function, you get a new function that takes one argument and returns the original function with that one argument fixed. (Curry is named for Haskell Curry, an American logician best known for his work in combinatory logic.) If Clojure had a curry, it might be implemented like this:

```
; almost a curry
(defn faux-curry [& args] (apply partial partial args))
```

One use of curry is partial application. Here is partial application in Clojure:

```
(def add-3 (partial + 3))
(add-3 7)
-> 10
```

And here is partial application using our faux-curry:

```
(def add-3 ((faux-curry +) 3))
(add-3 7)
-> 10
```

If all you want is partial application, currying is just an intermediate step. Our faux-curry is not a real curry. A real curry would return a result, not a function of no arguments, once all the arguments were fixed. We can see the difference here, using the function true?, which takes only one argument:

```
; faux curry
((faux-curry true?) (= 1 1))

; if the curry were real
((curry true?) (= 1 1))
-> true
```

Since Clojure functions can have variable-length argument lists, Clojure can't know when all the arguments are fixed. But you, the programmer, do know when you're done adding arguments. When you've curried as many arguments as you want, just invoke the function. That amounts to adding an extra set of parentheses around the earlier expression:

```
(((faux-curry true?) (= 1 1)))
-> true
```

The absence of curry from Clojure is not a major problem, since partial is available, and that's what people generally want out of curry anyway. In fact, some programmers use the terms *currying* and *partial application* interchangeably.

You've seen a lot of new forms in this section. Don't let all the details obscure the key idea: by combining existing functions from the sequence library, you were able to create a solution that was both simpler and more general than the direct approach. And you didn't have to worry about laziness or recursion at all. Instead, you worked at a higher level of abstraction and let Clojure deal with laziness and recursion for you.

Recursion Revisited

Clojure works very hard to balance the power of functional programming with the reality of the Java Virtual Machine. One example of this is the well-motivated choice of explicit TCO through loop/recur.

But blending the best of two worlds always runs the risk of unpleasant compromises, and it makes sense to ask the question, "Does Clojure contain hidden design compromises that, while not obvious on day one, will bite me later?"

This question is *never* fully answerable for any language, but let's consider it by exploring some more complex recursions. First, we'll look at *mutual recursion.*

A mutual recursion occurs when the recursion bounces between two or more functions. Instead of A calls A calls A, we have A calls B calls A again. As a simple example, you could define my-odd? and my-even? using mutual recursion:

src/examples/functional.clj
```
(declare my-odd? my-even?)

(defn my-odd? [n]
  (if (= n 0)
    false
    (my-even? (dec n))))
(defn my-even? [n]
  (if (= n 0)
    true
    (my-odd? (dec n))))
```

Because my-odd? and my-even? each call the other, you need to create both vars before you define the functions. You could do this with def, but the declare macro lets you create both vars (with no initial binding) in a single line of code.

Verify that my-odd? and my-even? work for small values:

```
(map my-even? (range 10))
-> (true false true false true false true false true false)
(map my-odd? (range 10))
-> (false true false true false true false true false true)
```

my-odd? and my-even? consume stack frames proportional to the size of their argument, so they will fail with large numbers.

```
(my-even? (* 1000 1000 1000))
-> StackOverflowError clojure.lang.Numbers$LongOps.equiv (Numbers.java:490)
```

This is similar to the problem that motivated the introduction of recur. But you can't use recur to fix it, because recur works with self-recursion, not mutual recursion. Of course, odd/even can be implemented more efficiently *without* recursion anyway. Clojure's implementation uses bit-and (bitwise and) to implement odd? and even?:

```
; from core.clj
(defn even? [n] (zero? (bit-and n 1)))
(defn odd? [n] (not (even? n)))
```

We picked odd/even for its simplicity. Other recursive problems are not so simple and don't have an elegant nonrecursive solution. We'll examine four approaches you can use to solve such problems:

- Converting to self-recursion
- Trampolining a mutual recursion
- Replacing recursion with laziness
- Shortcutting recursion with memoization

Converting to Self-recursion

Mutual recursion is often a nice way to model separate but related concepts. For example, oddness and evenness are separate concepts but clearly related to one another.

You can convert a mutual recursion to a self-recursion by coming up with a single abstraction that deals with multiple concepts simultaneously. For example, you can think of oddness and evenness in terms of a single concept: *parity*. Define a parity function that uses recur and returns 0 for even numbers and 1 for odd numbers:

src/examples/functional.clj
```
(defn parity [n]
  (loop [n n par 0]
    (if (= n 0)
      par
      (recur (dec n) (- 1 par)))))
```

Test that parity works for small values:

```
(map parity (range 10))
-> (0 1 0 1 0 1 0 1 0 1)
```

At this point, you can trivially implement my-odd? and my-even? in terms of parity:

src/examples/functional.clj
```
(defn my-even? [n] (= 0 (parity n)))
(defn my-odd? [n] (= 1 (parity n)))
```

Parity is a straightforward concept. Unfortunately, many mutual recursions will not simplify into an elegant self-recursion. If you try to convert a mutual recursion into a self-recursion and you find the resulting code to be full of conditional expressions that obfuscate the definition, then don't use this approach.

Trampolining Mutual Recursion

A *trampoline* is a technique for optimizing mutual recursion. A trampoline is like an after-the-fact recur, imposed by the *caller* of a function instead of the *implementer*. Since the caller can call more than one function inside a trampoline, trampolines can optimize mutual recursion.

Clojure's trampoline function invokes one of your mutually recursive functions:

```
(trampoline f & partial-args)
```

If the return value is not a function, then a trampoline works just like calling the function directly. Try trampolining a few simple Clojure functions:

```
(trampoline list)
-> ()
(trampoline + 1 2)
-> 3
```

If the return value *is* a function, then trampoline assumes you want to call it recursively and calls it for you. trampoline manages its own recur, so it will keep calling your function until it stops returning functions.

Back in *Tail Recursion*, on page 87, you implemented a tail-fibo function. You saw how the function consumed stack space and replaced the tail recursion with a recur. Now we have another option. You can take the code of tail-fibo and prepare it for trampolining by wrapping the recursive return case inside a function.

```
src/examples/trampoline.clj
; Example only. Don't write code like this.
(defn trampoline-fibo [n]
  (let [fib (fn fib [f-2 f-1 current]
              (let [f (+ f-2 f-1)]
                (if (= n current)
                  f
                  #(fib f-1 f (inc current)))))]
    (cond
      (= n 0) 0
      (= n 1) 1
      :else (fib 0N 1 2))))
```

The only difference between this and the original version of tail-fibo is the initial # on line 7. Try bouncing trampoline-fibo on a trampoline:

```
(trampoline trampoline-fibo 9)
-> 34N
```

Since trampoline does a recur, it can handle large inputs just fine, without throwing a StackOverflowError:

```
(rem (trampoline trampoline-fibo 1000000) 1000)
-> 875N
```

We've ported tail-fibo to use trampoline to compare and contrast trampoline and recur. For self-recursions like trampoline-fibo, trampoline offers no advantage, and you should prefer recur. But with mutual recursion, trampoline comes into its own.

Consider the mutually recursive definition of my-odd? and my-even?, which we presented at the beginning of *Recursion Revisited*, on page 98. You can convert these broken, stack-consuming implementations to use trampoline, with the same approach you used to convert tail-fibo: prepend a # to any recursive tail calls so that they return a function to produce the value, rather than the value itself:

src/examples/trampoline.clj
```
Line 1  (declare my-odd? my-even?)

        (defn my-odd? [n]
          (if (= n 0)
     5      false
            #(my-even? (dec n))))

        (defn my-even? [n]
          (if (= n 0)
    10      true
            #(my-odd? (dec n))))
```

The only difference from the original implementation is the function wrappers on lines 6 and 11. With this change in place, you can trampoline large values of n without blowing the stack:

```
(trampoline my-even? 1000000)
-> true
```

A trampoline is a special-purpose solution to a specific problem. It requires doctoring your original functions to return a different type to indicate recursion. If one of the other techniques presented here provides a more elegant implementation for a particular recursion, that's great. If not, you'll be happy to have trampoline in your box of tools. In practice, many Clojure programmers never encounter a case requiring trampoline at all.

Replacing Recursion with Laziness

Of all the techniques for eliminating or optimizing recursion discussed in this chapter, laziness is the one you'll probably use most often.

For our example, we'll implement the replace function developed by Eugene Wallingford to demonstrate mutual recursion. (See http://www.cs.uni.edu/~wallingf/patterns/recursion.html.)

replace works with an *s-list* data structure, which is a list that can contain both symbols and lists of symbols. replace takes an s-list, an oldsym, and a newsym and replaces all occurrences of oldsym with newsym. For example, this call to replace replaces all occurrences of b with a:

```
(replace '((a b) (((b g r) (f r)) c (d e)) b) 'b 'a)
-> ((a a) (((a g r) (f r)) c (d e)) a)
```

The following is a fairly literal translation of the Scheme implementation from Wallingford's paper. We've converted from Scheme functions to Clojure functions, changed the name to replace-symbol to avoid collision with Clojure's replace, and shortened names to better fit the printed page, but otherwise, we've preserved the structure of the original:

src/examples/wallingford.clj
```
; overly-literal port, do not use
(declare replace-symbol replace-symbol-expression)
(defn replace-symbol [coll oldsym newsym]
  (if (empty? coll)
    ()
    (cons (replace-symbol-expression
            (first coll) oldsym newsym)
          (replace-symbol
            (rest coll) oldsym newsym))))
(defn replace-symbol-expression [symbol-expr oldsym newsym]
  (if (symbol? symbol-expr)
    (if (= symbol-expr oldsym)
      newsym
      symbol-expr)
    (replace-symbol symbol-expr oldsym newsym)))
```

The two functions replace-symbol and replace-symbol-expression are mutually recursive, so a deeply nested structure could blow the stack. To demonstrate the problem, create a deeply-nested function that builds deeply nested lists containing a single bottom element:

src/examples/replace_symbol.clj
```
(defn deeply-nested [n]
  (loop [n n
         result '(bottom)]
    (if (= n 0)
      result
      (recur (dec n) (list result)))))
```

Try deeply-nested for a few small values of n:

```
(deeply-nested 5)
-> ((((((bottom))))))
```

```
(deeply-nested 25)
-> ((((((((((((((((((((((((((bottom))))))))))))))))))))))))))
```

Clojure provides a *print-level* that controls how deeply the Clojure printer will go into a nested data structure. Set the *print-level* to a modest value so that the printer doesn't go crazy trying to print a deeply nested structure. You'll see that when we nest deeper, the printer simply prints a # and stops:

```
(set! *print-level* 25)
-> 25
```

```
(deeply-nested 5)
-> ((((((bottom))))))
```

```
(deeply-nested 25)
-> ((((((((((((((((((((((((((#))))))))))))))))))))))))))
```

Now, try to use replace-symbol to change bottom to deepest for different levels of nesting. You'll see that large levels blow the stack. Depending on your JVM implementation, you may need a larger value than the 10000 shown here:

```
(replace-symbol (deeply-nested 5) 'bottom 'deepest)
-> ((((((deepest))))))
```

```
(replace-symbol (deeply-nested 10000) 'bottom 'deepest)
-> java.lang.StackOverflowError
```

All of the recursive calls to replace-symbol are inside a cons. To break the recursion, all you have to do is wrap the recursion with lazy-seq. *It's really that simple.* You can break a sequence-generating recursion by wrapping it with a lazy-seq. Here's the improved version. Since the transition to laziness was so simple, we couldn't resist the temptation to make the function more Clojure-ish in another way as well:

src/examples/replace_symbol.clj
```
Line 1  (defn- coll-or-scalar [x & _] (if (coll? x) :collection :scalar))
     2  (defmulti replace-symbol coll-or-scalar)
     3  (defmethod replace-symbol :collection [coll oldsym newsym]
     4    (lazy-seq
     5      (when (seq coll)
     6        (cons (replace-symbol (first coll) oldsym newsym)
     7              (replace-symbol (rest coll) oldsym newsym)))))
     8  (defmethod replace-symbol :scalar [obj oldsym newsym]
     9    (if (= obj oldsym) newsym obj))
```

On line 4, the lazy-seq breaks the recursion, preventing stack overflow on deeply nested structures. The other improvement is on line 2. Rather than have two different functions to deal with symbols and lists, there's a single multimethod replace-symbol with one method for lists and another for symbols. (Multimethods are covered in detail in Chapter 9, *Multimethods*, on page 209.) This gets rid of an if form and improves readability.

Make sure the improved replace-symbol can handle deep nesting:

```
(replace-symbol (deeply-nested 10000) 'bottom 'deepest)
-> (((((((((((((((((((((((((((((#))))))))))))))))))))))))))))))
```

Laziness is a powerful ally. You can often write recursive and even mutually recursive functions and then break the recursion with laziness.

Shortcutting Recursion with Memoization

To demonstrate a more complex mutual recursion, let's look at the Hofstadter Female and Male sequences. The first Hofstadter sequences were described in *Gödel, Escher, Bach: An Eternal Golden Braid [Hof99]*. The Female and Male sequences are defined as follows:[6]

$F(0) = 1; M(0) = 0$

$F(n) = n - M(F(n-1)), n > 0$

$M(n) = n - F(M(n-1)), n > 0$

This suggests a straightforward definition in Clojure:

```
src/examples/male_female.clj
; do not use these directly
(declare m f)
(defn m [n]
  (if (zero? n)
    0
    (- n (f (m (dec n)))))))
(defn f [n]
  (if (zero? n)
    1
    (- n (m (f (dec n)))))))
```

The Clojure definition is easy to read and closely parallels the mathematical definition. However, it performs *terribly* for large values of n. Each value in the sequence requires calculating two other values from scratch, which in turn requires calculating two other values from scratch. On one of our MacBook Pro computers,[7] it takes more than half a minute to calculate (m 250):

---

6. http://en.wikipedia.org/wiki/Hofstadter_sequence
7. 3.06 GHz Intel Core 2 Duo, 4 GB 667 MHz DDR2 SDRAM, Ubuntu 10.10, SSD

```
(time (m 250))
"Elapsed time: 38443.902083 msecs"
-> 155
```

Is it possible to preserve the clean, mutually recursive definition *and* have decent performance? Yes, with a little help from *memoization*. Memoization trades space for time by caching the results of past calculations. When you call a memoized function, it first checks your input against a map of previous inputs and their outputs. If it finds the input in the map, it can return the output immediately, without having to perform the calculation again.

Rebind m and f to memoized versions of themselves, using Clojure's memoize function:

src/examples/memoized_male_female.clj
```
(def m (memoize m))
(def f (memoize f))
```

Now Clojure needs to calculate *F* and *M* only once for each *n*. The speedup is enormous. Calculating (m 250) is thousands of times faster:

```
(time (m 250))
"Elapsed time: 5.190739 msecs"
-> 155
```

And, of course, once the memoization cache is built, "calculation" of a cached value is almost instantaneous:

```
(time (m 250))
"Elapsed time: 0.065877 msecs"
-> 155
```

Memoization alone is not enough, however. Memoization shortcuts the recursion only if the memoization cache is already populated. If you start with an empty cache and ask for m or f of a large number, you'll blow the stack before the cache can be built:

```
(m 10000)
-> java.lang.StackOverflowError
```

The final trick is to guarantee that the cache is built from the ground up by exposing *sequences*, instead of *functions*. Create m-seq and f-seq by mapping m and f over the whole numbers:

src/examples/male_female_seq.clj
```
(def m-seq (map m (iterate inc 0)))
(def f-seq (map f (iterate inc 0)))
```

Now callers can get *M(n)* or *F(n)* by taking the nth value from a sequence:

```
(nth m-seq 250)
-> 155
```

The approach is quite fast, even for larger values of n:

```
(time (nth m-seq 10000))
"Elapsed time: 0.735 msecs"
-> 6180
```

The approach we used here is as follows:

- Define a mutually recursive function in a natural way.

- Use memoization to shortcut recursion for values that have already been calculated.

- Expose a sequence so that dependent values are cached before they're needed.

This approach *is* heap consuming, in that it caches all previously seen values. If this is a problem, in some situations, you can eliminate it by selecting a more complex caching policy.

We've spent much of this chapter exploring different techniques for implementing and leveraging laziness. However, Clojure also provides a range of solutions for *eager* evaluation of transformations over collections. Next, we'll explore when these are preferred and how to perform eager transformations.

Eager Transformations

While lazy sequences are the right solution in many cases, they're not the best answer in every case. An eager approach can be better when we wish to construct an output collection rather than a sequence, optimize memory and performance for transformations of large collections, or control external resources.

Producing Output Collections

Sequence transformations produce output only as needed, which allows us to avoid unnecessary work and even to work with infinite sequences. However, it's also common to encounter situations where we want our output to be a persistent collection, not a sequence. In this case, we want all of the transformation to be completed, so we won't get any advantage from laziness.

For example, consider applying a function to a sequence to produce an output vector. In this case we'd need to apply a final vec function to transfer the elements of the sequence back into a collection:

src/examples/eager.clj
```
(defn square [x] (* x x))

(defn sum-squares-seq [n]
  (vec (map square (range n))))
```

Recall that sequences cache the result of their evaluation so that they're safe, immutable values, just like collections. This example will produce an input sequence (from the range), which stores the values in memory, then the output of the map, which stores another sequence of values, and then the final output vector. Sequences will share values if they are the same across sequences (as they are immutable), but you'll have three times as much sequence overhead for the objects holding the values.

Instead, we can perform the intermediate transformation on the input collection values and place the result directly into the output vector using into with a *map transducer*. Let's first see what that looks like before we discuss what it means:

src/examples/eager.clj
```
(defn sum-squares
  [n]
  (into [] (map square) (range n)))
```

Here the call to into takes three arguments: the output collection, the transformation, and the input collection. The transformation here is a *transducer*. Many of the sequence functions (like map) can be called without their input collection argument to return a transducer. A transducer is a function that captures the essence of a collection transformation without tying it to the form of either the input collection or the output collection.

The into provides the elements from the input range to the map transformation and then adds the results directly into the output collection. This happens eagerly and returns the final vector, avoiding the creation of the intermediate lazy sequences, which are just overhead if we know the output target is a collection.

In the next section, we'll see a more complicated example and examine the performance implications more closely.

Optimizing Performance

In the previous example we saw the difference between a single sequence transformation and a single transducer. We can also compose transducers and apply multiple transformations within into in a single pass over the input.

Imagine you want to find all of the predicate functions in the namespaces we've loaded so far. Predicate functions typically end in ?, so we can find all the loaded namespaces, then find their public vars, filter down to just those ending in ?, and finally convert them to friendly names. Using sequences, we often chain transformations together with ->>:

```
src/examples/eager.clj
(defn preds-seq []
  (->> (all-ns)
    (map ns-publics)
    (mapcat vals)
    (filter #(clojure.string/ends-with? % "?"))
    (map #(str (. sym %)))
    vec))
```

Each step of this transformation creates a sequence, which caches the intermediate values of the sequence. Finally, at the end we collect the result into a vector.

Transducers can be composed in a similarly pipelined fashion using comp. Transducers are composed in a stack-like fashion, which means that comp combines them left-to-right, just like ->>. Using chained transducers with into looks like this equivalent function:

```
src/examples/eager.clj
(defn preds []
  (into []
    (comp (map ns-publics)
      (mapcat vals)
      (filter #(clojure.string/ends-with? % "?"))
      (map #(str (.-sym %))))
    (all-ns)))
```

The sequence implementation creates four intermediate sequences. The transducer implementation composes the four transformations into a single combined transformation and applies it during a single traversal of the (all-ns) input sequence. It then places the results directly into the output vector. Removing the intermediate sequences can result in a significant reduction in memory usage, particularly if the size of the input collection is large or the number of transformations is large.

The transducer version can also take advantage of some extra optimizations. First, if the input collection is *reducible* (that is, it knows how to perform a reduce on itself), then the resulting compiled code is often far more efficient. Here we can't take advantage of this, but in the sum of squares example, range was a reducible collection.

Secondly, some Clojure collections can be more efficiently bulk loaded using *transients*. Transients temporarily make an immutable collection mutable while adding values, then switch the collection back to a normal immutable collection when done. This happens in a constrained scope such that users are never exposed to the mutable version. into (and some other transducer aware functions) automatically takes advantage of this optimization.

Now that you've seen some of the performance advantages of doing eager transformations with transducers, let's consider how laziness complicates managment of external resources and how eager transformation can help.

Managing External Resources

When data is read from external resources like files, databases, or web services, it's tempting to return a lazy sequence so we can begin processing the data as it's read:

src/examples/eager.clj

```
(defn non-blank? [s]
  (not (clojure.string/blank? s)))

(defn non-blank-lines-seq [file-name]
  (let [reader (clojure.java.io/reader file-name)]
    (filter non-blank? (line-seq reader))))
```

The problem here is that the reader is not being closed. This resource is being left open and stranded in this code. Beyond that, it's not clear when it could be closed, because we need to wait for the processing of the last line in the lazy sequence of lines. Another approach is to eagerly process all of the lines, then close the resource before returning:

src/examples/eager.clj

```
(defn non-blank-lines [file-name]
  (with-open [reader (clojure.java.io/reader file-name)]
    (into [] (filter non-blank?) (line-seq reader))))
```

This solves the dangling resource problem but only by eagerly creating the entire vector of non-blank lines and returning it. That's fine for small files but is a recipe for an eventual OutOfMemoryError with a sufficiently large file. What we really want is to process the file, without the caching aspects of lazy sequences, and to know when the input has been exhausted so that the reader can be closed.

First let's refactor the non-blank-lines function to take a reader and return an *eduction*:

src/examples/eager.clj
```
(defn non-blank-lines-eduction [reader]
  (eduction (filter non-blank?) (line-seq reader)))
```

An eduction is a suspended transformation (like a sequence), but it processes the entire input each time its asked (usually just once). Because it's processed anew each time, there's no caching as with a sequence. Instead, the transformation is just applied to the input to produce an output in a full pass through the data, usually performed with a reduce (when the output is a collection) or an into (when the output is a single computed value). For example, we can use non-blank-lines-eduction to count lines:

src/examples/eager.clj
```
(defn line-count [file-name]
  (with-open [reader (clojure.java.io/reader file-name)]
    (reduce (fn [cnt el] (inc cnt)) 0 (non-blank-lines-eduction reader))))
```

In line-count, we first create the reader in a with-open block, which will automatically close the reader before returning the result of the body. Next we process the eduction in the context of a reduce. The eduction processes each line and then releases the associated memory, so the eduction will hold only one line in memory at a time.

Transducers and eductions allow us to choose exactly when an input source is processed and thus know when the external resource is done and ready to release. With lazy sequences, it's much harder to know when processing is "done" and it's time to release.

Wrapping Up

In this chapter you've seen how Clojure's support for functional programming strikes a well-motivated balance between academic purity and effectiveness on the Java Virtual Machine. Clojure provides a wide variety of techniques including self-recursion with recur, mutual recursion with trampoline, lazy sequences, and memoization.

Better still, for a wide variety of everyday programming tasks, you can use the sequence library without ever having to define your own explicit recursions of lazy sequences. Functions like partition create clean, expressive solutions that are much easier to write.

Finally, we saw how Clojure provides eager approaches as a companion to lazy sequences for use cases where eager evaluation is better suited. Transducers provide fast, composable transformations that can be used in a variety of situations to produce output collections, improve performance, and manage external resources.

At this point, you've seen the core of Clojure—the syntax, immutable collections, the sequence abstraction, functional programming, and recursion. With the next chapter, we'll begin adding additional features. These features all build on top of the core ideas of immutable data and functional transformation. We'll start with *spec*, a Clojure library for describing the structure of data and functions.

CHAPTER 5

Specifications

Statically typed languages like Java create unique, named data structures (classes) for every unit of data in a program. Clojure is dynamically typed and instead relies on reusing a few generic collection types (vectors, maps, sets, lists, and sequences) to represent a program's data. This approach yields tremendous opportunities for code reuse, simplicity, generality, and extension.

However, one consequence of this approach is that functions in a Clojure program lack the explicit types that programmers in a statically typed language rely on as signposts to understand a piece of code.

For example, a Java program might have a function that takes a recipe ingredient and scales the quantity for a larger recipe. In Java, we would define an Ingredient class and Unit class, and the method might look like this:

```java
public class Ingredient {
  private String name;
  private double quantity;
  private Unit unit;

  // ...

  public static Ingredient scale(Ingredient ingredient, double factor) {
    ingredient.setQuantity(ingredient.getQuantity() * factor);
    return ingredient;
  }
}
```

In a Clojure program, an ingredient might just be a map with some well-known keys. A scale function would then take and return a map without ever mentioning any explicit types:

src/examples/spec.clj
```clojure
(defn scale-ingredient [ingredient factor]
  (update ingredient :quantity * factor))
```

This code is preferable to the Java version in several ways. It takes and returns immutable values, rather than update mutable state, so it's easier to reason about and inherently thread-safe by default. Also, the ingredient maps are just collections of attributes that can easily evolve over the life of a program, rather than being trapped behind the custom API of a Java class. However, one thing the Clojure code is lacking is explicit information about the expected structure of ingredient. We need to infer the structure from documentation or other parts of the program.

In Clojure 1.9, Clojure introduced the *spec* library, which allows us to create "specs" that describe the structure of our data, and the inputs and outputs of our functions. The actual code we write is the same—it still uses generic collections and generic operations on those collections. Adding specs to your code can make the implicit structure explicit.

For example, we could annotate this code with the following specs (s here is an alias for the clojure.spec.alpha namespace):

src/examples/spec.clj
```
;; Specs describing an ingredient
(s/def ::ingredient (s/keys :req [::name ::quantity ::unit]))
(s/def ::name      string?)
(s/def ::quantity  number?)
(s/def ::unit      keyword?)

;; Function spec for scale-ingredient
(s/fdef scale-ingredient
  :args (s/cat :ingredient ::ingredient :factor number?)
  :ret  ::ingredient)
```

These specs give us a precise description of the shape of an ingredient map, its fields, and their contents. The function spec gives us an explicit definition of the arguments and return value of scale-ingredient. These specs don't just serve as documentation. The spec library uses them to provide several additional tools that operate on specs—data validation, explanations of invalid data, generation of example data, and even automatically created generative tests for functions with a spec.

We'll start by considering how to define specs in our code and use them at runtime, followed by how we combine specs and validate data. Finally, we'll see how to use s/fdef to define function specs for argument checking and generative testing.

Defining Specs

Specs are logical compositions of predicates (functions returning a logical true/false value) used to describe a set of data values. The spec library provides operations to create, combine, and register specs.

To work with spec, you'll need to load the namespace clojure.spec.alpha, which is commonly aliased to s. All spec examples in this chapter use the s alias to refer to functions or macros from the clojure.spec library.

```
(require '[clojure.spec.alpha :as s])
```

The s/def macro names and registers a spec in the global registry of specs accessible in the current Clojure program. The syntax for s/def is:

```
(s/def name spec)
```

Spec names are qualified keywords. For example, a simple spec definition using a predicate spec looks like:

```
(s/def :my.app/company-name string?)
```

Place this spec definition in your Clojure source file at the top level, just like var definitions made with the special form def. When creating function specs, most developers place them before the function they describe or sometimes collect all of the function specs into a separate namespace. For example, clojure.core itself has specs in a separate namespace clojure.core.specs.alpha.

At runtime, specs are read and evaluated like function definitions. The global spec registry stores the spec, keyed by name.

Spec names must be fully qualified keywords. As a Clojure developer, it's your responsibility to use sufficiently qualified keywords as names so that your code will work with other code in the greater ecosystem. If you're writing a library for public reuse, you should follow rules similar to those used when choosing the project group ID and artifact ID when deploying the project artifact. Namely, the qualified part of the keyword should start with a domain name or a product or project name for which you control the trademark or mindshare in the market. For example, :cognitect.transit.handler/name would be sufficient.

When these qualified keywords are cumbersome in code, we can use aliases and auto-resolved keywords to simplify their names. Auto-resolved keywords start with ::. If no qualifier is specified (::ingredient), then the current namespace is used as the qualifier. Since project namespaces are often sufficiently qualified, this is a great way to piggieback on good choices we've already made.

If a qualifier is specified, then it can refer to an alias defined in the current namespace. For example, ::recipe/ingredient might expand to the namespace aliased to recipe, perhaps :cookingco.recipe/ingredient. In this chapter, we often use auto-resolved keywords for brevity in the code examples.

Next, we'll look at how to create and combine specs to validate data, which we can choose to do during development or even at runtime.

Validating Data

Any time you receive a value from a user or an external source, that data may contain values that break your expectations. Instead, Clojure specs precisely describe those expectations, check whether the data is valid, and determine how it conforms to the specification. In the case where data is invalid, you may want to know what parts are invalid and why.

Predicates are the simplest kind of spec—they check whether a predicate matches a single value. Other specs compose predicates (and other specs) to create more complicated specifications. Some of the tools we'll discuss include range specs, logical connectors like and and or, and collection specs. These specs combine to cover any data structure you need to describe.

Predicates

Predicate functions that take a single value and return a logical true or false value are valid specs. Clojure provides dozens of predicates (many of these functions end in ?); you can use any of those or ones in your own project. Some example predicates in clojure.core are functions like boolean?, string?, and keyword?. These predicates check for a single underlying type.

Other predicates combine several types together, such as rational?, which returns true for a value that is an integer, a decimal, or a ratio. Many predicates verify a property of the value itself, like pos?, zero?, empty?, any?, and some?.

Consider a simple predicate spec for a company name:

```
(s/def :my.app/company-name string?)
```

We've registered the specification for a company name in our application, so let's use it to validate incoming data:

```
(s/valid? :my.app/company-name "Acme Moving")
-> true

(s/valid? :my.app/company-name 100)
-> false
```

Now that we've created the spec and registered it with a name (:my.app/company-name), other parts of our program can use it as well. As we code, we build and record the semantics of our domain.

Next, we'll consider the common case of writing a spec that matches a set of enumerated values.

Enumerated values

If we're in the business of selling marbles, we might stock three colors—red, green, and blue. When defining a spec for the color, we want to match any of those three values (declared as a keyword). Clojure sets are a perfect match for this—they allow us to store a set of non-duplicate items with a fast check for containment. Even better, sets implement the function interface and are valid specs as well:

```
(s/def :marble/color #{:red :green :blue})

(s/valid? :marble/color :red)
-> true

(s/valid? :marble/color :pink)
-> false
```

Consider writing a spec to match a bowling roll, where 0–10 pins could be knocked down. We can write such a spec like this:

```
(s/def ::bowling/roll #{0 1 2 3 4 5 6 7 8 9 10})

(s/valid? ::bowling/roll 5)
-> true
```

This works fine, but it seems silly to need to say all those numbers in order. We should make our computer take care of that instead, and range specs provide this functionality.

Range Specs

Clojure spec provides several range specs for just the purpose of validating a range of values, like a bowling roll. Let's rewrite our spec using the provided s/int-in spec. We provide this spec with beginning (inclusive) and end (exclusive) integer values.

```
(s/def ::bowling/ranged-roll (s/int-in 0 11))

(s/valid? ::bowling/ranged-roll 10)
-> true
```

In addition to s/int-in, s/double-in and s/inst-in are for ranges of doubles and time instants. All of these cases define value ranges with lower and upper bounds.

The details vary slightly depending on the data type, so check the doc string for each function for proper use using (doc s/double-in) or (doc s/inst-in). Now let's see how specs handle the special case of nil values.

Handling nil

Most predicates in Clojure will return false for the nil value; however, there are many cases where you'll want to take an existing spec and extend it to also include the nil value. You can use the special s/nilable operation to extend an existing spec.

For example we could define our company name field as accepting either strings or nil:

```
(s/def ::my.app/company-name-2 (s/nilable string?))
```

```
(s/valid? ::my.app/company-name-2 nil)
-> true
```

The s/nilable predicate provides optimal performance and is preferred over equivalent specs that you might construct with s/or or other operations.

One case you might encounter is spec'ing the set of values true, false, or nil. It's tempting to use an explicit set for this #{true, false, nil}. However, when you ask whether a set contains a value, it returns the matching value—in this case, possibly false or nil. Spec interprets this as the predicate rejecting the value, rather than accepting it. Instead, use s/nilable to add nil as a valid value to the boolean? predicate:

```
(s/def ::nilable-boolean (s/nilable boolean?))
```

This will give you the correct behavior and the best performance.

Now that we know the basics of working with predicates and sets, we can consider writing more interesting compound specs that combine specs using logical operations.

Logical Specs

Logical specs create composite specs from other specs using s/and or s/or. For example, to create a spec for an odd integer, combine the predicates int? and odd?:

```
(s/def ::odd-int (s/and int? odd?))
(s/valid? ::odd-int 5)
-> true
(s/valid? ::odd-int 10)
-> false
(s/valid? ::odd-int 5.2)
-> false
```

In this example, we're combining predicates, but s/and can take any kind of spec.

Similarly, we use s/or to combine multiple alternatives. For instance, to add 42 as a valid value in our last spec:

```
(s/def ::odd-or-42 (s/or :odd ::odd-int :42 #{42}))
```

With s/or, we see that things are a bit different—each option in the s/or contains a keyword tag used to report how a value matches (or doesn't match) the spec.

If we want to know how a value matched a spec, we can use s/conform, which returns the value annotated with information about optional choices or the components of the value. We call this a *conformed value.*

For all of the specs we've seen until this point, there were no options or components, and so the conformed value was the same as the original value. The s/or contains a choice, and the conformed value tags the choice taken with the key (either :42 or :odd):

```
(s/conform ::odd-or-42 42)
-> [:42 42]
(s/conform ::odd-or-42 19)
-> [:odd 19]
```

The conformed value for an s/or is a map entry, and the key and val functions extract the tag and value, respectively. The s/conform operation parses a value and describes the parse structure using the tags.

Conversely, the s/explain function describes all of the ways an *invalid* value didn't match its spec:

```
(s/explain ::odd-or-42 0)
| val: 0 fails spec: :user/odd-int at: [:odd] predicate: odd?
| val: 0 fails spec: :user/odd-or-42 at: [:42] predicate: #{42}
```

Here, spec has found and reported two problems with the value. The first problem is that the value is not odd. Note that it passed the int? check inside ::odd-int, so the report only includes the failing predicates. In each problem line, we see the failing value, the spec being checked, the tag path to the failing spec, and the failing predicate.

The explain messages print to the console, but we can alternately retrieve this info as a string with s/explain-str or as data with s/explain-data.

Now that we've started to compose specs, you may be looking at your own data and thinking about how to write specs for it. Most Clojure data is not made of individual values but of collections, and there are a number of ways to write collection specs.

Collection Specs

The two most common collection specs you'll use are s/coll-of and s/map-of. The s/coll-of spec describes lists, vectors, sets, and seqs. You provide a spec that members of the collection must satisfy, and spec checks all members.

```
(s/def ::names (s/coll-of string?))
(s/valid? ::names ["Alex" "Stu"])
-> true
(s/valid? ::names #{"Alex" "Stu"})
-> true
(s/valid? ::names '("Alex" "Stu"))
-> true
```

The s/coll-of spec also comes with many additional options supplied as keyword arguments at the end of the spec.

- :kind - a predicate checked at the beginning of the spec. Common examples are vector? and set?.

- :into - one of these literal collections: [], (), or #{}. Conformed values collect into the specified collection.

- :count - an exact count for the collection.

- :min-count - a minimum count for the collection.

- :max-count - a maximum count for the collection.

- :distinct - true if the elements of the collection must be unique.

As you can see, these options allow for specifying many common collection shapes and constraints. For example, we can choose to match just int sets with at least two values with a spec like this:

```
(s/def ::my-set (s/coll-of int? :kind set? :min-count 2))
(s/valid? ::my-set #{10 20})
```

Similar to s/coll-of, s/map-of specs a lookup map where the keys and values each follow a spec, such as a mapping from player names to scores:

```
(s/def ::scores (s/map-of string? int?))
(s/valid? ::scores {"Stu" 100, "Alex" 200})
-> true
```

All of the s/coll-of options also apply, although you won't typically need to use :into or :kind because they default to map-specific settings.

If you recall, the s/conform function tells how a value was parsed according to a spec. s/map-of conforms to a map and always conforms values. Keys are not conformed by default, but you can change that using the :conform-keys flag.

In cases of large collections or large maps, you might not want to validate or conform all values. For these cases, you can use the sampling specs s/every and s/every-kv instead.

Collection Sampling

The sampling collection specs are s/every and s/every-kv for collections and maps, respectively. They are similar in operation to s/coll-of and s/map-of, except they check up to only s/*coll-check-limit* elements (by default, 101).

Because these specs validate only a limited subset of values and conform no elements, large collections and maps have much better validation performance.

Tuples

Tuples are vectors with a known structure where each fixed element has its own spec. For example, a vector of x and y coordinates can represent a point:

```
(s/def ::point (s/tuple float? float?))
(s/conform ::point [1.3 2.7])
-> [1.3 2.7]
```

Tuples do not name or tag the returned fields. Later in this chapter, we'll see another approach to handling sequential collections with well-known internal structure (using s/cat).

It's common to use maps to represent information with well-known fields. Clojure spec provides a number of tools for handling these kinds of maps, which we'll look at next.

Information Maps

It's common in Clojure to represent domain objects as maps with well-known fields; for example, we might be managing data related to bands and music albums. We might represent a particular release like this:

```
{::music/id #uuid "40e30dc1-55ac-33e1-85d3-1f1508140bfc"
 ::music/artist "Rush"
 ::music/title "Moving Pictures"
 ::music/date #inst "1981-02-12"}
```

We start with describing specs for the attributes:

src/examples/spec.clj
```
(s/def ::music/id uuid?)
(s/def ::music/artist string?)
(s/def ::music/title string?)
(s/def ::music/date inst?)
```

Many validation libraries define the structure of a map of attributes by including definitions of the attributes. This approach introduces important long-term problems. Attributes have independent semantics and may be reused across different structures where they should have the identical meaning without needing to be redefined.

By contrast, Clojure spec requires attributes to be defined independently and then defines map specs as open collections of attributes with no need for restatement of attribute definitions. This approach easily supports subsets of maps, evolution of maps over time, and the transfer of maps through subsystems where not all attributes need to be understood by the intermediary.

To specify a map of attributes, we use s/keys, which describes both required and optional attributes:

```
src/examples/spec.clj
(s/def ::music/release
  (s/keys :req [::music/id]
          :opt [::music/artist
                ::music/title
                ::music/date]))
```

Here we define a ::music/release map to require only a ::music/id attribute, and all other attributes are optional.

An important additional feature of s/keys is that it will validate the values of all registered keys, even if they're not listed as required or optional. For example, if new optional attributes for ::music/release are added in the future, the s/keys spec will automatically validate those as well. This approach encourages the uniform validation of registered attributes and the growth of systems over time.

In the case where you have existing maps that don't use qualified keys, the variant options :req-un and :opt-un take a spec identifier but find the value to check by using the unqualified name of the spec. For example, if our map instead looked like this:

```
{:id #uuid "40e30dc1-55ac-33e1-85d3-1f1508140bfc"
 :artist "Rush"
 :title "Moving Pictures"
 :date #inst "1981-02-12"}
```

we could use our existing attribute specs to create an unqualified version of the spec:

```
src/examples/spec.clj
(s/def ::music/release-unqualified
  (s/keys :req-un [::music/id]
          :opt-un [::music/artist
                   ::music/title
                   ::music/date]))
```

This version of the spec will match the spec for ::music/id with the unqualified attribute :id and so on for the other attributes as well. Specs for records also use the same approach with unqualified attributes.

You've now seen an overview of the basic tools for specifying the structure of our data. In the next section, we take things to the next level by specifying the inputs and outputs of our functions using specs. When we do that, we'll need some way to specify the syntax for function calls, and that will bring in one final set of specs we've not yet examined—*regex ops*.

Validating Functions

A function spec describes the operation of a function. It thus contains up to three specs: an "args" spec for the arguments of the function, a "ret" spec describing the return value, and a "fn" spec used to relate the arguments to the return value. Creating function specs unlocks many of the most useful capabilities of the spec library, like instrumentation and generative testing.

The argument spec defines the collection of arguments that you can use to invoke the function being spec'ed. The spec operations we've seen so far allowed us to create specs for collections, but we need more power to represent the broad range of variability we see in function arguments—repeated arguments, optional arguments, and other structured collections. For these, spec provides *regex op* specs.

Most languages have support for matching the characters in a string according to a *regular expression*,[1] which defines the structure of the string (including repeated or optional patterns). Similarly, regex op specs apply one or more specs to match the values in a collection.

Let's see how we can use regex op specs to define the arguments in a function spec and then *instrument* our code to automatically validate the arguments of a function call.

---

1.   https://en.wikipedia.org/wiki/Regular_expression

Sequences With Structure

String regular expressions match the characters in a string. For example, the regular expression abc* describes strings like "ab", "abc", and "abcc". In string regular expressions, placing two matching expressions next to each other indicates concatentation. The special operator * represents the repetition of 0 or more times of the prior matching expression (in this case, c).

Regex op specs provide a similar function, but instead of matching characters in a string, they match any arbitrary value in a collection. Like string regular expressions, regex op specs can match concatenated, repeated, and optional patterns.

Perhaps the most common regex op spec is s/cat, which specifies a concatenation (a series of elements, in order), where each element is simply another spec. s/cat specs also name each component for use in conforming valid values or explaining invalid values.

For example, a spec to describe a sequential collection taking a string and an integer looks like:

```
(s/def ::cat-example (s/cat :s string? :i int?))
-> :user/cat-example
```

```
(s/valid? ::cat-example ["abc" 100])
-> true
```

In the s/cat, each component has a keyword tag naming the component in the conformed result:

```
(s/conform ::cat-example ["abc" 100])
-> {:s "abc", :i 100}
```

There is also a regex op spec s/alt for indicating alternatives within the sequential structure. The conformed value is an entry with the matched tag and value.

```
(s/def ::alt-example (s/alt :i int? :k keyword?))
-> :user/alt-example
```

```
(s/valid? ::alt-example [100])
-> true
```

```
(s/valid? ::alt-example [:foo])
-> true
```

```
(s/conform ::alt-example [:foo])
-> [:k :foo]
```

Just like string regular expressions, spec also contains operators for the repetition of a spec, which we'll dive into next.

Repetition Operators

There are three repetition operators—s/? for 0 or 1, s/* for 0 or more, and s/+ for 1 or more.

All of the regex operators can be combined and nested arbitrarily along with predicates, sets, and other specs. The key thing to remember is that all connected regex ops describe the structure of a single sequential collection.

Consider the example of a collection that contains one or more odd numbers and an optional trailing even number:

```
(s/def ::oe (s/cat :odds (s/+ odd?) :even (s/? even?)))
-> :user/oe

(s/conform ::oe [1 3 5 100])
-> {:odds [1 3 5], :even 100}
```

Note how the nested s/+ and s/? don't describe nested collections like [[1 3 5] [100]]. All regex op specs combine to describe the structure of a single top-level collection. This also applies to named regex ops, which allows us to factor regex op specs into smaller reusable pieces:

```
(s/def ::odds (s/+ odd?))
-> :user/odds

(s/def ::optional-even (s/? even?))
-> :user/optional-even

(s/def ::oe2 (s/cat :odds ::odds :even ::optional-even))
-> :user/oe2

(s/conform ::oe2 [1 3 5 100])
-> {:odds [1 3 5], :even 100}
```

Variable Argument Lists

Consider now how we might spec the arguments for a function that took multiple arguments. For example, println takes zero or more objects and prints them as a string with spaces between them. We can use the any? predicate to specify each object and s/* to indicate the repetition:

```
(s/def ::println-args (s/* any?))
```

We might also have both some fixed arguments and a variable argument at the end. For example, in the clojure.set namespace, the intersection function takes at least one initial set, followed by any number of sets to intersect:

```
(doc clojure.set/intersection)
| -------------------------
| clojure.set/intersection
| ([s1] [s1 s2] [s1 s2 & sets])
|   Return a set that is the intersection of the input sets
-> nil

(clojure.set/intersection #{1 2} #{2 3} #{2 5})
-> #{2}
```

We can spec the arguments to intersection as follows.

```
(s/def ::intersection-args
  (s/cat :s1 set?
         :sets (s/* set?)))

(s/conform ::intersection-args '[#{1 2} #{2 3} #{2 5}])
-> {:s1 #{1 2}, :sets [#{3 2} #{2 5}]}
```

To conform the args, we pass them in a vector, just as if we were invoking apply on the function and passing this vector of args. The conformed value returns the map describing each argument.

In this case, because each argument is the same spec, we could also use just s/+:

```
(s/def ::intersection-args-2 (s/+ set?))
-> :user/intersection-args-2

(s/conform ::intersection-args-2 '[#{1 2} #{2 3} #{2 5}])
-> [#{1 2} #{3 2} #{2 5}]
```

Another common case in Clojure is the use of optional keyword arguments. For example, looking at the atom function, it has a signature (atom x & options) with options named :meta or :validator. Clojure supports the destructuring of these keyword options as if they were a map. Clojure spec can also create a regex spec as if these were a map using s/keys*, which has the identical structure to s/keys.

You can spec atom's args like this (some of these args are deliberately under-specified for demonstration purposes):

```
(s/def ::meta map?)
-> :user/meta

(s/def ::validator ifn?)
-> :user/validator

(s/def ::atom-args
  (s/cat :x any? :options (s/keys* :opt-un [::meta ::validator])))
-> :user/atom-args
```

```
(s/conform ::atom-args [100 :meta {:foo 1} :validator int?])
-> {:x 100,
    :options {:meta {:foo 1},
              :validator #object[clojure.core$int_QMARK_ ...]}}
```

The atom function follows a typical pattern of having two arities—one with options and one without. This is the most common case for multi-arity functions. However, it's also typical to encounter functions with an optional first argument, multiple invocation styles, or an argument that is repeated many times. Regex specs can cover all of these cases, and we'll look at another example in the next section.

Multi-arity Argument Lists

You can see another case of multi-arity argument lists in the repeat function, which has two arities, one with and one without the length n, which is the first argument, not the second. The spec can simply declare that first argument as optional:

```
(doc repeat)
| -----------------------
| clojure.core/repeat
| ([x] [n x])
|  Returns a lazy (infinite!, or length n if supplied) sequence of xs.
-> nil

(s/def ::repeat-args
  (s/cat :n (s/? int?) :x any?))
-> :user/repeat-args

(s/conform ::repeat-args [100 "foo"])
-> {:n 100, :x "foo"}

(s/conform ::repeat-args ["foo"])
-> {:x "foo"}
```

In some relatively rare cases, the arities are sufficiently different that it makes more sense to use s/alt to fully describe each arity.

Now that we've examined how to spec the arguments of a function, it's time to spec the function itself.

Specifying Functions

Function specs are a combination of three different specs for the arguments, the return value, and the "fn" spec that describes the relationship between the arguments and return.

Let's start with a function spec for rand:

```
clojure.core/rand
([] [n])
  Returns a random floating point number between 0 (inclusive) and
  n (default 1) (exclusive).
```

We can first create an argument spec that is either empty or takes an optional number:

src/examples/spec.clj
```
(s/def ::rand-args (s/cat :n (s/? number?)))
```

The docstring states the function's return value is a floating point number, but we can more precisely state that it will be a double:

src/examples/spec.clj
```
(s/def ::rand-ret double?)
```

We then need to consider the :fn spec, which receives a map containing the conformed args and the conformed return value based on their specs. In this case, the docs state that the random number must be >= 0 and <= n. Let's state that as a predicate:

src/examples/spec.clj
```
(s/def ::rand-fn
  (fn [{:keys [args ret]}]
    (let [n (or (:n args) 1)]
      (cond (zero? n) (zero? ret)
            (pos? n) (and (>= ret 0) (< ret n))
            (neg? n) (and (<= ret 0) (> ret n))))))
```

We can now tie all these together using s/fdef, which takes a fully-qualified function name and one or more of the specs (we'll supply all three):

src/examples/spec.clj
```
(s/fdef clojure.core/rand
  :args ::rand-args
  :ret  ::rand-ret
  :fn   ::rand-fn)
```

In a moment we'll see how to use these specs, but first, let's take a slight detour to talk about spec'ing anonymous functions.

Anonymous Functions

Higher order functions (ones that take and return functions) are common in Clojure. Use s/fspec to define the spec of an anonymous function. The syntax is the same as s/fdef but omits the function name. For instance, consider a function opposite, which takes a predicate function and creates the opposite predicate function:

src/examples/spec.clj
```
(defn opposite [pred]
  (comp not pred))
```

The function opposite accepts a predicate function, which we can describe using s/fspec. We can use that function spec in both the :args and :ret spec for opposite.

src/examples/spec.clj
```
(s/def ::pred
  (s/fspec :args (s/cat :x any?)
           :ret  boolean?))

(s/fdef opposite
  :args (s/cat :pred ::pred)
  :ret ::pred)
```

It's also worth considering a simpler spec for anonymous functions—they don't always need to be fully spec'd, and sometimes simply using ifn? as the spec is sufficient. Now that we've seen how to spec functions, let's consider what we can do with them.

Instrumenting Functions

During development and testing, we can use *instrumentation* (stest/instrument) to wrap a function with a version that uses spec to verify that the incoming arguments to a function conform to the function's spec.

Instrumentation is for :args Only

Note that instrumentation does not check the :ret or :fn specs—the purpose of instrumentation is for verifying correct invocation, not correct implementation. We'll see more on testing implementations later with stest/check.

Once you've defined a spec for a function with s/fdef, call stest/instrument on the fully qualified function symbol to enable it:

```
(require '[clojure.spec.test.alpha :as stest])
(stest/instrument 'clojure.core/rand)
-> [clojure.core/rand]
```

You can also use stest/enumerate-namespace to enumerate a collection of all symbols in a namespace to pass to stest/instrument:

```
(stest/instrument (stest/enumerate-namespace 'clojure.core))
-> [clojure.core/rand]
```

Note that instrument returns a collection of all symbols that were successfully instrumented. Check the return value to ensure it contains your intended symbols.

Instrumenting a function replaces its var with a new var that will check args and invoke the old function via its var. In the following, an invalid call to rand triggers an error:

```
(rand :boom)
| ExceptionInfo Call to #'clojure.core/rand did not conform to spec:
| In: [0] val: :boom fails spec: :user/rand-args
|   at: [:args :n] predicate: number?
| :clojure.spec.alpha/args  (:boom)
| :clojure.spec.alpha/failure  :instrument
| :clojure.spec.test.alpha/caller  {...}
```

Here we see an explain failure for the rand args spec. It expected a number? but received the value :boom, clearly not a number.

Instrumentation is not designed for production-time usage (there is an overhead in validating the spec and invoking a secondary var), but instrumentation is a valuable tool for catching errors faster at development or test time.

Let's move from catching invalid calls to a function to instead using a function's specs to test the function itself with stest/check.

Generative Function Testing

Classic *example-based unit testing* relies on the programmer to test a function by writing a series of example inputs, then writing assertions about the return value when the function is invoked with each input.

In comparison, *generative testing* is a technique that produces thousands of random inputs, runs a procedure, and verifies a set of properties for each output. Generative testing is a great technique for getting broader test coverage of your code.

Spec can automatically perform generative testing for functions that have function specs. Let's see how that's done and then explore ways to influence those tests for more accurate coverage.

Checking Functions

Spec implements automated generative testing with the function check in the namespace clojure.spec.test.alpha (commonly aliased as stest). You can run stest/check on any symbol or symbols that have been spec'ed with s/fdef.

Including the test.check Library

All invocations of spec generators (either directly or within stest/instrument, stest/check, etc.) require including the test.check library as a dependency, typically as either a test or dev profile dependency, so that it's not included at production runtime.

When you invoke check, it generates 1000 sets of arguments that are valid according to the function's :args spec. For each argument set, check invokes the function, then checks that the return value is valid according to the :ret spec and that the :fn spec is valid for the arguments and return value.

Let's see how it works with a spec for the Clojure core function symbol, which takes a name and an optional namespace:

```
(doc symbol)
| ---------- ---------------
| clojure.core/symbol
| ([name] [ns name])
|   Returns a Symbol with the given namespace and name.
```

First we need to define the function spec:

src/examples/spec.clj
```
(s/fdef clojure.core/symbol
  :args (s/cat :ns (s/? string?) :name string?)
  :ret symbol?
  :fn (fn [{:keys [args ret]}]
        (and (= (name ret) (:name args))
          (= (namespace ret) (:ns args)))))
```

And then we can run the test as follows:

```
(stest/check 'clojure.core/symbol)
-> ({:sym clojure.core/symbol
     :spec #object[clojure.spec.alpha$fspec_impl$reify__14282 ...],
     :clojure.spec.test.check/ret {
            :result true,
            :num-tests 1000,
            :seed 1485241441400}})
```

You can see from the output that stest/check ran 1000 tests on clojure.core/symbol and found no problems. When an error occurs, the test.check library goes the extra step of "shrinking" the error to the least complicated possible input that still fails. In complex tests, this is a crucial step to produce tractable input for reproduction and fixing.

One step that we glossed over is *how* spec generated 1000 random input arguments. While we haven't mentioned it before, every spec is both a validator and a data generator for values that match the spec. Once we created a spec for the function arguments, check was able to use it to generate random arguments.

Generating Examples

The argument spec we used above was (s/cat :ns (s/? string?) :name string?). To simulate how check generates random arguments from that spec, we can use the s/exercise function, which produces pairs of examples and their conformed values:

```
(s/exercise (s/cat :ns (s/? string?) :name string?))
-> ([("" "") {:ns "", :name ""}]
    [("F" "") {:ns "F", :name ""}]
       [("s" "73") {:ns "s", :name "73"}]
       [("u") {:name "u"}]
       [("") {:name ""}]
       [("" "3y") {:ns "", :name "3y"}]
       [("t" "9pudu") {:ns "t", :name "9pudu"}]
       [("Xhw25" "nPR7C9C") {:ns "Xhw25", :name "nPR7C9C"}]
       [("FXs3E" "N") {:ns "FXs3E", :name "N"}]
       [("UhUN5dZK1" "le8") {:ns "UhUN5dZK1", :name "le8"}])
```

This example works, but sometimes spec can't automatically create a valid generator, or you need to create a custom generator for related arguments. In the following sections, we'll see how to address these issues. First, let's consider a case where an s/and spec doesn't produce any values.

Combining Generators With s/and

One of the most common ways to compose specs is with s/and. The s/and operation uses the generator of its first component spec, then filters the values by each subsequent component spec.

For example, consider the following spec for an odd number greater than 100:

```
(defn big? [ ] (> x 100))
```

```
(s/def ::big-odd (s/and odd? big?))
```

This would work as a spec, but its automatic generator doesn't work:

```
(s/exercise ::big-odd)
-> Unable to construct gen at: [] for: odd?
```

The problem is that while many common Clojure predicates have automatically mapped generators, the predicates we're using here do not. The odd? predicate works on more than one numeric type and so is not mapped to a generator. The big? predicate is a custom predicate that will never have mappings.

To fix this, we need to add an initial predicate that has a mapped genera-tor—the type-oriented predicates are all good choices for that. Let's insert int? at the beginning:

```
(s/def ::big-odd-int (s/and int? odd? big?))
-> ::big-odd-int

(s/exercise ::big-odd-int)
-> ([1367 1367]
    [7669 7669]
    [171130765 171130765]
    ... )
```

When you debug generators for s/and specs, remember that only the first compo-nent spec's generator is used. Another related problem with s/and generators is when the component specs after the first one are too "sparse", filtering so many values that the generator would have to work for a long time to generate a valid one. The best way to solve this problem is with a custom generator.

Creating Custom Generators

There are many cases where the automatic generator is either inefficient or will not produce related values that are useful. For example, a function might take two arguments—a collection and an element from that collection. An automatic generator is unlikely to independently produce valid combinations of values. Instead, you need to supply your own custom generator that satisfies this constraint.

You have a number of opportunities in spec to replace the automatically created generator with your own implementation. Some specs like s/coll-of, s/map-of, s/every, s/every-kv, and s/keys accept a custom generator option.

Also, you can explicitly add a replacement generator to any existing spec with s/with-gen. And you can temporarily override a generator by name or path with generator overrides in some functions like s/exercise, stest/instrument, and stest/check—those overrides take effect only for the duration of the call.

We can create generators in several ways. The simplest way is to first create a different spec, then use s/gen to retrieve its generator. Alternately, the clo-jure.spec.gen.alpha namespace, typically aliased as gen, contains other generators and functions to combine generators. The generators in this namespace are wrappers around the test.check library, so you need that library on your classpath to do any work with generators.

Let's look at how we can supply a replacement generator for :marble/color to hard-code exactly the color to return. Occasionally this is useful to reduce the randomness of your inputs or to directly supply a complex input that would be difficult to generate.

Here we use s/with-gen to override the default generator for :marble/color (which produces marbles of all colors) and replace it with a generator that only produces red marbles:

```
(s/def :marble/color-red
  (s/with-gen :marble/color #(s/gen #{:red})))
-> :marble/color-red

(s/exercise :marble/color-red)
-> ([:red :red] [:red :red] [:red :red] ...)
```

The clojure.spec.gen.alpha namespace contains many functions to generate all of the standard Clojure types, collections, and more. One function it provides (gen/fmap) allows you to start from a source generator, then modify each generated value by applying another function.

For example, to generate strings that start with a standard prefix, you can generate the random suffix, then concatenate the prefix. The generator itself might look like this:

```
(require '[clojure.string :as str])

(s/def ::sku
  (s/with-gen (s/and string? #(str/starts-with? % "SKU-"))
    (fn [] (gen/fmap #(str "SKU-" %) (s/gen string?)))))
```

Here, gen/fmap starts with a source generator (the generator for any valid string), then applies a function to the generated values to prefix the random string with "SKU-". That generator is then attached to the spec. Let's try exercising it:

```
(s/exercise ::sku)
-> (["SKU-" "SKU-"] ["SKU-P" "SKU-P"] ["SKU-L56" "SKU-L56"] ...)
```

You now know how to adjust your specs to create better generators, and when necessary, how to replace your generators with your own custom implementations. With these tools, you can create good argument specs for your functions and automatically test your functions with generative testing.

Wrapping Up

In this chapter we've looked at how to specify the structure of both our data and our functions. You learned how to validate your data using a spec with s/valid?, as well as how to discover how it conformed with s/conform or how it failed with s/explain.

Additionally, you learned how to check for invalid calls with stest/instrument when working at the REPL or in tests, and how to automatically test a properly spec'd function using stest/check.

The spec library requires a fair amount of extra effort in the code you write, particularly if you take the extra step to ensure that the :args spec of any function generates high-quality inputs for testing. However, you also gain lots of leverage by doing so, and it's entirely up to you how much of your code to spec.

Next, we change our focus to consider the management of state and how to write concurrent programs using Clojure.

CHAPTER 6

State and Concurrency

A *state* is the value of an identity at a point in time.

Quite a lot is packed into the previous sentence. Let's unpack the word *value* first. A value is an immutable, persistent data structure. When you can program entirely with values, life is easy, as we saw in Chapter 4, *Functional Programming*, on page 81.

The flow of time makes things substantially more difficult. Are the New York Yankees the same now as they were last year? In 1927? The roster of the Yankees is an *identity* whose value changes over time.

Updating an identity does not destroy old values. In fact, updating an identity has no impact on existing values whatsoever. The Yankees could trade every player, or disband in a fit of boredom, without in any way altering our ability to think about any past Yankees we happen to care about.

Clojure's reference model clearly separates identities from values. Almost everything in Clojure is a value. For identities, Clojure provides four reference types:

- Refs manage *coordinated, synchronous* changes to shared state.
- Atoms manage *uncoordinated, synchronous* changes to shared state.
- Agents manage *asynchronous* changes to shared state.
- Vars manage *thread-local* state.

Each of these APIs is discussed in this chapter. At the end of the chapter, we'll develop a sample application. The Snake game demonstrates how to divide an application model into immutable and mutable components.

Before we start, let's review the intersection of state with concurrency and parallelism, as well as look at the difficulty with traditional lock-based approaches.

Concurrency, Parallelism, and Locking

A concurrent program models more than one thing happening simultaneously. A parallel program takes an operation that could be sequential and chooses to break it into separate pieces that can execute concurrently to speed overall execution.

There are many reasons to write concurrent or parallel programs:

- For decades, performance improvements have come from packing more power into cores. Now, and for the near future, performance improvements will come from using more cores. Our hardware is itself more concurrent than ever, and systems must be concurrent to take advantage of this power.

- Expensive computations may need to execute in parallel on multiple cores (or multiple boxes) to complete in a timely manner.

- Tasks that are blocked waiting for a resource should stand down and let other tasks use available processors.

- User interfaces need to remain responsive while performing long-running tasks.

- Operations that are logically independent are easier to implement if the platform can recognize and take advantage of their independence.

Concurrency makes it glaringly obvious that more than one observer (e.g., thread) may be looking at your data. This is a big problem for languages that complect[1] value and identity. Such languages treat a piece of data as a bank ledger with only one line. Each new operation erases history, potentially corrupting the work of every other thread on the system.

While concurrency makes the challenges more obvious, it's a mistake to assume that multiple observers come into play only with concurrency. If your program ever has two variables that refer to the same data, those variables are different observers. If your program allows mutability at all, then you must think carefully about state.

Mutable languages tend to tackle the challenge by locking and defensive copying. Continuing the ledger analogy: the bank hires guards (locks) to supervise the activities of anybody using a ledger, and nobody is allowed to modify a ledger while anybody else is using it.

---

1. http://www.infoq.com/presentations/Simple-Made-Easy

When the performance becomes really bad, the bank may even ask ledger readers to make their own private copies of the ledger so they can get out of the way and let transactions continue. These copies must still be supervised by the guards!

As irritating as this model sounds, it gets worse at the level of implementation detail. Choosing what and where to lock is a difficult task. If you get it wrong, all sorts of bad things can happen. *Race conditions* between threads can corrupt data. *Deadlocks* can stop an entire program from functioning at all. *Java Concurrency in Practice [Goe06]* covers these and other problems, plus their solutions, in detail. It's a terrific book, but it's difficult to read it and not ask yourself, "Is there another way?"

Clojure's model for state and identity solves these problems. The bulk of program code is functional. The small parts of the codebase that truly benefit from mutability are distinct and must explicitly select one of four reference models. Using these models, you can split your models into two layers:

- A *functional model* that has no mutable state. Most of your code will normally be in this layer, which is easier to read, easier to test, and easier to parallelize.

- *Reference models* for the parts of the application that you find more convenient to deal with using mutable state (despite its disadvantages).

Let's get started working with state in Clojure, using the most notorious of Clojure's reference models: software transactional memory.

Refs and Software Transactional Memory

Most objects in Clojure are immutable. When you really want mutable data, you must be explicit about it, such as by creating a mutable *reference* (ref) to an immutable object. You create a ref with this:

```
(ref initial-state)
```

For example, you could create a reference to the current song in your music playlist:

```
(def current-track (ref "Mars, the Bringer of War"))
-> #'user/current-track
```

The ref wraps and protects access to its internal state. To read the contents of the reference, you can call deref:

```
(deref reference)
```

The deref function can be shortened to the @ reader macro. Try using both deref and @ to dereference current-track:

```
(deref current-track)
-> "Mars, the Bringer of War"
```

```
@current-track
-> "Mars, the Bringer of War"
```

Notice how in this example the Clojure model fits the real world. A track is an immutable entity. It doesn't change into another track when you're finished listening to it. But the *current* track is a reference to an entity, and it does change.

ref-set

You can change where a reference points with ref-set:

```
(ref-set reference new-value)
```

Call ref-set to listen to a different track:

```
(ref-set current-track "Venus, the Bringer of Peace")
-> java.lang.IllegalStateException: No transaction running
```

Oops. Because refs are mutable, you must protect their updates. In many languages, you would use a *lock* for this purpose. In Clojure, you can use a *transaction*. Transactions are wrapped in a dosync:

```
(dosync & exprs)
```

Wrap your ref-set with a dosync, and all is well.

```
(dosync (ref-set current-track "Venus, the Bringer of Peace"))
-> "Venus, the Bringer of Peace"
```

The current-track reference now refers to a different track.

Transactional Properties

Like database transactions, Software Transactional Memory (STM) allows programmers to describe reads and writes to stateful references in the scope of a transaction. These transactions guarantee some important properties:

- Updates are *atomic*. If you update more than one ref in a transaction, the cumulative effect of all the updates will appear as a single instantaneous event to anyone not inside your transaction.

- Updates are *consistent*. Refs can specify validation functions. If any of these functions fail, the entire transaction will fail.

- Updates are *isolated*. Running transactions can't see partially completed results from other transactions.

Databases provide the additional guarantee that updates are *durable*. Because Clojure's transactions are in-memory transactions, Clojure does not guarantee that updates are durable. If you want a durable transaction in Clojure, you should use a database.

Together, the four transactional properties are called ACID. Databases provide ACID; Clojure's STM provides ACI.

If you change more than one ref in a single transaction, the changes are all coordinated to "happen at the same time" from the perspective of any code outside the transaction. So, you can make sure that updates to current-track and current-composer are *coordinated*:

```
(def current-track (ref "Venus, the Bringer of Peace"))
-> #'user/current-track
(def current-composer (ref "Holst"))
-> #'user/current-composer

(dosync
  (ref-set current-track "Credo")
  (ref-set current-composer "Byrd"))
▶ "Byrd"
```

Because the updates are in a transaction, no other thread will ever see an updated track with an out-of-date composer, or vice versa.

alter

The current-track example is deceptively easy, because updates to the ref are totally independent of any previous state. Let's build a more complex example, where transactions need to update existing information. A simple chat application fits the bill. First, create a message record that has a sender and some text:

src/examples/chat.clj
```
(defrecord Message [sender text])
```

Now, you can create messages by instantiating the record:

```
(->Message "Aaron" "Hello")
-> #:user.Message{:sender "Aaron", :text "Hello"}
```

Users of the chat application want to see the most recent message first, so a list is a good data structure. Create a messages reference that points to an initially empty list:

```
(def messages (ref ()))
```

Now you need a function to add a new message to the front of messages. You could simply deref to get the list of messages, cons the new message, and then ref-set the updated list back into messages:

```
; bad idea
(defn naive-add-message [msg]
  (dosync (ref-set messages (cons msg @messages))))
```

But there's a better option. Why not perform the read and update in a single step? Clojure's alter will apply an update function to a referenced object within a transaction:

```
(alter ref update-fn & args...)
```

alter returns the new value of the ref within the transaction. When a transaction successfully completes, the ref will take on its last in-transaction value. Using alter instead of ref-set makes the code more readable:

```
(defn add-message [msg]
  (dosync (alter messages conj msg)))
```

Notice that the update function is conj (short for "conjoin"), not cons. This is because conj takes arguments in an order suitable for use with alter:

```
(cons item sequence)
(conj sequence item)
```

The alter function calls its update-fn with the current reference value as its first argument, as conj expects. If you plan to write your own update functions, they should follow the same structure as conj:

```
(your-func thing-that-gets-updated & optional-other-args)
```

Try adding a few messages to see that the code works as expected:

```
(add-message (->Message "user 1" "hello"))
-> (#:user.Message{:sender "user 1", :text "hello"})

(add-message (->Message "user 2" "howdy"))
-> (#:user.Message{:sender "user 2", :text "howdy"}
    #:user.Message{:sender "user 1", :text "hello"})
```

alter is the workhorse of Clojure's STM and the primary means of updating refs. But if you know a little about how the STM works, you may be able to optimize your transactions in certain scenarios.

How STM Works: MVCC

Clojure's STM uses a technique called Multiversion Concurrency Control (MVCC), which is also used in several major databases. Here's how MVCC works in Clojure.

Transaction A begins by taking a *point*, which is simply a number that acts as a unique timestamp in the STM world. Transaction A has access to its own *effectively private* copy of any reference it needs, associated with the point. Clojure's persistent data structures (*Persistent Data Structures*, on page 82) make it cheap to provide these effectively private copies.

During Transaction A, operations on a ref work against (and return) the transaction's private copy of the ref's data, called the *in-transaction value*.

If at any point the STM detects that another transaction has already set/altered a ref that Transaction A wants to set/alter, Transaction A is forced to retry. If you throw an exception out of the dosync block, then Transaction A aborts *without* a retry.

If and when Transaction A commits, its heretofore private writes will become visible to the world, associated with a single point in the transaction timeline.

Sometimes the approach implied by alter is too cautious. What if you *don't care* that another transaction altered a reference in the middle of your transaction? If in such a situation you'd be willing to commit your changes anyway, you can beat alter's performance with commute.

commute

commute is a specialized variant of alter allowing for more concurrency:

```
(commute ref update-fn & args...)
```

Of course, there's a trade-off. Commutes are so named because they must be *commutative*. That is, updates must be able to occur in any order. This gives the STM system freedom to reorder commutes.

To use commute, replace alter with commute in your implementation of add-message:

```
(defn add-message-commute [msg]
  (dosync (commute messages conj msg)))
```

commute returns the new value of the ref. However, the last in-transaction value you see from a commute will *not* always match the end-of-transaction value of a ref, because of reordering. If another transaction sneaks in and alters a ref that you're trying to commute, the STM will not restart your transaction. Instead, it will run your commute function again, out of order. Your transaction will *never even see* the ref value that your commute function finally ran against.

Since Clojure's STM can reorder commutes behind your back, you can only use them when you don't care about ordering. Literally speaking, this isn't true for a chat application. The list of messages most certainly has an order, so if two message adds get reversed, the resulting list will not show correctly the order in which the messages arrived.

Practically speaking, chat message updates are *commutative enough*. STM-based reordering of messages will likely happen on time scales of microseconds or less. For users of a chat application, there are already reorderings on much larger time scales due to network and human latency. (Think about times that you have "spoken out of turn" in an online chat because another speaker's message hadn't reached you yet.) Since these larger reorderings are unfixable, it's reasonable for a chat application to ignore the smaller reorderings that might bubble up from Clojure's STM.

Prefer alter

Many updates are not commutative. For example, consider a counter that returns an increasing sequence of numbers. You might use such a counter to build unique IDs in a system. The counter can be a simple reference to a number:

src/examples/concurrency.clj
```
(def counter (ref 0))
```

You should not use commute to update the counter. commute returns the in-transaction value of the counter at the time of the commute, but reorderings could cause the actual end-of-transaction value to be different. This could lead to more than one caller getting the same counter value. Instead, use alter:

```
(defn next-counter [] (dosync (alter counter inc)))
```

Try calling next-counter a few times to verify that the counter works as expected:

```
(next-counter)
-> 1

(next-counter)
-> 2
```

In general, you should prefer alter over commute. Its semantics are easy to understand and error proof. commute, on the other hand, requires that you think carefully about transactional semantics. If you use alter when commute would suffice, the worst thing that might happen is performance degradation. But if you use commute when alter is required, you'll introduce a subtle bug that's difficult to detect with automated tests.

Adding Validation to Refs

Database transactions maintain consistency through various integrity checks. You can do something similar with Clojure's transactional memory, by specifying a validation function when you create a ref:

```
(ref initial-state options*)
; options include:
;   :validator validate-fn
;   :meta metadata-map
```

The options to ref include an optional validation function that can throw an exception to prevent a transaction from completing. Note that options is *not* a map; it's a sequence of key/value pairs spliced into the function call.

Continuing the chat example, add a validation function to the messages reference that guarantees that all messages have non-nil values for :sender and :text:

```
src/examples/chat.clj
(defn valid-message? [msg]
  (and (:sender msg) (:text msg)))

(def validate-message-list #(every? valid-message? %))

(def messages (ref () :validator validate-message-list))
```

This validation acts like a key constraint on a table in a database transaction. If the constraint fails, the entire transaction rolls back. Try adding an ill-formed message such as a simple string:

```
(add-message "not a valid message")
-> java.lang.IllegalStateException: Invalid reference state

@messages
-> ()
```

Messages that match the constraint are no problem:

```
(add-message (->Message "Aaron" "Real Message"))
-> (#:user.Message{:sender "Aaron", :text "Real Message"})
```

Refs are great for coordinated access to shared state, but not all tasks require such coordination. For updating a single piece of isolated data, prefer an atom.

Use Atoms for Uncoordinated, Synchronous Updates

Atoms are a lighter-weight mechanism than refs. Where multiple ref updates can be coordinated in a transaction, atoms allow updates of a single value, uncoordinated with anything else.

You create atoms with atom, which has a signature similar to ref:

```
(atom initial-state options?)
; options include:
;    :validator validate-fn
;    :meta metadata-map
```

Returning to our music player example, you could store the current-track in an atom instead of a ref:

```
(def current-track (atom "Venus, the Bringer of Peace"))
-> #'user/current-track
```

You can dereference an atom to get its value, just as you would a ref:

```
(deref current-track)
-> "Venus, the Bringer of Peace"

@current-track
-> "Venus, the Bringer of Peace"
```

Atoms don't participate in transactions and thus do not require a dosync. To set the value of an atom, just call reset!.

```
(reset! an-atom newval)
```

For example, you can set current-track to "Credo":

```
(reset! current-track "Credo")
-> "Credo"
```

What if you want to coordinate an update of both current-track and current-composer with an atom? The short answer is, "You can't." That's the difference between refs and atoms. If you need coordinated access, use a ref.

The longer answer is, "You can...if you're willing to change the way you model the problem." What if you store the track title and composer in a map and then store the whole map in a single atom?

```
(def current-track (atom {:title "Credo" :composer "Byrd"}))
-> #'user/current-track
```

Now you can update both values in a single reset!.

```
(reset! current-track {:title "Spem in Alium" :composer "Tallis"})
-> {:title "Spem in Alium", :composer "Tallis"}
```

Maybe you like to listen to several tracks in a row by the same composer. If so, you want to change the track title but keep the same composer. swap! will do the trick:

```
(swap! an-atom f & args)
```

swap! updates an-atom by calling function f on the current value of an-atom, plus any additional args.

To change just the track title, use swap! with assoc to update only the :title:

```
(swap! current-track assoc :title "Sancte Deus")
-> {:title "Sancte Deus", :composer "Tallis"}
```

swap! returns the new value. Calls to swap! might be retried, if other threads are attempting to modify the same atom. So, the function you pass to swap! should have no side effects.

Both refs and atoms perform synchronous updates. When the update function returns, the value is already changed. If you don't need this level of control and can tolerate updates happening asynchronously at some later time, prefer an agent.

Use Agents for Asynchronous Updates

Some applications have tasks that can proceed independently with minimal coordination between tasks. Clojure *agents* support this style of task.

Agents have much in common with refs. Like refs, you create an agent by wrapping some piece of initial state:

```
(agent initial-state)
```

Create a counter agent that wraps an initial count of zero:

```
(def counter (agent 0))
-> #'user/counter
```

Once you have an agent, you can send the agent a function to update its state. send queues an update-fn to run later, on a thread in a thread pool:

```
(send agent update-fn & args)
```

Sending to an agent is much like commuting a ref. Tell the counter to inc:

```
(send counter inc)
-> #object[clojure.lang.Agent 0x7ae288e1 {:status :ready, :val 1}]
```

Notice that the call to send doesn't return the new value of the agent, returning instead the agent itself. That's because send *does not know* the new value. After send queues the inc to run later, it returns immediately.

Although send does not know the new value of an agent, the REPL *might* know. Depending on whether the agent thread or the REPL thread runs first, you might see a 1 or a 0 for the :val in the previous output.

You can check the current value of an agent with deref/@, just as you would a ref. By the time you get around to checking the counter, the inc will almost certainly have completed on the thread pool, raising the value to 1:

```
@counter
-> 1
```

If the race condition between the REPL and the agent thread bothers you, there is a solution. If you want to be sure that the agent has completed the actions *you sent* to it, you can call await or await-for:

```
(await & agents)
```

```
(await-for timeout-millis & agents)
```

These functions cause the current thread to block until all actions sent from the current thread or agent have completed. await-for returns nil if the timeout expires and returns a non-nil value otherwise. await has no timeout, so be careful: await is willing to wait forever.

Validating Agents and Handling Errors

Agents have other points in common with refs. They also can take a validation function:

```
(agent initial-state options*)
; options include:
;   :validator validate-fn
;   :meta metadata-map
;   :error-handler handler-fn
;   :error-mode mode-keyword (:continue or :fail)
```

Recreate the counter with a validator that ensures it's a number:

```
(def counter (agent 0 :validator number?))
-> #'user/counter
```

Try to set the agent to a value that's not a number by passing an update function that ignores the current value and simply returns a string:

```
(send counter (fn [_] "boo"))
-> #object[clojure.lang.Agent 0x3a46c14f {:status :ready, :val 0}]
```

Everything looks fine (so far) because send still returns immediately. When the agent tries to update itself on a pooled thread, it encounters an exception while applying the action. Agents have two possible error modes—:fail and :continue. If no :error-handler is supplied when the agent is created, the error mode is set to :fail, and any exception that occurs during an action or during valida-tion puts the agent into an exceptional state.

When an agent is in this failed state, it can still be dereferenced and will return the last value from before the failed action. To discover the last error on an agent, call agent-error which returns either the failure or nil if not in a failed state:

```
(agent-error counter)
-> #error {
    :cause "Invalid reference state"
    :via [{:type java.lang.IllegalStateException
          :message "Invalid reference state"
          :at [clojure.lang.ARef validate "ARef.java" 33]}]
          :trace
            [[clojure.lang.ARef validate "ARef.java" 33]
             ... ]}]}
```

All new actions are queued until the agent is restarted using restart-agent. Once an agent has errors, all subsequent attempts to query the agent return an error. You can make the agent active again by calling restart-agent:

```
(restart-agent counter 0)
-> nil

@counter
-> 0
```

If an :error-handler is supplied when the agent is created, the agent will instead be in error mode :continue. When an error occurs, the error handler is invoked and the agent then continues as if no error occurred.

```
(defn handler [agent err]
  (println "ERR!" (.getMessage err)))
-> #'user/handler

(def counter2 (agent 0 :validator number? :error-handler handler))
-> #'user/counter2
```

```
(send counter2 (fn [_] "boo"))
| ERR! Invalid reference state
-> #object[clojure.lang.Agent 0x5ba87f7f {:status :ready, :val 0}]

(send counter2 inc)
-> #object[clojure.lang.Agent 0x5ba87f7f {:status :ready, :val 0}]

@counter2
-> 1
```

Now that you know the basics of agents, let's use them in conjunction with refs and transactions.

Including Agents in Transactions

Transactions should not have side effects, because Clojure may retry a transaction an arbitrary number of times. However, sometimes you *want* a side effect when a transaction succeeds. Agents provide a solution. If you send an action to an agent from within a transaction, that action is sent exactly once, if and only if the transaction succeeds.

As an example of where this would be useful, consider an agent that writes to a file when a transaction succeeds. You could combine such an agent with the chat example from *commute*, on page 143, to automatically back up chat messages. First, create a backup-agent that stores the filename to write to:

src/examples/concurrency.clj
```
(def backup-agent (agent "output/messages-backup.clj"))
```

Then, create a modified version of add-message. The new function add-message-with-backup should do two additional things:

- Grab the return value of commute, which is the current database of messages, in a let binding.

- While still inside a transaction, send an action to the backup agent that writes the message database to filename. For simplicity, have the action function return filename so that the agent uses the same filename for the next backup.

```
(defn add-message-with-backup [msg]
  (dosync
    (let [snapshot (commute messages conj msg)]
      (send-off backup-agent (fn [filename]
                               (spit filename snapshot)
                               filename))
      snapshot)))
```

The new function has one other critical difference: it calls send-off instead of send to communicate with the agent. send-off is a variant of send for actions that expect to block, as a file write might do. send-off actions get their own expandable thread pool. Never send a blocking function, or you may unnecessarily prevent other agents from making progress.

Try adding some messages using add-message-with-backup:

```
(add-message-with-backup (->Message "John" "Message One"))
-> (#:user.Message{:sender "John", :text "Message One"})

(add-message-with-backup (->Message "Jane" "Message Two"))
-> (#:user.Message{:sender "Jane", :text "Message Two"}
     #:user.Message{:sender "John", :text "Message One"})
```

You can check both the in-memory messages as well as the backup file messages-backup to verify that they contain the same structure.

You could enhance the backup strategy in this example in various ways. You could provide the option to back up less often than on every update or back up only information that has changed since the last backup.

Since Clojure's STM provides the ACI properties of ACID, and since writing to a file provides the D ("durability"), it's tempting to think that STM plus a backup agent equals a database. This is *not* the case. A Clojure transaction promises only to send/send-off an action to the agent; it does not actually perform the action under the ACI umbrella. So for example, a transaction could complete, and then someone could unplug the power cord before the agent writes to the database. The moral is simple. If your problem calls for a real database, use a real database.

The Unified Update Model

As you've seen, refs, atoms, and agents all provide functions for updating their state by applying a function to their previous state. This unified model for handling shared state is one of the central concepts of Clojure. The unified functions for each reference type are summarized in the following table.

Update Mechanism	Ref Function	Atom Function	Agent Function
Function application	alter	swap!	send-off
Function (commutative)	commute	N/A	N/A
Function (nonblocking)	N/A	N/A	send
Simple setter	ref-set	reset!	N/A

The unified update model is by far the most important way to update refs, atoms, and agents. The ancillary functions, on the other hand, are optimizations and options that stem from the semantics peculiar to each API:

- The opportunity for the commute optimization arises when coordinating updates. Since only refs provide coordinated updates, commute makes sense only for refs.

- Updates to refs and atoms take place on the thread they are called on, so they provide no scheduling options. Agents update later, on a thread pool, making blocking/nonblocking a relevant scheduling option.

Clojure's final reference type, the var, is a different beast entirely. Vars do not participate in the unified update model and are instead used to manage thread-local, private state.

Managing Per-Thread State with Vars

When you call def or defn, you create a *var*. In all the examples so far in the book, you pass an initial value to def, which becomes the *root binding* for the var. For example, the following code creates a root binding for foo of 10:

```
(def ^:dynamic foo 10)
-> #'user/foo
```

The binding of foo is shared by all threads. You can check the value of foo on your own thread:

```
foo
-> 10
```

You can also verify the value of foo from another thread. Create a new thread, passing it a function that prints foo. Don't forget to start the thread:

```
user=> (.start (Thread. (fn [] (println foo))))
-> nil
| 10
```

In the previous example, the call to start() returns nil, and then the value of foo is printed from a new thread.

Most vars are content to keep their root bindings forever. However, you can create a *thread-local* binding for a var with the binding macro:

```
(binding [bindings] & body)
```

Bindings have *dynamic scope*. In other words, a binding is visible anywhere a thread's execution takes it, until the thread exits the scope where the binding began. A binding is not visible to any other threads.

Structurally, a binding looks a lot like a let. Create a thread-local binding for foo and check its value:

```
(binding [foo 42] foo)
-> 42
```

To see the difference between binding and let, create a simple function that prints the value of foo:

```
(defn print-foo [] (println foo))
-> #'user/print-foo
```

Now, try calling print-foo from both a let and a binding:

```
(let [foo "let foo"] (print-foo))
| 10
```

```
(binding [foo "bound foo"] (print-foo))
| bound foo
```

As you can see, the let has no effect outside its own form, so the first print-foo prints the root binding 10. The binding, on the other hand, stays in effect through any nested function invocations, so the second print-foo prints bound foo.

Acting at a Distance

Vars intended for dynamic binding are sometimes called *special* variables. It's good style to name them with leading and trailing asterisks. For example, Clojure uses dynamic binding for thread-wide options, such as the standard I/O streams *in*, *out*, and *err*. Dynamic bindings enable *action at a distance*. When you change a dynamic binding, you can change the behavior of distant functions without changing any function arguments.

One kind of action at a distance is temporarily augmenting the behavior of a function. In some languages this would be classified as aspect-oriented programming; in Clojure it's a side effect of dynamic binding. As an example, imagine that you have a function that performs an expensive calculation. To simulate this, write a function named slow-double that sleeps for a 10th of a second and then doubles its input.

```
(defn ^:dynamic slow-double [n]
  (Thread/sleep 100)
  (* n 2))
```

Next, write a function named calls-slow-double that calls slow-double for each item in [1 2 1 2 1 2]:

```
(defn calls-slow-double []
  (map slow-double [1 2 1 2 1 2]))
```

Time a call to calls-slow-double. With six internal calls to slow-double, it should take a little over six-tenths of a second. Note that you'll have to run through the result with dorun; otherwise, Clojure's map will outsmart you by immediately returning a lazy sequence.

```
(time (dorun (calls-slow-double)))
"Elapsed time: 601.418 msecs"
```

Reading the code, you can tell that calls-slow-double is slow because it does the same work over and over again. One times two is two, no matter how many times you ask.

Calculations such as slow-double are good candidates for *memoization*, which we explored in *Shortcutting Recursion with Memoization*, on page 105. When you memoize a function, it keeps a cache mapping past inputs to past outputs. If subsequent calls hit the cache, they return almost immediately. Thus, you're trading space (the cache) for time (calculating the function again for the same inputs).

Clojure provides memoize, which takes a function and returns a memoization of that function:

```
(memoize function)
```

slow-double is a great candidate for memoization, but it isn't memoized yet, and clients like calls-slow-double already use the slow, unmemoized version. With dynamic binding, this is no problem. Create a binding to a memoized version of slow-double and call calls-slow-double from within the binding.

```
(defn demo-memoize []
  (time
    (dorun
      (binding [slow-double (memoize slow-double)]
        (calls-slow-double)))))
```

With the memoized version of slow-double, calls-slow-double runs three times faster, completing in about two-tenths of a second:

```
(demo-memoize)
"Elapsed time: 203.115 msecs"
```

This example demonstrates the power and the danger of action at a distance. By dynamically rebinding a function such as slow-double, you change the behavior of *other* functions such as calls-slow-double without their knowledge or consent. With lexical binding forms such as let, it's easy to see the entire range of your changes. Dynamic binding is not so simple. It can change the behavior of other forms in other files, far from the point in your source where the binding occurs.

Used occasionally, dynamic binding has great power. But it should not become your primary mechanism for extension or reuse. Functions that use dynamic bindings are not pure functions and can quickly lose the benefits of Clojure's functional style.

Working with Java Callback APIs

Several Java APIs depend on callback event handlers. UI frameworks such as Swing use event handlers to respond to user input. XML parsers such as SAX depend on the user implementing a callback handler interface.

These callback handlers are written with mutable objects in mind. Also, they tend to be single threaded. In Clojure, the best way to meet such APIs halfway is to use dynamic bindings. This involves mutable references that feel almost like variables, but because they're used in a single-threaded setting, they don't present any concurrency problems.

Clojure provides the set! special form for setting a thread-local dynamic binding:

```
(set! var-symbol new-value)
```

set! should be used rarely. One of the only places in the entire Clojure core that uses set! is the Clojure implementation of a SAX ContentHandler.

A ContentHandler receives callbacks as a parser encounters various bits of an XML stream. In nontrivial scenarios, the ContentHandler needs to keep track of *where it is* in the XML stream: the current stack of open elements, current character data, and so on.

In Clojure-speak, you can think of a ContentHandler's current position as a mutable pointer to a specific spot in an immutable XML stream. It's unnecessary to use references in a ContentHandler, since everything happens on a single thread. Instead, Clojure's ContentHandler uses dynamic variables and set!. Here is the relevant detail:

```
; redacted from Clojure's xml.clj to focus on dynamic variable usage
(startElement
  [uri local-name q-name #^Attributes atts]
  ; details omitted
  (set! *stack* (conj *stack* *current*))
  (set! *current* e)
  (set! *state* :element))
nil)
```

```
(endElement
 [uri local-name q-name]
 ; details omitted
 (set! *current* (push-content (peek *stack*) *current*))
 (set! *stack* (pop *stack*))
 (set! *state* :between)
nil)
```

A SAX parser calls startElement when it encounters an XML start tag. The callback handler updates three thread-local variables. The *stack* is a stack of all the elements the current element is nested inside. The *current* is the current element, and the *state* keeps track of what kind of content is inside. (This is important primarily when inside character data, which is not shown here.)

endElement reverses the work of startElement by popping the *stack* and placing the top of the *stack* in *current*.

It's worth noting that this style of coding is the industry norm: objects are mutable, and programs are single-threadedly oblivious to the possibility of concurrency. Clojure permits this style as an explicit special case, and you should use it for interop purposes only.

The ContentHandler's use of set! does not leak mutable data into the rest of Clojure. Clojure uses the ContentHandler implementation to build an immutable Clojure structure.

You have now seen four different models for dealing with state. And since Clojure is built atop Java, you can also use Java's lock-based model. The models and their uses are summarized in the following table.

Model	Usage	Functions
Refs and STM	Coordinated, synchronous updates	Pure
Atoms	Uncoordinated, synchronous updates	Pure
Agents	Uncoordinated, asynchronous updates	Any
Vars	Thread-local dynamic scopes	Any
Java locks	Coordinated, synchronous updates	Any

Let's put these models to work in designing a small but complete application.

A Clojure Snake

The Snake game features a player-controlled snake that moves around a game grid hunting for an apple. When your snake eats an apple, it grows longer by a segment, and a new apple appears. If your snake reaches a certain length, you win. But if your snake crosses over its own body, you lose.

Before you start building your own snake, take a minute to try the completed version. Follow the instructions in the README file at the root of the sample code for the book to start a REPL, then enter the following:

```
(require '[examples.snake :refer :all])
```

```
(game)
```

Select the Snake window and use the arrow keys to control your snake.

Our design for the snake takes advantage of Clojure's functional nature and its support for explicit mutable state by dividing the game into three layers:

- The *functional model* will use pure functions to model as much of the game as possible.

- The *mutable model* will handle the mutable state of the game. The mutable model will use one or more of the reference models discussed in this chapter. Mutable state is much harder to test, so we'll keep this part small.

- The *GUI* will use Swing to draw the game and to accept input from the user.

These layers will make the Snake easy to build, test, and maintain.

As you work through this example, add your code to the file reader/snake.clj in the sample code. When you open the file, you'll see that it already imports/uses the Swing classes and Clojure libraries that you'll need:

src/reader/snake.clj
```
(ns reader.snake
  (:import (java.awt Color Dimension)
           (javax.swing JPanel JFrame Timer JOptionPane)
           (java.awt.event ActionListener KeyListener))
  (:refer examples.import-static :refer :all))
(import-static java.awt.event.KeyEvent VK_LEFT VK_RIGHT VK_UP VK_DOWN)
```

Now you're ready to build the functional model.

Other Snake Implementations

There's more than one way to skin a snake. You may enjoy comparing the snake presented here with these other snakes:

- David Van Horn's Snake,[a] written in Typed Scheme, has no mutable state.

- Dale Vaillancourt's Worm Game[b] includes some verifications using the theorem prover ACL2.

- Mark Volkmann wrote a Clojure Snake[c] designed for readability.

Each of the snake implementations has its own distinctive style. What would *your* style look like?

_____

a. http://planet.plt-scheme.org/package-source/dvanhorn/snake.plt/1/0/main.ss
b. http://dracula-lang.github.io/worm.html
c. http://www.ociweb.com/mark/programming/ClojureSnake.html

The Functional Model

First, create a set of constants to describe time, space, and motion:

```
(def width 75)
(def height 50)
(def point-size 10)
(def turn-millis 75)
(def win-length 5)
(def dirs { VK_LEFT  [-1  0]
            VK_RIGHT [ 1  0]
            VK_UP    [ 0 -1]
            VK_DOWN  [ 0  1]})
```

width and height set the size of the game board, and point-size is used to convert a game point into screen pixels. turn-millis is the heartbeat of the game, controlling how many milliseconds pass before each update of the game board. win-length is how many segments your snake needs before you win the game. (Five is a small number suitable for testing.) The dirs maps symbolic constants for the four directions to their vector equivalents. Since Swing already defines the VK_ constants for different directions, we'll reuse them here rather than define our own.

Next, create some basic math functions for the game:

```
(defn add-points [& pts]
  (vec (apply map + pts)))

(defn point-to-screen-rect [pt]
  (map #(* point-size %)
       [(pt 0) (pt 1) 1 1]))
```

The add-points function adds points together. You can use add-points to calculate the new position of a moving game object. For example, you can move an object at [10, 10] left by one:

```
(add-points [10 10] [-1 0])
-> [9 10]
```

point-to-screen-rect converts a point in game space to a rectangle on the screen:

```
(point-to-screen-rect [5 10])
-> (50 100 10 10)
```

Next, let's write a function to create a new apple:

```
(defn create-apple []
  {:location [(rand-int width) (rand-int height)]
   :color (Color. 210 50 90)
   :type :apple})
```

Apples occupy a single point, the :location, which is guaranteed to be on the game board. Snakes are a bit more complicated:

```
(defn create-snake []
  {:body (list [1 1])
   :dir [1 0]
   :type :snake
   :color (Color. 15 160 70)})
```

Because a snake can occupy multiple points on the board, it has a :body, which is a list of points. Also, snakes are always in motion in some direction expressed by :dir.

Next, create a function to move a snake. This should be a pure function, returning a new snake. Also, it should take a grow option, allowing the snake to grow after eating an apple.

```
(defn move [{:keys [body dir] :as snake} & grow]
  (assoc snake :body (cons (add-points (first body) dir)
                           (if grow body (butlast body)))))
```

move uses a fairly complex binding expression. The {:keys [body dir]} part makes the snake's body and dir available as their own bindings, and the :as snake part binds snake to the entire snake. The function proceeds as follows:

1. add-points creates a new point, which is the head of the original snake offset by the snake's direction of motion.

2. cons adds the new point to the front of the snake. If the snake is growing, the entire original snake is kept. Otherwise, it keeps all the original snake except the last segment (butlast).

3. assoc returns a new snake, which is a copy of the old snake but with an updated :body.

Test move by moving and growing a snake:

```
(move (create-snake))
-> {:body ([2 1]), ; etc.

(move (create-snake) :grow)
-> {:body ([2 1] [1 1]), ; etc.
```

Write a win? function to test whether a snake has won the game:

```
(defn win? [{body :body}]
  (>= (count body) win-length))
```

Test win? against different body sizes. Note that win? binds only the :body, so you don't need a "real" snake, just anything with a body:

```
(win? {:body [[1 1]]})
-> false

(win? {:body [[1 1] [1 2] [1 3] [1 4] [1 5]]})
-> true
```

A snake loses if its head ever comes into contact with the rest of its body. Write a head-overlaps-body? function to test for this, and use it to define lose?:

```
(defn head-overlaps-body? [{[head & body] :body}]
  (contains? (set body) head))

(def lose? head-overlaps-body?)
```

Test lose? against overlapping and nonoverlapping snake bodies:

```
(lose? {:body [[1 1] [1 2] [1 3]]})
-> false

(lose? {:body [[1 1] [1 2] [1 1]]})
-> true
```

A snake eats an apple if its head occupies the apple's location. Define an eats? function to test this:

```
(defn eats? [{[snake-head] :body} {apple :location}]
  (= snake-head apple))
```

Notice how clean the body of the eats? function is. All the work is done in the bindings: {[snake-head] :body} binds snake-head to the first element of the snake's :body, and {apple :location} binds apple to the apple's :location. Test eats? from the REPL:

```
(eats? {:body [[1 1] [1 2]]} {:location [2 2]})
-> false

(eats? {:body [[2 2] [1 2]]} {:location [2 2]})
-> true
```

Finally, you need some way to turn the snake, updating its :dir:

```
(defn turn [snake newdir]
  (assoc snake :dir newdir))
```

turn returns a new snake, with an updated direction:

```
(turn (create-snake) [0 -1])
-> {:body ([1 1]), :dir [0 -1], ; etc.
```

All of the code you've written so far is part of the functional model of the Snake game. It's easy to understand in part because it has no local variables and no mutable state. As you'll see in the next section, the amount of *mutable* state in the game is quite small. (It's even possible to implement the Snake with *no* mutable state, but that's not the purpose of this demo.)

Building a Mutable Model with STM

The mutable state of the Snake game can change in only three ways:

- A game can be reset to its initial state.

- Every turn, the snake updates its position. If it eats an apple, a new apple is placed.

- A snake can turn.

We'll implement each of these changes as functions that modify Clojure refs inside a transaction. That way, changes to the position of the snake and the apple will be synchronous and coordinated.

reset-game is trivial:

```
(defn reset-game [snake apple]
  (dosync (ref-set apple (create-apple))
          (ref-set snake (create-snake)))
  nil)
```

You can test reset-game by passing in some refs and then checking that they dereference to a snake and an apple:

```
(def test-snake (ref nil))
(def test-apple (ref nil))
```

```
(reset-game test-snake test-apple)
-> nil
```

```
@test-snake
-> {:body ([1 1]), :dir [1 0], ; etc.
```

```
@test-apple
-> {:location [52 8], ; etc.
```

update-direction is even more simpler than that; it's just a trivial wrapper around the functional turn:

```
(defn update-direction [snake newdir]
  (when newdir (dosync (alter snake turn newdir))))
```

Try turning your test-snake to move in the "up" direction:

```
(update-direction test-snake [0 -1])
-> {:body ([1 1]), :dir [0 -1], ; etc.
```

The most complicated mutating function is update-positions. If the snake eats the apple, a new apple is created, and the snake grows. Otherwise, the snake simply moves:

```
(defn update-positions [snake apple]
  (dosync
   (if (eats? @snake @apple)
     (do (ref-set apple (create-apple))
         (alter snake move :grow))
     (alter snake move)))
  nil)
```

To test update-positions, reset the game:

```
(reset-game test-snake test-apple)
-> nil
```

Then, move the apple into harm's way, under the snake:

```
(dosync (alter test-apple assoc :location [1 1]))
-> {:location [1 1], ; etc.
```

Now, after you update-positions, you should have a bigger, two-segment snake:

```
(update-positions test-snake test-apple)
-> nil
```

```
(:body @test-snake)
-> ([2 1] [1 1])
```

And that is all the mutable state of the Snake world: three functions, about a dozen lines of code.

The Snake GUI

The Snake GUI consists of functions that paint screen objects, respond to user input, and set up the various Swing components. Since snakes and apples are drawn from simple points, the painting functions are simple. The fill-point function fills in a single point:

```
(defn fill-point [g pt color]
  (let [[x y width height] (point-to-screen-rect pt)]
    (.setColor g color)
    (.fillRect g x y width height)))
```

The paint multimethod knows how to paint snakes and apples:

```
Line 1  (defmulti paint (fn [g object & _] (:type object)))
     2
     3  (defmethod paint :apple [g {:keys [location color]}]
     4    (fill-point g location color))
     5
     6  (defmethod paint :snake [g {:keys [body color]}]
     7    (doseq [point body]
     8      (fill-point g point color)))
```

paint takes two required arguments: g is a java.awt.Graphics instance, and object is the object to be painted. The defmulti includes an optional rest argument so that future implementations of paint have the option of taking more arguments. (See *Defining Multimethods*, on page 211 for an in-depth description of defmulti.) On line 3, the :apple method of paint binds the location and color of the apple and uses them to paint a single point on the screen. On line 6, the :snake method binds the snake's body and color and then uses doseq to paint each point in the body.

The meat of the UI is the game-panel function, which creates a Swing JPanel with handlers for painting the game, updating on each timer tick, and responding to user input:

```
Line 1  (defn game-panel [frame snake apple]
     -    (proxy [JPanel ActionListener KeyListener] []
     -      (paintComponent [g]
     -        (proxy-super paintComponent g)
     5        (paint g @snake)
     -        (paint g @apple))
     -      (actionPerformed [e]
     -        (update-positions snake apple)
     -        (when (lose? @snake)
    10          (reset-game snake apple)
     -          (JOptionPane/showMessageDialog frame "You lose!"))
     -        (when (win? @snake)
     -          (reset-game snake apple)
     -          (JOptionPane/showMessageDialog frame "You win!"))
```

```
15        (.repaint this))
  -     (keyPressed [e]
  -       (update-direction snake (dirs (.getKeyCode e))))
  -     (getPreferredSize []
  -       (Dimension. (* (inc width) point-size)
20                    (* (inc height) point-size)))
  -     (keyReleased [e])
  -     (keyTyped [e])))
```

game-panel is long but simple. It uses proxy to create a panel with a set of Swing callback methods.

- Swing calls paintComponent (line 3) to draw the panel. paintComponent calls proxy-super to invoke the normal JPanel behavior, and then it paints the snake and the apple.

- Swing will call actionPerformed (line 7) on every timer tick. actionPerformed updates the positions of the snake and the apple. If the game is over, the program displays a dialog and resets the game. Finally, it triggers a repaint with (.repaint this).

- Swing calls keyPressed (line 16) in response to keyboard input. keyPressed calls update-direction to change the snake's direction. (If the keyboard input is not an arrow key, the dirs function returns nil and update-direction does nothing.)

- The game panel ignores keyReleased and keyTyped.

The game function creates a new game:

```
Line 1  (defn game []
  -     (let [snake (ref (create-snake))
  -           apple (ref (create-apple))
  -           frame (JFrame. "Snake")
5             panel (game-panel frame snake apple)
  -           timer (Timer. turn-millis panel)]
  -       (doto panel
  -         (.setFocusable true)
  -         (.addKeyListener panel))
10        (doto frame
  -         (.add panel)
  -         (.pack)
  -         (.setVisible true))
  -       (.start timer)
15        [snake, apple, timer]))
```

On line 2, game creates all the necessary game objects: the mutable model objects snake and apple and the UI components frame, panel, and timer. Lines 7 and 10 perform boilerplate initialization of the panel and frame. Line 14 starts the game by kicking off the timer.

Line 15 returns a vector with the snake, apple, and time. This is for convenience when testing at the REPL; you can use these objects to move the snake and apple or to start and stop the game.

To start the game, use the snake library at the REPL, and run game. If you entered the code yourself, you can use the library name you picked (examples.reader in the instructions); otherwise, you can use the completed sample at examples.snake:

```
(require '[examples.snake :refer :all])
(game)
```

The game window may appear behind your REPL window. If this happens, use your local operating system fu to locate the game window.

There are many possible improvements to the Snake game. If the snake reaches the edge of the screen, perhaps it should turn to avoid disappearing from view. Or maybe you just lose the game. Sorry! Make the Snake game your own by improving it to suit your personal style.

Snakes Without Refs

We chose to implement the Snake game's mutable model using refs so we could coordinate the updates to the snake and the apple. Other approaches are also valid. For example, you could combine the snake and apple state into a single game object. With only one object, coordination is no longer required, and you can use an atom instead.

The file examples/atom-snake.clj demonstrates this approach. Functions like update-positions become part of the functional model and return a new game object with updated state:

```
src/examples/atom_snake.clj
(defn update-positions [{snake :snake, apple :apple, :as game}]
  (if (eats? snake apple)
    (merge game {:apple (create-apple) :snake (move snake :grow)})
    (merge game {:snake (move snake)})))
```

Notice how destructuring makes it easy to get at the internals of the game: both snake and apple are bound by the argument list.

The actual mutable updates are now all atom swap!s. We found these to be simple enough to leave them in the UI function game-panel, as this excerpt shows:

```
(actionPerformed [e]
  (swap! game update-positions)
  (when (lose? (@game :snake))
    (swap! game reset-game)
    (JOptionPane/showMessageDialog frame "You lose!")))
```

There are other possibilities as well. Chris Houser's fork of the book's sample code[2] demonstrates using an agent that Thread/sleeps instead of a Swing timer, as well as using a new agent per game turn to update the game's state.

Wrapping Up

Clojure's reference model is the most innovative part of the language. The combination of software transactional memory, agents, atoms, and dynamic binding that you've seen in this chapter gives Clojure powerful abstractions for all sorts of stateful systems. It also makes Clojure one of the few languages suited to the coming generation of multicore computer hardware.

Next, we'll look at one of Clojure's newer features. Some call it a solution to the "expression problem."[3] We call it a protocol.

---

2. http://github.com/Chouser/programming-clojure
3. http://en.wikipedia.org/wiki/Expression_problem

CHAPTER 7

Protocols and Datatypes

Abstractions lay at the foundation of reusable code. The Clojure language itself has abstractions for sequences, collections, and callability. Traditionally, these abstractions were described with Java interfaces and implemented using Java classes. In the beginning, Clojure provided proxy and gen-class, removing the need to drop all the way to Java to achieve this, but that changed with the introduction of protocols.

- Protocols provide an alternative to Java interfaces for high-performance polymorphic method dispatch.

- Datatypes provide an alternative to Java classes for creating implementations of abstractions defined with either protocols or interfaces.

Protocols and datatypes provide a high-performance, flexible mechanism for abstraction and concretion that removes the need to write Java interfaces and classes when programming in Clojure. With protocols and datatypes, you can create new abstractions and new types that implement those abstractions and even extend new abstractions to existing types.

In this chapter, we'll explore Clojure's approach to abstraction using protocols and datatypes. First, we will implement our own version of Clojure's built-in spit and slurp functions. Then, we'll take a short detour to build a CryptoVault, where you'll learn about extending some of Java's standard library. Finally, we'll put everything together using records and protocols to define musical notes and sequences. After working through these exercises, you will certainly see the power of Clojure's composable abstractions.

Programming to Abstractions

Clojure's spit and slurp I/O functions are built on two abstractions, reading and writing. This means you can use them with a variety of source and destination types, including files, URLs, and sockets, and they can be extended to support new types by anybody, whether they're existing types or newly defined.

- The slurp function takes an input source, reads the contents, and returns it as a string.

- The spit function takes an output destination and a value, converts the value to a string, and writes it to the output destination.

We'll start by writing basic versions of the two functions that can read from and write to files only. We'll then refactor the basic versions several times as we explore different approaches to supporting additional datatypes. Working through this will give you a good feel for the usefulness of programming to abstractions in general and the flexibility and power of Clojure's protocols and datatypes in particular.

After writing our versions of spit and slurp, called expectorate and gulp, respectively, which work with several existing datatypes, we'll create a new datatype, Crypto-Vault, which can be used with our versions of the functions as well as the originals.

The gulp function is a simplified version of Clojure's slurp function, and expectorate, despite its highfalutin name, is a dumbed-down version of Clojure's spit function. Let's write a basic version of gulp that can read from a java.io.File only.

src/examples/gulp.clj
```
(ns examples.gulp
  (:import (java.io FileInputStream InputStreamReader BufferedReader)))
(defn gulp [src]
  (let [sb (StringBuilder.)]
    (with-open [reader (-> src
                           FileInputStream.
                           InputStreamReader.
                           BufferedReader.)]
      (loop [c (.read reader)]
        (if (neg? c)
          (str sb)
          (do
            (.append sb (char c))
            (recur (.read reader))))))))
```

The gulp function creates a BufferedReader from a given File object and then loops/recurs over it, reading a character at a time and appending each to a StringBuilder until it reaches the end of the input where it returns a string. The basic expectorate function is even smaller:

```
src/examples/expectorate.clj
(ns examples.expectorate
  (:import (java.io FileOutputStream OutputStreamWriter BufferedWriter)))

(defn expectorate [dst content]
  (with-open [writer (-> dst
                         FileOutputStream.
                         OutputStreamWriter.
                         BufferedWriter.)]
    (.write writer (str content))))
```

It creates a BufferedWriter file, converts the value of the content parameter to a string, and writes it out to the BufferedWriter.

But what if we want to support additional types like Sockets, URLs, and basic input and output streams? We need to update gulp and expectorate to be able to make BufferedReaders and BufferedWriters from datatypes other than files. So, let's create two new functions, make-reader and make-writer, that will be responsible for this behavior.

- The make-reader function makes a BufferedReader from an input source.
- The make-writer makes a BufferedWriter from an output destination.

```
(defn make-reader [src]
  (-> src FileInputStream. InputStreamReader. BufferedReader.))

(defn make-writer [dst]
  (-> dst FileOutputStream. OutputStreamWriter. BufferedWriter.))
```

Like our basic gulp and expectorate functions, make-reader and make-writer work only on files, but that will change shortly. Now let's refactor gulp and expectorate to use the new functions:

```
src/examples/protocols.clj
(defn gulp [src]
  (let [sb (StringBuilder.)]
    (with-open [reader (make-reader src)]
      (loop [c (.read reader)]
        (if (neg? c)
          (str sb)
          (do
            (.append sb (char c))
            (recur (.read reader))))))))

(defn expectorate [dst content]
  (with-open [writer (make-writer dst)]
    (.write writer (str content))))
```

We can now add support for additional source and destination types to gulp and expectorate just by updating make-reader and make-writer. One approach to supporting additional types is to use a cond or condp statement to process different types appropriately. For example, the following version of make-reader replaces the call to the FileInputStream constructor with a condp statement that creates an InputStream from the given input, whether it's a File, Socket, or URL or already is an InputStream.

```
(defn make-reader [src]
  (-> (condp = (type src)
        java.io.InputStream src
        java.lang.String (FileInputStream. src)
        java.io.File (FileInputStream. src)
        java.net.Socket (.getInputStream src)
        java.net.URL (if (= "file" (.getProtocol src))
                         (-> src .getPath FileInputStream.)
                         (.openStream src)))
      InputStreamReader.
      BufferedReader.))
```

Here's a version of make-writer using the same strategy:

```
(defn make-writer [dst]
  (-> (condp = (type dst)
        java.io.OutputStream dst
        java.io.File (FileOutputStream. dst)
        java.lang.String (FileOutputStream. dst)
        java.net.Socket (.getOutputStream dst)
        java.net.URL (if (= "file" (.getProtocol dst))
                         (-> dst .getPath FileOutputStream.)
                         (throw (IllegalArgumentException.
                                  "Can't write to non-file URL"))))
      OutputStreamWriter.
      BufferedWriter.))
```

The problem with this approach is that it's closed: nobody else can come along and add support for new source and destination types without rewriting make-reader and make-writer. What we need is an open solution, one where support for new types can be added after the fact and by different parties. What we need is two abstractions, one for reading and one for writing.

Interfaces

In Java, the usual mechanism for supporting this form of abstraction is the interface. The interface mechanism provides a means for dispatching calls to an abstract function, specified in an interface definition, to a specific implementation based on the datatype of the first parameter passed in the call. In Java, the first parameter is implicit; it's the object that implements the interface.

Following are the strengths of interfaces:

• Datatypes can implement multiple interfaces.

- Interfaces provide only specification, not implementation, which allows implementation of multiple interfaces without the problems associated with multiple class inheritance.

The weakness of interfaces is that existing datatypes cannot be extended to implement new interfaces without rewriting them.

We can create Java interfaces in Clojure with the definterface macro. This takes a name and one or more method signatures:

```
(definterface name & sigs)
```

Let's create our abstraction for things-that-can-be-read-from-and-be-written-to as an interface, which we'll call IOFactory.

```
(definterface IOFactory
  (^java.io.BufferReader make-reader [this])
  (^java.io.BufferedWriter make-writer [this]))
```

This will create an interface called IOFactory that includes two abstract functions, make-reader and make-writer. Any class that implements this interface must include make-reader and make-writer functions that take a single parameter and an instance of the datatype itself and return a BufferedReader and BufferedWriter, respectively.

Unfortunately, the interfaces that a class supports are determined at design time by the author; once a Java class is defined, it cannot be updated to support new interfaces without rewriting it. Therefore, we can't extend the File, Socket, and URL classes to implement the IOFactory interface.

Like the versions of make-reader and make-writer we based on condp, our interface is closed to extension by parties other than the author. This is part of what is called the *expression problem.*[1] Fortunately, Clojure has a solution to it.[2]

Protocols

One piece of Clojure's solution to the expression problem is the protocol. Protocols provide a flexible mechanism for abstraction that leverages the best parts of interfaces by providing only specification, not implementation, and by letting datatypes implement multiple protocols. Additionally, protocols address the key weaknesses of interfaces by allowing nonintrusive extension of existing types to support new protocols.

---

1.   http://lambda-the-ultimate.org/node/2232
2.   http://www.ibm.com/developerworks/java/library/j-clojure-protocols/?ca=drs-

Following are the strengths of protocols:

- Datatypes can implement multiple protocols.

- Protocols provide only specification, not implementation, which allows implementation of multiple interfaces without the problems associated with multiple-class inheritance.

- Existing datatypes can be extended to implement new interfaces with no modification to the datatypes.

- Protocol method names are namespaced, so there's no risk of name collision when multiple parties choose to extend the same extant type.

The defprotocol macro works just like definterface, but now we're able to extend existing datatypes to implement our new abstraction.

```
(defprotocol name & opts+sigs)
```

Let's redefine IOFactory as a protocol, instead of an interface.

```
(defprotocol IOFactory
  "A protocol for things that can be read from and written to."
  (make-reader [this] "Creates a BufferedReader.")
  (make-writer [this] "Creates a BufferedWriter."))
```

Notice we can include a document string for the protocol as a whole, as well as for each of its methods. Now let's extend java.io.InputStream and java.io.OutputStream to implement our IOFactory protocol.

We use the extend function to associate an existing type to a protocol and to provide the required function implementations, usually referred to as *methods* in this context. The parameters to extend are the name of the type to extend, the name of the protocol to implement, and a map of method implementations, where the keys are keywordized versions of the method names.

```
(extend type & proto+mmaps)
```

The make-reader implementation for an InputStream just wraps the value passed to it in a BufferedReader.

```
src/examples/protocols.clj
(extend InputStream
  IOFactory
  {:make-reader (fn [src]
                  (-> src InputStreamReader. BufferedReader.))
   :make-writer (fn [dst]
                  (throw (IllegalArgumentException.
                          "Can't open as an InputStream.")))})
```

Similarly, the implementation of make-writer for an OutputStream wraps its given input in a BufferedWriter. And since you can't write to an InputStream or read from an OutputStream, the respective implementations of make-writer and make-reader throw IllegalArgumentExceptions.

```
(extend OutputStream
  IOFactory
  {:make-reader (fn [src]
                  (throw
                   (IllegalArgumentException.
                    "Can't open as an OutputStream.")))
   :make-writer (fn [dst]
                  (-> dst OutputStreamWriter. BufferedWriter.))})
```

We can extend the java.io.File type to implement our IOFactory protocol with the extend-type macro, which provides a slightly cleaner syntax than extend.

```
(extend-type type & specs)
```

It takes the name of the type to extend and one or more specs, which includes a protocol name and its respective method implementations.

```
(extend-type File
  IOFactory
  (make-reader [src]
    (make-reader (FileInputStream. src)))
  (make-writer [dst]
    (make-writer (FileOutputStream. dst))))
```

Notice that we create an InputStream, specifically, a FileInputStream, from our file and then make a recursive call to make-reader, which will be dispatched to the implementation defined earlier for InputStreams. We use the same recursive pattern for the make-writer method, as well as for the methods of the following remaining types.

We can extend the remaining types all at once with the extend-protocol macro:

```
(extend-protocol protocol & specs)
```

This takes the name of the protocol followed by one or more type names with their respective method implementations.

```
(extend-protocol IOFactory
  Socket
  (make-reader [src]
    (make-reader (.getInputStream src)))
  (make-writer [dst]
    (make-writer (.getOutputStream dst)))
```

```
  URL
  (make-reader [src]
    (make-reader
     (if (= "file" (.getProtocol src))
       (-> src .getPath FileInputStream.)
       (.openStream src))))

  (make-writer [dst]
    (make-writer
     (if (= "file" (.getProtocol dst))
       (-> dst .getPath FileInputStream.)
       (throw (IllegalArgumentException.
               "Can't write to non-file URL"))))))
```

Now let's put it all together.

```
(ns examples.io
  (:import (java.io File FileInputStream FileOutputStream
                    InputStream InputStreamReader
                    OutputStream OutputStreamWriter
                    BufferedReader BufferedWriter)
           (java.net Socket URL)))

(defprotocol IOFactory
  "A protocol for things that can be read from and written to."
  (make-reader [this] "Creates a BufferedReader.")
  (make-writer [this] "Creates a BufferedWriter."))

(defn gulp [src]
  (let [sb (StringBuilder.)]
    (with-open [reader (make-reader src)]
      (loop [c (.read reader)]
        (if (neg? c)
          (str sb)
          (do
            (.append sb (char c))
            (recur (.read reader))))))))

(defn expectorate [dst content]
  (with-open [writer (make-writer dst)]
    (.write writer (str content))))

(extend-protocol IOFactory
  InputStream
  (make-reader [src]
    (-> src InputStreamReader. BufferedReader.))

  (make-writer [dst]
    (throw
     (IllegalArgumentException.
      "Can't open as an InputStream.")))

  OutputStream
  (make-reader [src]
```

```
(throw
 (IllegalArgumentException.
  "Can't open as an OutputStream.")))
(make-writer [dst]
  (-> dst OutputStreamWriter. BufferedWriter.))
File
(make-reader [src]
  (make-reader (FileInputStream. src)))

(make-writer [dst]
  (make-writer (FileOutputStream. dst)))
Socket
(make-reader [src]
  (make-reader (.getInputStream src)))

(make-writer [dst]
  (make-writer (.getOutputStream dst)))
URL
(make-reader [src]
  (make-reader
   (if (= "file" ( getProtocol src))
     (-> src .getPath FileInputStream.)
     (.openStream src))))

(make-writer [dst]
  (make-writer
   (if (= "file" (.getProtocol dst))
     (-> dst .getPath FileInputStream.)
     (throw (IllegalArgumentException.
             "Can't write to non-file URL")))))))
```

Datatypes

We've shown how to extend existing types to implement new abstractions with protocols, but what if we want to create a new type in Clojure? That's where datatypes come in.

A datatype provides the following:

- A unique class, either named or anonymous
- Structure, either explicitly as fields or implicitly as a closure
- Fields that can have type hints and can be primitive
- Immutability on by default
- Unification with maps (via records)
- Optional implementations of abstract methods specified in protocols or interfaces

We will use the deftype macro to define a new datatype, called CryptoVault, that will implement two protocols, including IOFactory.

Now that gulp and expectorate support several existing Java classes, let's create a new supported type, CryptoVault. You'll create an instance of a CryptoVault by passing in an argument that implements the clojure.java.io.IOFactory protocol (not the one we've defined here), a path to a cryptographic key store, and a password. The contents expectorated into the CryptoVault will be encrypted and written to the IOFactory object and then decrypted when gulped back in.

We'll use deftype to create the new type.

```
(deftype name [& fields] & opts+specs)
```

It takes the name of the type and a vector of fields contained by the type. The naming convention for datatypes is the same as used by Java classes, i.e., CamelCase.

```
user=> (deftype CryptoVault [filename keystore password])
user.CryptoVault
```

Once the type has been defined, we can create an instance of our CryptoVault:

```
user=> (def vault (->CryptoVault "vault-file" "keystore" "toomanysecrets"))
#'user/vault
```

And its fields can be accessed using the same prefix-dot syntax used to access fields in Java objects.

```
user=> (.filename vault)
"vault-file"
```

```
user=> (.keystore vault)
"keystore"
```

```
user=> (.password vault)
"toomanysecrets"
```

Now that we've defined the basic CryptoVault type, let's add behavior with some methods. Datatypes can implement only those methods that have been specified in either a protocol or an interface, so let's first create a Vault protocol.

```
(defprotocol Vault
  (init-vault [vault])
  (vault-output-stream [vault])
  (vault-input-stream [vault]))
```

The protocol includes three functions—init-vault, vault-output-stream, and vault-input-stream—that every Vault must implement.

We can define our new type's methods inline with deftype; we just pass the type name and vector of fields as before, followed by a protocol name and one or more method bodies:

```
src/examples/cryptovault.clj
(ns examples.cryptovault
  (:require [examples.io :refer [IOFactory make-reader make-writer]])
  (:require [clojure.java.io :as io])
  (:import (java.security KeyStore KeyStore$SecretKeyEntry
                          KeyStore$PasswordProtection)
           (javax.crypto KeyGenerator Cipher CipherOutputStream
                          CipherInputStream)
           (java.io FileOutputStream)))
(deftype CryptoVault [filename keystore password]
  Vault
  (init-vault [vault]
    ... define method body here ...)

  (vault-output-stream [vault]
    ... define method body here ...)

  (vault-input-stream [vault]
    ... define method body here ...)

  IOFactory
  (make-reader [vault]
    (make-reader (vault-input-stream vault)))
  (make-writer [vault]
    (make-writer (vault-output-stream vault))))
```

Notice that the methods for more than one protocol can be defined inline; we've defined the methods for the Vault and IOFactory protocols together, although the bodies of the Vault methods have been elided and will be described next.

The init-vault method will generate an Advanced Encryption Standard (AES) key, place it in a java.security.KeyStore, write the keystore data to the file specified by the keystore field in the CryptoVault, and then password-protect it.

```
(init-vault [vault]
  (let [password (.toCharArray (.password vault))
        key (.generateKey (KeyGenerator/getInstance "AES"))
        keystore (doto (KeyStore/getInstance "JCEKS")
                   (.load nil password)
                   (.setEntry "vault-key"
                              (KeyStore$SecretKeyEntry. key)
                              (KeyStore$PasswordProtection. password)))]
    (with-open [fos (FileOutputStream. (.keystore vault))]
      (.store keystore fos password))))
```

Both the vault-output-stream and vault-input-stream methods will use a function, vault-key, to load the keystore associated with the CryptoVault and extract the AES key used to encrypt and decrypt the contents of the vault.

```
(defn vault-key [vault]
  (let [password (.toCharArray (.password vault))]
    (with-open [fis (FileInputStream. (.keystore vault))]
      (-> (doto (KeyStore/getInstance "JCEKS")
            (.load fis password))
          (.getKey "vault-key" password)))))
```

The vault-output-stream method uses the vault-key method to initialize an AES cipher object, creates an OutputStream from the Vault's filename, and then uses the cipher and OutputStream to create an instance of a CipherOutputStream.

```
(vault-output-stream [vault]
  (let [cipher (doto (Cipher/getInstance "AES")
                 (.init Cipher/ENCRYPT_MODE (vault-key vault)))]
    (CipherOutputStream. (io/output-stream (.filename vault)) cipher)))
```

vault-input-stream works like vault-output-stream, but returns a CipherInputStream.

```
(vault-input-stream [vault]
  (let [cipher (doto (Cipher/getInstance "AES")
                 (.init Cipher/DECRYPT_MODE (vault-key vault)))]
    (CipherInputStream. (io/input-stream (.filename vault)) cipher)))
```

To create an instance of a CryptoVault, just pass the location where data should be stored, the keystore filename, and the password protecting the keystore. If the keystore hasn't been initialized, then call the init-vault method:

```
user=> (def vault (->CryptoVault "vault-file" "keystore" "toomanysecrets"))
#'user/vault

user=> (init-vault vault)
nil
```

Then use the CryptoVault like any other source/destination used by gulp and expectorate.

```
user=> (expectorate vault "This is a test of the CryptoVault")
nil

user=> (gulp vault)
"This is a test of the CryptoVault"
```

We can use the CryptoVault with the built-in spit and slurp functions by extending it to support the clojure.java.io/IOFactory protocol. This version of the IOFactory has four methods, instead of two like ours, and there are default method implementations defined in a map called default-streams-impl. We'll override just two of its methods, make-input-stream and make-output-stream, by assoc'ing our new implementations into this map and passing it to the extend function.

```
(extend CryptoVault
  clojure.java.io/IOFactory
  (assoc clojure.java.io/default-streams-impl
    :make-input-stream (fn [x opts] (vault-input-stream x))
    :make-output-stream (fn [x opts] (vault-output-stream x))))
```

That's it; now we can read and write to a CryptoVault using slurp and spit.

```
user=> (spit vault "This is a test of the CryptoVault using spit and slurp")
nil

user=> (slurp vault)
"This is a test of the CryptoVault using spit and slurp"
```

Let's put all the pieces together in a .clj file. Make a src/examples/datatypes subdirectory within your project directory, and create a file called vault.clj.

src/examples/cryptovault_complete.clj
```
(ns examples.cryptovault-complete
  (:require [clojure.java.io :as io]
            [examples.protocols.io :as proto])
  (:import (java.security KeyStore KeyStore$SecretKeyEntry
                          KeyStore$PasswordProtection)
           (javax.crypto Cipher KeyGenerator CipherOutputStream
                         CipherInputStream)
           (java.io FileInputStream FileOutputStream)))
(defprotocol Vault
  (init-vault [vault])
  (vault-output-stream [vault])
  (vault-input-stream [vault]))
(defn vault-key [vault]
  (let [password (.toCharArray (.password vault))]
    (with-open [fis (FileInputStream. (.keystore vault))]
      (-> (doto (KeyStore/getInstance "JCEKS")
            (.load fis password))
          (.getKey "vault-key" password)))))
(deftype CryptoVault [filename keystore password]
  Vault
  (init-vault [vault]
    (let [password (.toCharArray (.password vault))
          key (.generateKey (KeyGenerator/getInstance "AES"))
          keystore (doto (KeyStore/getInstance "JCEKS")
                     (.load nil password)
                     (.setEntry "vault-key"
                                (KeyStore$SecretKeyEntry. key)
                                (KeyStore$PasswordProtection. password)))]
      (with-open [fos (FileOutputStream. (.keystore vault))]
        (.store keystore fos password))))
```

```
(vault-output-stream [vault]
  (let [cipher (doto (Cipher/getInstance "AES")
                 (.init Cipher/ENCRYPT_MODE (vault-key vault)))]
    (CipherOutputStream. (io/output-stream (.filename vault)) cipher)))

(vault-input-stream [vault]
  (let [cipher (doto (Cipher/getInstance "AES")
                 (.init Cipher/DECRYPT_MODE (vault-key vault)))]
    (CipherInputStream. (io/input-stream (.filename vault)) cipher)))

proto/IOFactory
(make-reader [vault]
  (proto/make-reader (vault-input-stream vault)))
(make-writer [vault]
  (proto/make-writer (vault-output-stream vault))))
(extend CryptoVault
  clojure.java.io/IOFactory
  (assoc io/default-streams-impl
    :make-input-stream (fn [x opts] (vault-input-stream x))
    :make-output-stream (fn [x opts] (vault-output-stream x))))
```

Records

Classes in object-oriented programs tend to fall into two distinct categories: those that represent programming artifacts, such as String, Socket, InputStream, and OutputStream, and those that represent application domain information, such as Employee and PurchaseOrder.

Unfortunately, using classes to model application domain information hides it behind a class-specific micro-language of setters and getters. You can no longer take a generic approach to information processing, and you end up with a proliferation of unnecessary specificity and reduced reusability. See Clojure's documentation on datatypes[3] for more information.

For this reason, Clojure has always encouraged the use of maps for modeling such information, and that holds true even with datatypes, which is where records come in. A record is a datatype, like those created with deftype, that also implements PersistentMap and therefore can be used like any other map (mostly); and since records are also proper classes, they support type-based polymorphism through protocols. With records, we have the best of both worlds: maps that can implement protocols.

What could be more natural than using records to play music? So, let's create a record that represents a musical note, with fields for pitch, octave, and

---

3.   https://clojure.org/reference/datatypes

duration; then we'll use the JDK's built-in MIDI synthesizer to play sequences of these notes.

Since records are maps, we'll be able to change the properties of individual notes using the assoc and update-in functions, and we can create or transform entire sequences of notes using map and reduce. This gives us access to the entirety of Clojure's collection API.

We'll create a Note record with the defrecord macro, which behaves like deftype.

```
(defrecord name [& fields] & opts+specs)
```

A Note record has three fields: pitch, octave, and duration.

```
(defrecord Note [pitch octave duration])
-> user.Note
```

The pitch will be represented by a keyword like :C, :C#, and :Db, which represent the notes C, C♯ (C sharp), and D♭ (D flat), respectively. Each pitch can be played at different octaves; for instance, middle C is in the fourth octave. Duration indicates the note length; a whole note is represented by 1, a half note by 1/2, a quarter note by 1/4, and a 16th note by 1/16. For example, we can represent a D♯ half note in the fourth octave with this Note record:

```
(->Note :D# 4 1/2)
-> #user.Note{:pitch :D#, :octave 4, :duration 1/2}
```

We can treat records like any other datatype, accessing their fields with the dot syntax.

```
(.pitch (->Note :D# 4 1/2))
-> :D#
```

But records are also map-like:

```
(map? (->Note :D# 4 1/2))
-> true
```

so we can also access their fields using keywords:

```
(:pitch (->Note :D# 4 1/2))
-> :D#
```

We can create modified records with assoc and update-in.

```
(assoc (->Note :D# 4 1/2) :pitch :Db :duration 1/4)
-> #user.Note{:pitch :Db, :octave 4, :duration 1/4}

(update-in (->Note :D# 4 1/2) [:octave] inc)
-> #user.Note{:pitch :D#, :octave 5, :duration 1/2}
```

Records are open, so we can associate extra fields into a record:

```
(assoc (->Note :D# 4 1/2) :velocity 100)
-> #user.Note{:pitch :D#, :octave 4, :duration 1/2, :velocity 100}
```

Use the optional :velocity field to represent the force with which a note is played.

When used on a record, both assoc and update-in return a new record, but the dissoc function works a bit differently; it will return a new record if the field being dissociated is optional, like velocity in the previous example, but it will return a plain map if the field is mandated by the defrecord specification, like pitch, octave, or duration.

In other words, if you remove a required field from a record of a given type, it's no longer a record of that type, and it simply becomes a map.

```
(dissoc (->Note :D# 4 1/2) :octave)
-> {:pitch :D#, :duration 1/2}
```

Notice that dissoc returns a map, not a record. One difference between records and maps is that, unlike maps, records are not functions of keywords.

```
((->Note. :D# 4 1/2) :pitch)
-> user.Note cannot be cast to clojure.lang.IFn
```

ClassCastException is thrown because records do not implement the IFn interface like maps do. This is by design and drives a stylistic difference that makes code more readable.

When accessing a collection, you should place the collection first. When accessing a map that's acting (conceptually) as a data record, you should place the keyword first, even if the record is implemented as a plain map. Now that we have our basic Note record, let's add some methods so we can play them with the JDK's built-in MIDI synthesizer. We'll start by creating a MidiNote protocol with three methods:

```
src/examples/protocols.clj
(defprotocol MidiNote
  (to-msec [this tempo])
  (key-number [this])
  (play [this tempo midi-channel]))
```

To play our note with the MIDI synthesizer, we need to translate its pitch and octave into a MIDI key number and its duration into milliseconds. Here, we've defined to-msec, key-number, and play, which we will use to create our MidiNote.

- to-msec returns the duration of the note in milliseconds.
- key-number returns the MIDI key number corresponding to this note.
- play plays this note at the given tempo on the given channel.

Now let's extend our Note record to implement the MidiNote protocol.

```
(import 'javax.sound.midi.MidiSystem)
(extend-type Note
  MidiNote
  (to-msec [this tempo]
    (let [duration-to-bpm {1 240, 1/2 120, 1/4 60, 1/8 30, 1/16 15}]
      (* 1000 (/ (duration-to-bpm (:duration this))
                 tempo)))))
```

The to-msec function translates the note's duration from whole note, half note, quarter note, and so on, into milliseconds based on the given tempo, which is represented in beats per minute (bpm).

```
(key-number [this]
  (let [scale {:C 0,   :C# 1,  :Db 1,  :D 2,
               :D# 3,  :Eb 3,  :E 4,   :F 5,
               :F# 6,  :Gb 6,  :G 7,   :G# 8,
               :Ab 8,  :A 9,   :A# 10, :Bb 10,
               :B 11}]
    (+ (* 12 (inc (:octave this)))
       (scale (:pitch this)))))
```

The key-number function maps the keywords used to represent pitch into a number ranging from 0 to 11 [1] and then uses this number along with the given octave to find the corresponding MIDI key-number.

```
(play [this tempo midi-channel]
  (let [velocity (or (:velocity this) 64)]
    (.noteOn midi-channel (key-number this) velocity)
    (Thread/sleep (to-msec this tempo))))
```

Finally, the play method takes a note, a tempo, and a MIDI channel; sends a noteOn message to the channel; and then sleeps for the note's duration. The note continues to play even while the current thread is asleep, stopping only when the next note is sent to the channel.

Now we need a function that sets up the MIDI synthesizer and plays a sequence of notes:

```
(defn perform [notes & {:keys [tempo] :or {tempo 120}}]
  (with-open [synth (doto (MidiSystem/getSynthesizer) .open)]
    (let [channel (aget (.getChannels synth) 0)]
      (doseq [note notes]
        (play note tempo channel)))))
```

The perform function takes a sequence of notes and an optional tempo value, opens a MIDI synthesizer, gets a channel from it, and then calls each note's play method.

All the pieces are in place, so let's make music using a sequence of Note records:

```
(def close-encounters [(->Note :D 3 1/2)
                        (->Note :E 3 1/2)
                        (->Note :C 3 1/2)
                        (->Note :C 2 1/2)
                        (->Note :G 2 1/2)])
-> #'user/close-encounters
```

In this case, our "music" consists of the five notes used to greet the alien ships in the movie *Close Encounters of the Third Kind*. To play it, just pass the sequence to the perform function:

```
(perform close-encounters)
-> nil
```

We can also generate sequences of notes dynamically with the for macro.

```
(def jaws (for [duration [1/2 1/2 1/4 1/4 1/8 1/8 1/8 1/8]
                pitch [:E :F]]
            (Note. pitch 2 duration)))
-> #'user/jaws

(perform jaws)
-> nil
```

The result is the shark theme from *Jaws*—a sequence of alternating E and F notes progressively speeding up as they move from half notes to quarter notes to eighth notes.

Since notes are records and records are map-like, we can manipulate them with any Clojure function that works on maps. For instance, we can map the update-in function across the *Close Encounters* sequence to raise or lower its octave.

```
(perform (map #(update-in % [:octave] inc) close-encounters))
-> nil

(perform (map #(update-in % [:octave] dec) close-encounters))
-> nil
```

Or we can create a sequence of notes that have progressively larger values of the optional :velocity field:

```
(perform (for [velocity [64 80 90 100 110 120]]
           (assoc (Note. :D 3 1/2) :velocity velocity)))
-> nil
```

This results in a sequence of increasingly more forceful D notes. Manipulating sequences is a particular strength of Clojure, so there are endless possibilities for programmatically creating and manipulating sequences of Note records.

Let's put the MidiNote protocol, the Note record, and the perform function together in a Clojure source file called src/examples/midi.clj so we can use them in the future.

src/examples/midi.clj
```clojure
(ns examples.datatypes.midi
  (:import [javax.sound.midi MidiSystem]))
(defprotocol MidiNote
  (to-msec [this tempo])
  (key-number [this])
  (play [this tempo midi-channel]))

(defn perform [notes & {:keys [tempo] :or {tempo 88}}]
  (with-open [synth (doto (MidiSystem/getSynthesizer).open)]
    (let [channel (aget (.getChannels synth) 0)]
      (doseq [note notes]
        (play note tempo channel)))))

(defrecord Note [pitch octave duration]
  MidiNote
  (to-msec [this tempo]
    (let [duration-to bpm {1 240, 1/2 120, 1/4 60, 1/8 30, 1/16 15}]
      (* 1000 (/ (duration-to-bpm (:duration this))
                 tempo))))
  (key-number [this]
    (let [scale {:C 0,  :C# 1, :Db 1,  :D 2,
                 :D# 3, :Eb 3, :E 4,   :F 5,
                 :F# 6, :Gb 6, :G 7,   :G# 8,
                 :Ab 8, :A 9,  :A# 10, :Bb 10,
                 :B 11}]
      (+ (* 12 (inc (:octave this)))
         (scale (:pitch this)))))
  (play [this tempo midi-channel]
    (let [velocity (or (:velocity this) 64)]
      (.noteOn midi-channel (key-number this) velocity)
      (Thread/sleep (to-msec this tempo)))))
```

reify

The reify macro lets you create an anonymous instance of a datatype that implements either a protocol or an interface. Note that you get access by closure, not by declaration. This is because there are no declared members.

```clojure
(reify & opts+specs)
```

reify, like deftype and defrecord, takes the name of one or more protocols, or interfaces, and a series of method bodies. Unlike deftype and defrecord, it doesn't take a name or a vector of fields; datatype instances produced with reify don't have explicit fields, relying instead on closures.

Let's compose some John Cage–style[4] aleatoric music[5] or, better yet, create an aleatoric music generator. We'll use reify to create an instance of a MidiNote that will play a different random note each time its play method is called.

src/examples/generator.clj
```
(import '[examples.datatypes.midi MidiNote])
(let [min-duration 250
      min-velocity 64
      rand-note (reify
  MidiNote
  (to-msec [this tempo] (+ (rand-int 1000) min-duration))
  (key-number [this] (rand-int 100))
  (play [this tempo midi-channel]
    (let [velocity (+ (rand-int 100) min-velocity)]
      (.noteOn midi-channel (key-number this) velocity)
      (Thread/sleep (to-msec this tempo)))))))]
  (perform (repeat 15 rand-note)))
```

The first thing we need to do is import (not use or require) our MidiNote protocol from the examples.midi namespace. Next we bind two values, min-duration and min-velocity, that we will use in the MidiNote method implementations. Then we use reify to create an instance of an anonymous type, which implements the MidiNote protocol, that will select a random note, duration, and velocity each time its play method is called. Finally, we use the repeat function to create a sequence of 15 notes, consisting of a single instance of rand-note, and perform it. *Voila*, you now have a virtual John Cage!

Wrapping Up

We covered a lot of ground in this chapter, from the general use of abstraction in programming to some (but not all) of the specific abstraction mechanisms Clojure provides. We explored creating concrete abstractions using protocols in Clojure and had some fun in the process!

But there's still more. Clojure's macro implementation is easy to learn and use correctly for common tasks and yet powerful enough for the harder macro-related tasks. In the next chapter, you'll see how Clojure is bringing macros to mainstream programming.

---

4.   http://en.wikipedia.org/wiki/John_Cage
5.   http://en.wikipedia.org/wiki/Aleatoric_music

CHAPTER 8

Macros

Macros give Clojure great power. With most programming techniques, you build features *within* the language. When you write macros, it's more accurate to say that you're "adding features to" the language. This is a powerful capability, so you should follow the rules in this chapter until you have enough experience to decide for yourself when to deviate. We'll explore an example of how to use macros to add a new feature to Clojure.

While powerful, macros are not always simple. Clojure works to make macros as simple as is feasible by including conveniences to solve many common problems that occur when writing macros. We'll explain these problems and show how Clojure mitigates them.

Macros are so different from other programming idioms that you may struggle to know when to use them. There's no better guide than the shared experience of the community, so we'll close the chapter by introducing a taxonomy of Clojure macros, based on the macros in Clojure and contrib libraries.

When to Use Macros

In 1996, author Chuck Palahniuk released the novel "Fight Club", which was later made into a movie. The so-called fight club in the story had a set of rules. The first rule of fight club was, "You don't talk about fight club."

In a similar spirit, we introduce Macro Club. Macro Club has two rules, plus one exception. The first rule of Macro Club is Don't Write Macros. Macros are complex, and they require you to think carefully about the interplay of macro expansion time and compile time. If you can write it as a function, think twice before using a macro.

The second rule of Macro Club is Write Macros If That Is the Only Way to Encapsulate a Pattern. All programming languages provide some way to encapsulate patterns, but without macros these mechanisms are incomplete. In most languages, you sense that incompleteness whenever you say, "My life would be easier if only my language had feature X." In Clojure, you just implement feature X using a macro.

The exception to the rule is that *you can write any macro that makes life easier for your callers when compared with an equivalent function.* But to understand this exception, you need some practice writing macros and comparing them to functions. So, let's get started with an example.

Writing a Control Flow Macro

Clojure provides the if special form as part of the language:

```
(if (= 1 1) (println "yep, math still works today"))
| yep, math still works today
```

Some languages have an unless, which is (almost) the opposite of if. unless performs a test and then executes its body only if the test is logically false.

Clojure doesn't have unless, but it does have an equivalent macro called when-not. For the sake of having a simple example to start with, let's pretend that when-not doesn't exist and create an implementation of unless. To follow the rules of Macro Club, begin by trying to write unless as a function:

src/examples/macros.clj
```
; This is doomed to fail...
(defn unless [expr form]
  (if expr nil form))
```

Check that unless correctly evaluates its form when its test expr is false:

```
(unless false (println "this should print"))
| this should print
```

Things look fine so far. But let's be diligent and test the true case, too:

```
(unless true (println "this should not print"))
| this should not print
```

Clearly something has gone wrong. The problem is that Clojure evaluates all the arguments before passing them to a function, so the println is called before unless *ever sees it.* In fact, both calls to unless earlier call println too soon, before entering the unless function. To see this, add a println inside unless:

```
(defn unless [expr form]
  (println "About to test...")
  (if expr nil form))
```

Now you can clearly see that function arguments are always evaluated before they are passed to unless:

```
(unless false (println "this should print"))
| this should print
| About to test...

(unless true (println "this should not print"))
| this should not print
| About to test...
```

Macros solve this problem, because they don't evaluate their arguments immediately. Instead, you get to choose when (and if!) the arguments to a macro are evaluated.

When Clojure encounters a macro, it processes it in two steps. First, it expands (executes) the macro and substitutes the result back into the program. This is called *macro expansion time*. Then, it continues with the normal *compile time*.

To write unless, you need to write Clojure code to perform the following translation at macro expansion time:

```
(unless expr form) -> (if expr nil form)
```

Then, you need to tell Clojure that your code is a macro by using defmacro, which looks almost like defn:

```
(defmacro name doc-string? attr-map? [params*] body)
```

Because Clojure code is just Clojure data, you already have all the tools you need to write unless. Write the unless macro using list to build the if expression:

```
(defmacro unless [expr form]
  (list 'if expr nil form))
```

The body of unless executes at macro expansion time, producing an if form for compilation. If you enter this expression at the REPL:

```
(unless false (println "this should print"))
```

then Clojure will (invisibly to you) expand the unless form into the following:

```
(if false nil (println "this should print"))
```

Then, Clojure compiles and executes the expanded if form. Verify that unless works correctly for both true and false:

```
(unless false (println "this should print"))
| this should print
-> nil

(unless true (println "this should not print"))
-> nil
```

Congratulations, you have written your first macro. unless may seem pretty simple, but consider this: what you have just done is *impossible* in most languages. In languages without macros, special forms get in the way.

Special Forms, Design Patterns, and Macros

Clojure has no special syntax for code. Code is composed of data structures. This is true for normal functions but also for special forms and macros.

Consider a language with more syntactic variety, such as Java. In Java, the most flexible mechanism for writing code is the instance method. Imagine that you're writing a Java program. If you discover a recurring pattern in some instance methods, you have the entire Java language at your disposal to encapsulate that recurring pattern.

Good so far. But Java also has lots of "special forms" (although they're not normally called by that name). Unlike Clojure special forms, which are just Clojure data, each Java special form has its own syntax. For example, if is a special form in Java. If you discover a recurring pattern of usage involving if, there's *no way to encapsulate* that pattern. You can't create an unless, so you're stuck simulating unless with an idiomatic usage of if:

```
if (!something) ...
```

This may seem like a relatively minor problem. Java programmers can certainly learn to mentally make the translation from if (!foo) to unless (foo). But the problem is not just with if: *every distinct syntactic form* in the language inhibits your ability to encapsulate recurring patterns involving that form.

As another example, Java new is a special form. Polymorphism is not available for new, so you must simulate polymorphism, for example with an idiomatic usage of a class method:

```
Widget w = WidgetFactory.makeWidget(...)
```

This idiom is a little bulkier. It introduces a whole new class, WidgetFactory. This class is meaningless in the problem domain and exists only to work around the constructor special form. Unlike the unless idiom, the "polymorphic instantiation" idiom is complicated enough that there's more than one way to implement a solution. Thus, the idiom should more properly be called a *design pattern.*

Wikipedia defines a design pattern[1] to be a "general reusable solution to a commonly occurring problem in software design." It goes on to state that a "design pattern is not a finished design that can be transformed *directly* (emphasis added) into code."

That's where macros fit in. Macros provide a layer of *indirection* so that you can *automate the common parts of any recurring pattern*. Macros and code-as-data work together, enabling you to reprogram your language on the fly to encapsulate patterns.

Of course, this argument doesn't go entirely in one direction. Many people would argue that having a bunch of special syntactic forms makes a programming language easier to learn or read. We do not agree, but even if we did, we'd be willing to trade syntactic variety for a powerful macro system. Once you get used to code as data, the ability to automate design patterns is a huge payoff.

Expanding Macros

When you created the unless macro, you quoted the symbol If:

```
(defmacro unless [expr form]
  (list 'if expr nil form))
```

But you didn't quote any other symbols. To understand why, you need to think carefully about what happens at macro expansion time:

- By quoting if, you prevent Clojure from evaluating if at macro expansion time. Instead, evaluation strips off the quote, leaving if to be compiled.

- You don't want to quote expr and form, because they're macro arguments. Clojure will substitute them without evaluation at macro expansion time.

- You don't need to quote nil, since nil evaluates to itself.

Thinking about what needs to be quoted can get complicated quickly. Fortunately, you don't have to do this work in your head. Clojure includes diagnostic functions so that you can test macro expansions at the REPL.

The function macroexpand-1 shows you what happens at macro expansion time:

```
(macroexpand-1 form)
```

Use macroexpand-1 to prove that unless expands to a sensible if expression:

---

1. http://en.wikipedia.org/wiki/Design_pattern_(computer_science)

```
(macroexpand-1 '(unless false (println "this should print")))
-> (if false nil (println "this should print"))
```

Macros are complicated beasts, and we cannot overstate the importance of testing them with macroexpand-1. Let's go back and try some incorrect versions of unless. Here's one that incorrectly quotes the expr:

```
(defmacro bad-unless [expr form]
  (list 'if 'expr nil form))
```

When you expand bad-unless, you'll see that it generates the symbol expr, instead of the actual test expression:

```
(macroexpand-1 '(bad-unless false (println "this should print")))
-> (if expr nil (println "this should print"))
```

If you try to actually use the bad-unless macro, Clojure will complain that it can't resolve the symbol expr:

```
(bad-unless false (println "this should print"))
-> java.lang.Exception: Unable to resolve symbol: expr in this context
```

Sometimes macros expand into other macros. When this happens, Clojure will continue to expand all macros, until only normal code remains. For example, the .. macro expands recursively, producing a dot operator call, wrapped in another .. to handle any arguments that remain. You can see this with the following macro expansion:

```
(macroexpand-1 '(.. arm getHand getFinger))
-> (clojure.core/.. (. arm getHand) getFinger)
```

If you want to see .. expanded all the way, use macroexpand:

```
(macroexpand form)
```

If you macroexpand a call to .., it will recursively expand until only dot operators remain:

```
(macroexpand '(.. arm getHand getFinger))
-> (. (. arm getHand) getFinger)
```

(It's not a problem that arm, getHand, and getFinger don't exist. You're only expanding them, not attempting to compile and execute them.)

Another recursive macro is and. If you call and with more than two arguments, it will expand to include another call to and, with one less argument:

```
(macroexpand '(and 1 2 3))
-> (let* [and__3585__auto__ 1]
     (if and__3585__auto__ (clojure.core/and 2 3)
     and__3585__auto__))
```

This time, macroexpand does *not* expand all the way. macroexpand works only against the top level of the form you give it. Since the expansion of and creates a new and nested inside the form, macroexpand does not expand it.

when and when-not

Your unless macro could be improved slightly to execute multiple forms, avoiding this error:

```
(unless false (println "this") (println "and also this"))
-> java.lang.IllegalArgumentException: \
Wrong number of args passed to: macros$unless
```

Think about how you would write the improved unless. You'd need to capture a variable argument list and stick a do in front of it so that every form executes. Clojure provides exactly this behavior in its when and when-not macros:

```
(when test & body)
```

```
(when-not test & body)
```

when-not is the improved unless you're looking for:

```
(when-not false (println "this") (println "and also this"))
| this
| and also this
-> nil
```

Given your practice writing unless, you should now have no trouble reading the source for when-not:

```
; from Clojure core
(defmacro when-not [test & body]
  (list 'if test nil (cons 'do body)))
```

And, of course, you can use macroexpand-1 to see how when-not works:

```
(macroexpand-1 '(when-not false (print "1") (print "2")))
-> (if false nil (do (print "1") (print "2")))
```

when is the opposite of when-not and executes its forms only when its test is true. Note that when differs from if in two ways:

- if allows an else clause, and when does not. This reflects English usage, because nobody says "when … else."

- Since when does not have to use its second argument as an else clause, it's free to take a variable argument list and execute all the arguments inside a do.

You don't really need an unless macro. Just use Clojure's when-not. Always check to see whether somebody else has written the macro you need.

Making Macros Simpler

The unless macro is a great simple example, but most macros are more complex. In this section, we'll build a set of increasingly complex macros, introducing Clojure features as we go. For your reference, the following table summarizes the features introduced.

Form	Description
foo#	Auto-gensym: Inside a syntax-quoted section, create a unique name prefixed with foo.
(gensym prefix?)	Create a unique name, with optional prefix.
(macroexpand form)	Expand form with macroexpand-1 repeatedly until the returned form is no longer a macro.
(macroexpand-1 form)	Show how Clojure will expand form.
(list-frag? ~@form list-frag?)	Splicing unquote: Use inside a syntax quote to splice an unquoted list into a template.
`form	Syntax quote: Quote form, but allow internal unquoting so that form acts as a template. Symbols inside form are resolved to help prevent inadvertent symbol capture.
~form	Unquote: Use inside a syntax quote to substitute an unquoted value.

First let's build a replica of Clojure's .. macro. We'll call it chain, since it chains a series of method calls. Here are some sample expansions of chain:

Macro Call	Expansion
(chain arm getHand)	(. arm getHand)
(chain arm getHand getFinger)	(. (. arm getHand) getFinger)

Begin by implementing the simple case where the chain calls only one method. The macro needs only to make a simple list:

```
src/examples/macros/chain_1.clj
; chain reimplements Clojure's .. macro
(defmacro chain [x form]
  (list '. x form))
```

chain needs to support any number of arguments, so the rest of the implementation should define a recursion. The list manipulation becomes more complex, since you need to build two lists and concat them together:

```
src/examples/macros/chain_2.clj
(defmacro chain
  ([x form] (list '. x form))
  ([x form & more] (concat (list 'chain (list '. x form)) more)))
```

Test chain using macroexpand to make sure it generates the correct expansions:

```
(macroexpand '(chain arm getHand))
-> (. arm getHand)

(macroexpand '(chain arm getHand getFinger))
-> (. (. arm getHand) getFinger)
```

The chain macro works fine as written, but it's difficult to read the expression that handles more than one argument:

```
(concat (list 'chain (list '. x form)) more)))
```

The definition of chain oscillates between macro code and the body to be generated. The intermingling of the two makes the entire thing hard to read. And this is just a baby of a form, only one line in length. As macro forms grow more complex, assembly functions such as list and concat quickly obscure the meaning of the macro.

One solution to this kind of problem is a templating language. If macros were created from templates, you could take a "fill-in-the-blanks" approach to creating them. The definition of chain might look like this:

```
; hypothetical templating language
(defmacro chain
  ([x form] (. ${x} ${form}))
  ([x form & more] (chain (. ${x} ${form}) ${more})))
```

In this hypothetical templating language, the ${} lets you substitute arguments into the macro expansion.

Notice how much easier the definition is to read and how it clearly shows what the expansion will look like.

Syntax Quote, Unquote, and Splicing Unquote

Clojure macros support templating without introducing a separate language. The *syntax quote* character, which is a backquote (`` ` ``), works almost like normal quoting. But inside a syntax-quoted list, the *unquote character* (~, a tilde) turns quoting off again. The overall effect is templates that look like this:

src/examples/macros/chain_3.clj
```
(defmacro chain [x form]
  `(. ~x ~form))
```

Test that this new version of chain can correctly generate a single method call:

```
(macroexpand '(chain arm getHand))
-> (. arm getHand)
```

Unfortunately, the syntax quote/unquote approach won't quite work for the multiple-argument variant of chain:

src/examples/macros/chain_4.clj
```
; Does not quite work
(defmacro chain
  ([x form] `(. ~x ~form))
  ([x form & more] `(chain (. ~x ~form) ~more)))
```

When you expand this chain, the parentheses aren't quite right:

```
(macroexpand '(chain arm getHand getFinger))
-> (. (. arm getHand) (getFinger))
```

The last argument to chain is a list of more arguments. When you drop more into the macro "template," it has parentheses because it's a list. But you don't want these parentheses; you want more to be *spliced* into the list. This comes up often enough that there is a reader macro for it: *splicing unquote* (~@). Rewrite chain using splicing unquote to splice in more:

src/examples/macros/chain_5.clj
```
(defmacro chain
  ([x form] `(. ~x ~form))
  ([x form & more] `(chain (. ~x ~form) ~@more)))
```

Now, the expansion should be spot on:

```
(macroexpand '(chain arm getHand getFinger))
-> (. (. arm getHand) getFinger)
```

Many macros follow the pattern of chain, aka Clojure ..

1. Begin the macro body with a syntax quote (`` ` ``) to treat the entire thing as a template.

2. Insert individual arguments with an unquote (~).

3. Splice in more arguments with splicing unquote (~@).

The macros we've built so far have been simple enough to avoid creating any bindings with let or binding. Let's create such a macro next.

Creating Names in a Macro

Clojure has a time macro that times an expression, writing the elapsed time to the console:

```
(time (str "a" "b"))
| "Elapsed time: 0.06 msecs"
-> "ab"
```

Let's build a variant of time called bench, designed to collect data across many runs. Instead of writing to the console, bench will return a map that includes both the return value of the original expression and the elapsed time.

The best way to begin writing a macro is to write its desired expansion by hand. bench should expand like this:

```
; (bench (str "a" "b"))
; should expand to
(let [start (System/nanoTime)
      result (str "a" "b")]
  {:result result :elapsed (- (System/nanoTime) start)})

-> {:elapsed 61000, :result "ab"}
```

The let binds start to the start time and then executes the expression to be benched, binding it to result. Finally, the form returns a map including the result and the elapsed time since start.

With the expansion in hand, you can now work backward and write the macro to generate the expansion. Using the technique from the previous section, try writing bench using syntax quoting and unquoting:

src/examples/macros/bench_1.clj
```
; This won't work
(defmacro bench [expr]
  `(let [start (System/nanoTime)
         result ~expr]
     {:result result :elapsed (- (System/nanoTime) start)}))
```

If you try to call this version of bench, Clojure will complain:

```
(bench (str "a" "b"))
-> java.lang.Exception: Can't let qualified name: examples.macros/start
```

Clojure is accusing you of trying to let a qualified name, which is illegal. Calling macroexpand-1 confirms the problem:

```
(macroexpand-1 '(bench (str "a" "b")))
-> (clojure.core/let [examples.macros/start (System/nanoTime)
      examples.macros/result (str "a" "b")]
    {:elapsed (clojure.core/- (System/nanoTime) examples.macros/start)
     :result examples.macros/result})
```

When a syntax-quoted form encounters a symbol, it resolves the symbol to a fully qualified name. At the moment, this seems like an irritant, because you *want* to create local names, specifically start and result. But Clojure's approach protects you from a nasty macro bug called *symbol capture*.

What would happen if macro expansion *did* allow the unqualified symbols start and result, and then bench was later used in a scope where those names were already bound to something else? The macro would *capture* the names and bind them to different values, with bizarre results. If bench captured its symbols, it would appear to work fine most of the time. Adding 1 and 2 gives you 3:

```
(let [a 1 b 2]
  (bench (+ a b)))

->   {:result 3, :elapsed 39000}
```

...until the unlucky day that you picked a local name like start, which collided with a name inside bench:

```
(let [start 1 end 2]
  (bench (+ start end)))

->   {:result 1228277342451783002, :elapsed 39000}
```

bench captures the symbol start and binds it to (System/nanoTime). All of a sudden, "1 plus 2" seems to equal 1228277342451783002.

Clojure's insistence on resolving names in macros helps protect you from symbol capture, but you still don't have a working bench. You need some way to introduce local names, ideally *unique* ones that can't collide with any names used by the caller.

Clojure provides a reader form for creating unique local names. Inside a syntax-quoted form, you can append an octothorpe (#) to an unqualified name, and Clojure will create an autogenerated symbol, or *auto-gensym*: a symbol based on the name plus an underscore and a unique ID. Try it at the REPL:

```
`foo#
foo__1004
```

With automatically generated symbols at your disposal, it's easy to implement bench correctly:

```
(defmacro bench [expr]
  `(let [start# (System/nanoTime)
         result# ~expr]
     {:result result# :elapsed (- (System/nanoTime) start#)}))
```

Test it at the REPL:

```
(bench (str "a" "b"))
-> {:elapsed 63000, :result "ab"}
```

Clojure makes it easy to generate unique names, but if you're determined, you can still force symbol capture. The sample code for the book includes an evil-bench that shows a combination of syntax quoting, quoting, and unquoting that leads to symbol capture. Don't use symbol capture unless you have a thorough understanding of macros.

Taxonomy of Macros

Now that you've written several macros, we can restate the rules of Macro Club with more supporting detail.

The first rule of Macro Club is, Don't Write Macros. Macros are complex. If you can avoid that complexity, you should.

The second rule of Macro Club is, Write Macros If That Is the Only Way to Encapsulate a Pattern. As you've seen, the patterns that resist encapsulation tend to arise around special forms, which are irregularities in a language. So the second rule can also be called the Special Form Rule.

Special forms have special powers that you, the programmer, do not have:

- Special forms provide the most basic flow control structures, such as if and recur. All flow control macros must eventually call a special form.

- Special forms provide direct access to Java. When you call Java from Clojure, you're going through at least one special form, such as the . (dot) or new.

- Names are created and bound through special forms, whether defining a var with def, creating a lexical binding with let, or creating a dynamic binding with binding.

As powerful as they are, special forms are not functions. They can't do some things that functions can do. You cannot apply a special form, store a special form in a var, or use a special form as a filter with the sequence library. In short, special forms are not first-class citizens of the language.

The specialness of special forms could be a major problem and lead to repetitive, unmaintainable patterns in your code. But macros neatly solve the problem, because you can use macros to generate special forms. In a practical sense, *all language features are first-class features at macro expansion time.*

Macros that generate special forms are often the most difficult to write but also the most rewarding. As if by magic, such macros seem to *add new features to the language.*

The exception to the Macro Club rules is caller convenience: *you can write any macro that makes life easier for your callers when compared with an equivalent function.* Because macros don't evaluate their arguments, callers can pass raw code to a macro, instead of wrapping the code in an anonymous function. Or, callers can pass unescaped names, instead of quoted symbols or strings.

We have reviewed the macros in Clojure and contrib libraries, and almost all of them follow the rules of Macro Club. Also, they fit into one or more of the categories in the following table, which shows the taxonomy of Clojure macros.

Justification	Category	Examples
Special form	Conditional evaluation	when, when-not, and, or, comment
Special form	Defining vars	defn, defmacro, defmulti, defstruct, declare
Special form	Java interop	.., doto, import-static
Caller convenience	Postponing evaluation	lazy-cat, lazy-seq, delay
Caller convenience	Wrapping evaluation	with-open, dosync, with-out-str, time, assert
Caller convenience	Avoiding a lambda	*(Same as for "Wrapping evaluation")*

Let's examine each of the categories in turn.

Conditional Evaluation

Because macros do not immediately evaluate their arguments, they can be used to create custom control structures. You've already seen this with the unless example in *Writing a Control Flow Macro*, on page 188.

Macros that do conditional evaluation tend to be fairly simple to read and write. They follow a common form: evaluate some argument (the condition); then, based on that evaluation, pick which other arguments to evaluate, if any. A good example is Clojure's and:

```
Line 1  (defmacro and
     2    ([] true)
     3    ([x] x)
     4    ([x & rest]
     5      `(let [and# ~x]
     6        (if and# (and ~@rest) and#)))))
```

and is defined recursively. The zero- and one-argument bodies set up base cases:

- For no arguments, return true.
- For one argument, return that argument.

For two or more arguments, and uses the first argument as its condition, evaluating it on line 5. Then, if the condition is true, and proceeds to evaluate the remaining arguments by recursively anding the rest (line 6).

To short-circuit evaluation after the first non-true value is encountered, and must be a macro. Unsurprisingly, and has a close cousin macro, or. Their signatures are the same:

```
(and & exprs)
```

```
(or & exprs)
```

The difference is that and stops on the first logical false, while or stops on the first logical true:

```
(and 1 0 nil false)
-> nil

(or 1 0 nil false)
-> 1
```

The all-time, short-circuit evaluation champion is the comment macro:

```
(comment & exprs)
```

comment never evaluates *any* of its arguments and is sometimes used at the end of a source code file to demonstrate the usage of an API.

For example, the Clojure inspector library ends with the following comment, demonstrating the use of the inspector:

```
(comment

(load-file "src/inspector.clj")
(refer 'inspector)
(inspect-tree {:a 1 :b 2 :c [1 2 3 {:d 4 :e 5 :f [6 7 8]}]})
(inspect-table [[1 2 3][4 5 6][7 8 9][10 11 12]])

)
```

Notice the lack of indentation. This would be nonstandard in most Clojure code but is useful in comment, whose purpose is to draw attention to its body.

Creating Vars

Clojure vars are created by the def special form. Anything else that creates a var must eventually call def. So, for example, defn, defmacro, and defmulti are all themselves macros.

To demonstrate writing macros that create vars, we'll look at two macros that are also part of Clojure: defstruct and declare.

Clojure provides a low-level function for creating structs called create-struct. Note that structs are effectively deprecated now in favor of records, but defstruct is still an instructive macro example.

```
(create-struct & key-symbols)
```

Use create-struct to create a person struct:

```
(def person (create-struct :first-name :last-name))
-> #'user/person
```

create-struct works, but it's visually noisy. Given that you often want to immediately def a new struct, you'll typically call defstruct, which combines def and create-struct in a single operation:

```
(defstruct name & key-symbols)
```

defstruct is a simple macro, and it's already part of Clojure:

```
(defmacro defstruct
  [name & keys]
  `(def ~name (create-struct ~@keys)))
```

This macro takes advantage of several macro features: delayed evaluation of the symbol name, splicing of keys, and rewriting the expressions at compile time rather than a runtime invocation of def.

defstruct makes a single line easier to read, but some macros can also condense many lines into a single form. Consider the issue of forward declarations. You're writing a program that needs forward references to vars a, b, c, and d. You can call def with no arguments to define the var names without an initial binding:

```
(def a)
(def b)
(def c)
(def d)
```

But this is tedious and wastes a lot of vertical space. The declare macro takes a variable list of names and defs each name for you:

```
(declare & names)
```

Now you can declare all the names in a single compact form:

```
(declare a b c d)
-> #'user/d
```

The implementation of declare is built into Clojure:

```
(defmacro declare
  [& names] `(do ~@(map #(list 'def %) names)))
```

Let's analyze declare from the inside out. The anonymous function #(list 'def %) is responsible for generating a single def. Test this form alone at the REPL:

```
(#(list 'def %) 'a)
-> (def a)
```

The map invokes the inner function once for each symbol passed in. Again, you can test this form at the REPL:

```
(map #(list 'def %) '[a b c d])
-> ((def a) (def b) (def c) (def d))
```

The leading do makes the entire expansion into a single legal Clojure form:

```
`(do ~@(map #(list 'def %) '[a b c d]))
-> (do (def a) (def b) (def c) (def d))
```

Substituting '[a b c d] in the previous form is the manual equivalent of testing the entire macro with macroexpand-1:

```
(macroexpand-1 '(declare a b c d))
-> (do (def a) (def b) (def c) (def d))
```

Many of the most interesting parts of Clojure are macros that expand into special forms involving def. We've explored a few here, but you can read the source of any of them. Most of them live at src/clj/clojure/core.clj in the Clojure source distribution.

Java Interop

Clojure programs call into Java via the . (dot), new, and set! special forms. However, idiomatic Clojure code often uses macros such as .. (threaded member access) and doto to simplify forms that call Java.

You (or anyone else) can extend how Clojure calls Java by writing a macro. Consider the following scenario. You're writing code that uses several of the constants in java.lang.Math:

```
Math/PI
-> 3.141592653589793
(Math/pow 10 3)
-> 1000.0
```

In a longer segment of code, the Math/ prefix would quickly become distracting, so it would be nice if you could say simply PI and pow. Clojure doesn't provide a direct way to do this, but you could define a bunch of vars by hand:

```
(def PI Math/PI)
-> #'user/PI
(defn pow [b e] (Math/pow b e))
-> #'user/pow
```

Stuart Sierra[2] automated the boilerplate with the import-static macro:

```
(examples.import-static/import-static class & members)
```

import-static imports static members of a Java class as names in the local name-space. Use import-static to import the members you want from Math.

```
(require '[examples.import-static :refer [import-static]])
(import-static java.lang.Math PI pow)
-> nil

PI
-> 3.141592653589793

(pow 10 3)
-> 1000.0
```

Postponing Evaluation

Most sequences in Clojure are lazy. When you're building a lazy sequence, you often want to combine several forms whose evaluation is postponed until the sequence is forced. Since evaluation is not immediate, a macro is required.

You've already seen such a macro in *Lazy and Infinite Sequences*, on page 65: lazy-seq. Another example is delay:

```
(delay & exprs)
```

---

2. https://stuartsierra.com/

When you create a delay, it holds on to its exprs and does nothing with them until it's forced to. Try creating a delay that simulates a long calculation by sleeping:

```
(def slow-calc (delay (Thread/sleep 5000) "done!"))
-> #'user/slow-calc
```

To actually execute the delay, you must force it:

```
(force x)
```

Try forcing your slow-calc a few times:

```
(force slow-calc)
-> "done!"
(force slow-calc)
-> "done!"
```

The first time you force a delay, it executes its expressions and caches the result. Subsequent forces simply return the cached value.

The macros that implement lazy and delayed evaluation all call Java code in clojure.jar. In your own code, you should not call such Java APIs directly. Treat the lazy/delayed evaluation macros as the public API, and treat the Java classes as implementation detail that's subject to change.

Wrapping Evaluation

Many macros wrap the evaluation of a set of forms, adding some special semantics before and/or after the forms are evaluated. You've already seen several examples of this kind of macro:

- time starts a timer, evaluates forms, and then reports how long they took to execute.

- let and binding establish bindings, evaluate some forms, and then tear down the bindings.

- with-open takes an open file (or other resource), executes some forms, and then makes sure the resource is closed in a finally block.

- dosync executes forms within a transaction.

Another example of a wrapper macro is with-out-str:

```
(with-out-str & exprs)
```

with-out-str temporarily binds *out* to a new StringWriter, evaluates its exprs, and then returns the string written to *out*. with-out-str makes it easy to use print and println to build strings on the fly:

```
(with-out-str (print "hello, ") (print "world"))
-> "hello, world"
```

The implementation of with-out-str has a simple structure that can act as a template for writing similar macros:

```
Line 1  (defmacro with-out-str
     2    [& body]
     3    `(let [s# (new java.io.StringWriter)]
     4       (binding [*out* s#]
     5         ~@body
     6         (str s#))))
```

Wrapper macros usually take a variable number of arguments (line 2), which are the forms to be evaluated. They then proceed in three steps:

1. *Setup*: Create some special context for evaluation, introducing bindings with let (line 3) and bindings (line 4) as necessary.

2. *Evaluation*: Evaluate the forms (line 5). Since there is typically a variable number of forms, insert them via a splicing unquote: ~@.

3. *Teardown*: Reset the execution context to normal and return a value as appropriate (line 6).

When writing a wrapper macro, always ask yourself whether you need a finally block to implement the teardown step correctly. For with-out-str, the answer is No, because both let and binding take care of their own cleanup. If, however, you're setting some global or thread-local state via a Java API, you'll need a finally block to reset this state.

This talk of mutable state leads to another observation. Any code whose behavior changes when executed inside a wrapper macro is obviously *not* a pure function. print and println behave differently based on the value of *out* and so are not pure functions. Macros that set a binding, such as with-out-str, do so to alter the behavior of an impure function somewhere.

Not all wrappers change the behavior of the functions they wrap. You've already seen time, which times a function's execution. Another example is assert:

```
(assert expr)
```

assert tests an expression and raises an exception if it's not logically true:

```
(assert (= 1 1))
-> nil

(assert (= 1 2))
-> java.lang.Exception: Assert failed: (= 1 2)
```

Macros like assert and time violate the first rule of Macro Club to avoid unnecessary lambdas.

Avoiding Lambdas

For historical reasons, anonymous functions are often called *lambdas*. Sometimes a macro can be replaced by a function call, with the arguments wrapped in a lambda. For example, the bench macro from *Syntax Quote, Unquote, and Splicing Unquote*, on page 196 does not need to be a macro. You can write it as a function:

```
(defn bench-fn [f]
  (let [start (System/nanoTime)
        result (f)]
    {:result result :elapsed (- (System/nanoTime) start)}))
```

However, if you want to call bench-fn, you must pass it a function that wraps the form you want to execute. The following code shows the difference:

```
; macro
(bench (+ 1 2))
-> {:elapsed 44000, :result 3}

; function
(bench-fn (fn [] (+ 1 2)))
-> {:elapsed 53000, :result 3}
```

For things like bench, macros and anonymous functions are near substitutes. Both prevent immediate execution of a form. However, the anonymous function approach requires more work on the part of the caller, so it's OK to break the first rule and write a macro instead of a function.

Another reason to prefer a macro for bench is that bench-fn is not a perfect substitute; it adds the overhead of an anonymous function call at runtime. Since bench's purpose is to time things, you should avoid this overhead.

Wrapping Up

Clojure macros let you automate patterns in your code. Because they transform source code at macro expansion time, you can use macros to abstract away *any* kind of pattern in your code. You're not limited to working within Clojure. With macros, you can *extend* Clojure into your problem domain.

CHAPTER 9

Multimethods

Clojure multimethods provide a flexible way to associate a function with a set of inputs. This is similar to Java polymorphism but more general. When you call a Java method, Java selects a specific implementation to execute by examining the *type* of a *single object*. When you call a Clojure multimethod, Clojure selects a specific implementation to execute by examining the result of *any function you choose*, applied to *all* the function's arguments.

In this chapter, you'll develop a thirst for multimethods by first living without them. Then you'll build an increasingly complex series of multimethod implementations—first using multimethods to simulate polymorphism and then using multimethods to implement various ad hoc taxonomies.

Multimethods in Clojure are used much less often than polymorphism in object-oriented languages. But where they are used, they're often the key feature in the code. We'll close the chapter by looking at how multimethods are used in several open source Clojure projects and offer guidelines for when to use them in your own programs.

Living Without Multimethods

The best way to appreciate multimethods is to spend a few minutes living without them, so let's do that. Clojure can already print anything with print/println. But pretend for a moment that these functions don't exist and that you need to build a generic print mechanism. To get started, create a my-print function that can print a string to the standard output stream *out*:

```
src/examples/life_without_multi.clj
(defn my-print [ob]
  (.write *out* ob))
```

Next, create a my-println that calls my-print and then adds a line feed:

src/examples/life_without_multi.clj
```
(defn my-println [ob]
  (my-print ob)
  (.write *out* "\n"))
```

The line feed makes my-println's output easier to read when testing at the REPL. For the rest of this section, you'll make changes to my-print and test them by calling my-println. Test that my-println works with strings:

```
(my-println "hello")
| hello
-> nil
```

That's nice, but my-println doesn't work so well with nonstrings such as nil:

```
(my-println nil)
-> java.lang.NullPointerException
```

It's not a big deal though. Just use cond to add special-case handling for nil:

src/examples/life_without_multi.clj
```
(defn my-print [ob]
  (cond
    (nil? ob) (.write *out* "nil")
    (string? ob) (.write *out* ob)))
```

With the conditional in place, you can print nil with no trouble:

```
(my-println nil)
| nil
-> nil
```

Of course, there are still all kinds of types that my-println can't deal with. If you try to print a vector, neither of the cond clauses will match, and the program will print nothing at all:

```
(my-println [1 2 3])
-> nil
```

By now you know the drill. Just add another cond clause for the vector case. The implementation here is a little more complex, so you might want to separate the actual printing into a helper function, such as my-print-vector:

src/examples/life_without_multi.clj
```
(require '[clojure.string :as str])
(defn my-print-vector [ob]
  (.write *out*"[")
  (.write *out* (str/join " " ob))
  (.write *out* "]"))
```

```
(defn my-print [ob]
  (cond
    (vector? ob) (my-print-vector ob)
    (nil? ob) (.write *out* "nil")
    (string? ob) (.write *out* ob)))
```

Make sure that you can now print a vector:

```
(my-println [1 2 3])
| [1 2 3]
-> nil
```

my-println now supports three types: strings, vectors, and nil. And you have a road map for new types: just add new clauses to the cond in my-println. But it's a crummy road map, because it conflates two things: the decision process for selecting an implementation and the specific implementation detail.

You can improve the situation somewhat by pulling out helper functions like my-print-vector. But then you'll have to make two separate changes every time you want to a add new feature to my-println:

- Create a new type-specific helper function.
- Modify my-println to add a new cond invoking the feature-specific helper.

What you want is a way to add new features to the system by adding new code in a single place, without having to modify any existing code. Clojure offers this by way of protocols, covered in *Protocols*, on page 171, and multimethods.

Defining Multimethods

Multimethods capture the same pattern we explored in the previous section but support adding new cases without changing the existing code. Multimethods also provide some additional features that we'll look at later on. Multimethods consist of two parts: a *dispatch function* (created with defmulti) and a set of *methods* (created with defmethod).

To define a multimethod, use defmulti:

```
(defmulti name dispatch-fn)
```

name is the name of the new multimethod, and Clojure will invoke dispatch-fn against the method arguments to select one particular method (implementation) of the multimethod.

Consider my-print from the previous section. It takes a single argument, the thing to be printed, and you want to select a specific implementation based on the type of that argument. So dispatch-fn needs to be a function of one argument that returns the type of that argument. Clojure has a built-in function matching this description, namely, class. Use class to create a multimethod called my-print:

src/examples/multimethods.clj
```
(defmulti my-print class)
```

At this point, you've provided a description of how the multimethod will select a specific method but no actual specific methods. Unsurprisingly, attempts to call my-print will fail:

```
(my-println "foo")
-> java.lang.IllegalArgumentException: \
No method for dispatch value
```

To add a specific method implementation to my-println, use defmethod:

```
(defmethod name dispatch-val & fn-tail)
```

name is the name of the multimethod to which an implementation belongs. Clojure matches the result of defmulti's dispatch function with dispatch-val to select a method, and fn-tail contains arguments and body forms just like a normal function.

Create a my-print implementation that matches on strings:

src/examples/multimethods.clj
```
(defmethod my-print String [s]
  (.write *out* s))
```

Now, call my-println with a string argument:

```
(my-println "stu")
| stu
-> nil
```

Next, create a my-print that matches on nil:

src/examples/multimethods.clj
```
(defmethod my-print nil [s]
  (.write *out* "nil"))
```

Notice that you've solved the problem raised in the previous section. Instead of being joined in a big cond, each implementation of my-println is separate. Methods of a multimethod can live anywhere in your source, and you can add new ones any time, without having to touch the original code.

Dispatch Is Inheritance-Aware

Multimethod dispatch knows about Java inheritance. To see this, create a my-print that handles Number by printing a number's toString representation:

src/examples/multimethods.clj
```
(defmethod my-print Number [n]
  (.write *out* (.toString n)))
```

Test the Number implementation with an integer:

```
(my-println 42)
| 42
-> nil
```

42 is a Long, not a Number. Multimethod dispatch is smart enough to know that a long is a number and match anyway. Internally, dispatch uses the isa? function:

```
(isa? child parent)
```

isa? knows about Java inheritance, so it knows that an Integer is a Number:

```
(isa? Long Number)
-> true
```

isa? is not limited to inheritance. Its behavior can be extended dynamically at runtime, as you will see later in *Creating Ad Hoc Taxonomies*, on page 216.

Multimethod Defaults

It would be nice if my-print could have a fallback representation that you could use for any type you haven't specifically defined. You can use :default as a dispatch value to handle any methods that don't match anything more specific. Using :default, create a my-println that prints the Java toString value of objects, wrapped in #<>:

src/examples/multimethods.clj
```
(defmethod my-print :default [s]
  (.write *out* "#<")
  (.write *out* (.toString s))
  (.write *out* ">"))
```

Now test that my-println prints random things, using the default method:

```
(my-println (java.sql.Date. 0))
-> #<1969-12-31>

(my-println (java.util.Random.))
-> #<java.util.Random@1c398896>
```

In the unlikely event that :default already has some specific meaning in your domain, you can create a multimethod using this alternate signature:

```
(defmulti name dispatch-fn :default default-value)
```

The default-value lets you specify your own default. Maybe you'd like to call it :everything-else:

src/examples/multimethods/default.clj
```
(defmulti my-print class :default :everything-else)
(defmethod my-print String [s]
  (.write *out* s))
(defmethod my-print :everything-else [_]
  (.write *out* "Not implemented yet..."))
```

Any dispatch value that does not otherwise match will now match against :everything-else.

Dispatching a multimethod on the type of the first argument, as you've done with my-print, is by far the most common kind of dispatch. In many object-oriented languages, in fact, it's the *only* kind of dynamic dispatch, and it goes by the name *polymorphism*.

Clojure's dispatch is much more general. Let's add a few complexities to my-print and move beyond what's possible with plain ol' polymorphism.

Moving Beyond Simple Dispatch

Clojure's print function prints various "sequencey" things as lists. If you wanted my-print to do something similar, you could add a method that dispatched on a collection interface high in the Java inheritance hierarchy, such as Collection:

src/examples/multimethods.clj
```
(require '[clojure.string :as str])
(defmethod my-print java.util.Collection [c]
  (.write *out* "(")
  (.write *out* (str/join " " c))
  (.write *out* ")"))
```

Now, try various sequences to see that they get a nice print representation:

```
(my-println (take 6 (cycle [1 2 3])))
| (1 2 3 1 2 3)
-> nil

(my-println [1 2 3])
| (1 2 3)
-> nil
```

Perfectionist that you are, you cannot stand that vectors print with rounded braces, unlike their literal square-brace syntax. So add yet another my-print method, this time to handle vectors. Vectors all implement an IPersistentVector, so this should work:

src/examples/multimethods.clj
```
(defmethod my-print clojure.lang.IPersistentVector [c]
  (.write *out* "[")
  (.write *out* (str/join " " c))
  (.write *out* "]"))
```

But it doesn't work. Instead, printing vectors now throws an exception:

```
(my-println [1 2 3])
-> java.lang.IllegalArgumentException: Multiple methods match
dispatch value: class clojure.lang.LazilyPersistentVector ->
interface clojure.lang.IPersistentVector and
interface java.util.Collection,
and neither is preferred
```

The problem is that two dispatch values now match for vectors: Collection and IPersistentVector. Many languages constrain method dispatch to make sure these conflicts never happen, such as by forbidding multiple inheritance. Clojure takes a different approach. You can create conflicts, and you can resolve them with prefer-method:

```
(prefer-method multi-name loved-dispatch dissed-dispatch)
```

When you call prefer-method for a multimethod, you tell it to prefer the loved-dispatch value over the dissed-dispatch value whenever there's a conflict. Since you want the vector version of my-print to trump the collection version, tell the multimethod what you want:

src/examples/multimethods.clj
```
(prefer-method
 my-print clojure.lang.IPersistentVector java.util.Collection)
```

Now, you should be able to route both vectors and other sequences to the correct method implementation:

```
(my-println (take 6 (cycle [1 2 3])))
| (1 2 3 1 2 3)
-> nil

(my-println [1 2 3])
| [1 2 3]
-> nil
```

Many languages create complex rules, or arbitrary limitations, to resolve ambiguities in their systems for dispatching functions. Clojure allows a much simpler approach: just don't worry about it! If there's an ambiguity, use prefermethod to resolve it.

Creating Ad Hoc Taxonomies

Multimethods let you create ad hoc taxonomies, which can be helpful when you discover type relationships that are not explicitly declared as such.

For example, consider a financial application that deals with checking and savings accounts. Define a Clojure map for an account, using a tag to distinguish the two:

src/examples/multimethods/account.clj
```
(ns examples.multimethods.account)
```

Now, you're going to create two different checking accounts, tagged as ::checking and ::savings. The doubled :: causes the keywords to resolve in the current namespace. To see the namespace resolution happen, compare entering :checking and ::checking at the REPL:

```
:checking
-> :checking

::checking
-> :user/checking
```

Placing keywords in a namespace helps prevent name collisions with other people's code. When you want to use ::savings or ::checking from another namespace, you'll need to fully qualify them:

```
{:id 1, :tag :examples.multimethods.account/savings, :balance 100M}
```

Full names get tedious quickly, so you can use alias to specify a shorter alias for a long namespace name:

```
(alias short-name-symbol namespace-symbol)
```

Use alias to create the short name acc:

```
(alias 'acc 'examples.multimethods.account)
-> nil
```

Now that the acc alias is available, create two top-level test objects, a savings account and a checking account:

```
(def test-savings {:id 1, :tag ::acc/savings, ::balance 100M})
-> #'user/test-savings
```

```
(def test-checking {:id 2, :tag ::acc/checking, ::balance 250M})
-> #'user/test-checking
```

Note that the trailing M creates a BigDecimal literal and does not mean you have millions of dollars.

The interest rate is 0% for checking accounts and 5% for savings accounts. Create a multimethod interest-rate that dispatches based on :tag, like so:

src/examples/multimethods/account.clj
```
(defmulti interest-rate :tag)
(defmethod interest-rate ::acc/checking [_] 0M)
(defmethod interest-rate ::acc/savings [_] 0.05M)
```

Check your test-savings and test-checking to make sure that interest-rate works as expected.

```
(interest-rate test-savings)
-> 0.05M

(interest-rate test-checking)
-> 0M
```

Accounts have an annual service charge, with rules as follows:

- Normal checking accounts incur a $25 fee.
- Normal savings accounts incur a $10 fee.
- Premium accounts have no fee.
- Checking accounts with a balance of $5,000 or more are premium.
- Savings accounts with a balance of $1,000 or more are premium.

In a realistic example, the rules would be more complex. Premium status would be driven by average balance over time, and there would probably be other ways to qualify. But the previous rules are complex enough to demonstrate the point.

You could implement service-charge with a bunch of conditional logic, but premium feels like a type, although there's no explicit premium tag on an account. Create an account-level multimethod that returns ::premium or ::basic:

src/examples/multimethods/account.clj
```
(defmulti account-level :tag)
(defmethod account-level ::acc/checking [acct]
  (if (>= (:balance acct) 5000) ::acc/premium ::acc/basic))
(defmethod account-level ::acc/savings [acct]
  (if (>= (:balance acct) 1000) ::acc/premium ::acc/basic))
```

Test account-level to make sure that checking and savings accounts require different balance levels to reach ::premium status:

```
(account-level {:id 1, :tag ::acc/savings, :balance 2000M})
-> :examples.multimethods.account/premium
(account-level {:id 1, :tag ::acc/checking, :balance 2000M})
-> :examples.multimethods.account/basic
```

Now you might be tempted to implement service-charge using account-level as a dispatch function:

src/examples/multimethods/service_charge_1.clj
```
; bad approach
(defmulti service-charge account-level)
(defmethod service-charge ::basic [acct]
  (if (= (:tag acct) ::checking) 25 10))
(defmethod service-charge ::premium [_] 0)
```

The conditional logic in service-charge for ::basic is exactly the kind of type-driven conditional that multimethods should help us avoid. The problem here is that you're already dispatching by account-level, and now you need to be dispatching by :tag as well. No problem—you can dispatch on *both*. Write a service-charge whose dispatch function calls both account-level and :tag, returning the results in a vector:

src/examples/multimethods/service_charge_2.clj
```
(defmulti service-charge (fn [acct] [(account-level acct) (:tag acct)]))
(defmethod service-charge [::acc/basic ::acc/checking]   [_] 25)
(defmethod service-charge [::acc/basic ::acc/savings]    [_] 10)
(defmethod service-charge [::acc/premium ::acc/checking] [_] 0)
(defmethod service-charge [::acc/premium ::acc/savings]  [_] 0)
```

This version of service-charge dispatches against two different taxonomies: the :tag intrinsic to an account and the externally defined account-level. Try a few accounts to verify that service-charge works as expected:

```
(service-charge {:tag ::acc/checking :balance 1000})
-> 25

(service-charge {:tag ::acc/savings :balance 1000})
-> 0
```

There's one further improvement you can make to service-charge. Since all premium accounts have the same service charge, it seems redundant to have to define two separate service-charge methods for ::savings and ::checking accounts. It would be nice to have a parent type ::account so you could define a multimethod that matches ::premium for any kind of ::account. Clojure lets you define arbitrary parent-child relationships with derive:

```
(derive child parent)
```

Using derive, you can specify that both ::savings and ::checking are kinds of ::account:

```
src/examples/multimethods/service_charge_3.clj
(derive ::acc/savings ::acc/account)
(derive ::acc/checking ::acc/account)
```

When you start to use derive, isa? comes into its own. In addition to understanding Java inheritance, isa? knows all about derived relationships:

```
(isa? ::acc/savings ::acc/account)
-> true
```

Now that Clojure knows that savings and checking are accounts, you can define a service-charge using a single method to handle ::premium:

```
src/examples/multimethods/service_charge_3.clj
(defmulti service-charge (fn [acct] [(account-level acct) (:tag acct)]))
(defmethod service-charge [::acc/basic ::acc/checking]   [_] 25)
(defmethod service-charge [::acc/basic ::acc/savings]    [_] 10)
(defmethod service-charge [::acc/premium ::acc/account] [_] 0)
```

At first glance, you may think that derive and isa? duplicate functionality that's already available to Clojure via Java inheritance. This is not the case. Java inheritance relationships are forever fixed at the moment you define a class. derived relationships can be created when you need them and can be *applied to existing objects without their knowledge or consent*. So when you discover a useful relationship between existing objects, you can derive that relationship without touching the original objects' source code and without creating tiresome "wrapper" classes.

If the number of different ways you might define a multimethod has your head spinning, don't worry. In practice, most Clojure code uses multimethods sparingly. Let's take a look at some open source Clojure code to get a better idea of how multimethods are used.

When Should I Use Multimethods?

Multimethods are extremely flexible, and with that flexibility comes choices. How should you choose when to use multimethods, as opposed to some other technique? We approach this question from two directions, asking the following:

- Where do Clojure projects use multimethods?
- Where do Clojure projects *eschew* multimethods?

The most striking thing is that multimethods are *rare*—about one per 1,000 lines of code. So don't worry that you're missing something important if you build a Clojure application with few, or no, multimethods. A Clojure program that defines no multimethods isn't nearly as odd as an object-oriented program with no polymorphism.

Many multimethods dispatch on class. Dispatch-by-class is the easiest kind of dispatch to understand and implement. We already covered it in detail with the my-print example, so we'll say no more about it here.

Clojure multimethods that dispatch on something other than class are fairly rare. We can look directly in Clojure for some examples. The clojure.inspector and clojure.test libraries use unusual dispatch functions.

The Inspector

Clojure's inspector library uses Swing to create simple views of data. You can use it to get a tree view of your system properties:

```
(require '[clojure.inspector :refer [inspect inspect-tree]])
(inspect-tree (System/getProperties))
```

inspect-tree returns (and displays) a JFrame with a tree view of anything that's treeish. So you could also pass a nested map to inspect-tree:

```
(inspect-tree {:clojure {:creator "Rich" :runs-on-jvm true}})
```

Treeish things are made up of nodes that can answer two questions:

- Who are my children?
- Am I a leaf node?

The treeish concepts of "tree," "node," and "leaf" all sound like candidates for classes or interfaces in an object-oriented design. But the inspector doesn't work this way. Instead, it adds a "treeish" type system in an ad hoc way to existing types, using a dispatch function named collection-tag:

```
; from Clojure's clojure/inspector.clj
(defn collection-tag [x]
  (cond
    (map-entry? x) :entry
    (instance? java.util.Map x) :seqable
    (instance? java.util.Set x) :seqable
    (sequential? x) :seq
    (instance? clojure.lang.Seqable x) :seqable
    :else :atom))
```

collection-tag returns one of the keywords :entry, :map, :seqable, :seq, or :atom. These act as the type system for the treeish world. The collection-tag function is then used to dispatch three different multimethods that select specific implementations based on the treeish type system.

```
(defmulti is-leaf collection-tag)
(defmulti get-child
  (fn [parent index] (collection-tag parent)))
(defmulti get-child-count collection-tag)
; method implementations elided for brevity
```

The treeish type system is added around the existing Java type system. Existing objects don't have to *do* anything to become treeish; the Inspector library does it for them. Treeish demonstrates a powerful style of reuse. You can discover new type relationships in existing code and take advantage of these relationships simply, without having to modify the original code.

clojure.test

The clojure.test library in Clojure lets you write several different kinds of assertions using the is macro. You can assert that arbitrary functions are true. For example, 10 is not a string:

```
(require '[clojure.test :refer [is]])
(is (string? 10))

FAIL in () (NO_SOURCE_FILE:2)
expected: (string? 10)
actual: (not (string? 10))
-> false
```

Although you can use an arbitrary function, is knows about a few specific functions and provides more detailed error messages. For example, you can check that a string is not an instance? of Collection:

```
(is (instance? java.util.Collection "foo"))

FAIL in () (NO_SOURCE_FILE:3)
expected: (instance? java.util.Collection "foo")
actual: java.lang.String
-> false
```

is also knows about =. Verify that power does not equal wisdom.

```
(is (= "power" "wisdom"))

FAIL in () (NO_SOURCE_FILE:4)
expected: (= "power" "wisdom")
actual: (not (= "power" "wisdom"))
-> false
```

Internally, is uses a multimethod named assert-expr, which dispatches not on the type but on the actual *identity* of its first argument:

```
(defmulti assert-expr (fn [form message] (first form)))
```

Since the first argument is a symbol representing what function to check, this amounts to yet another ad hoc type system. This time, there are three types: =, instance?, and everything else.

The various assert-expr methods add specific error messages associated with different functions you might call from is. Because multimethods are open ended, you can add your own assert-expr methods with improved error messages for other functions you frequently pass to is.

Counterexamples

As you saw in the previous section, you can often use multimethods to hoist branches that are based on type out of the main flow of your functions. To find counterexamples where multimethods should not be used, we looked through Clojure's core to find type branches that had *not* been hoisted to multimethods.

A simple example is Clojure's class, which is a null-safe wrapper for the underlying Java getClass. Minus comments and metadata, class is as follows:

```
(defn class [x]
  (if (nil? x) x (.getClass x)))
```

You could write a version of class as a multimethod by dispatching on identity:

src/examples/multimethods.clj
```
(defmulti my-class identity)
(defmethod my-class nil [_] nil)
(defmethod my-class :default [x] (.getClass x))
```

Any nil-check could be rewritten this way. But we find the original class function easier to read than the multimethod version. This is a nice "exception that proves the rule." Even though class branches on type, the branching version is easier to read.

Use the following general rules when deciding whether to create a function or a multimethod:

- If a function branches based on a type, or multiple types, consider a multimethod.

- Types are whatever you discover them to be. They do not have to be explicit Java classes or data tags.

- You should be able to interpret the dispatch value of a defmethod without having to refer to the defmulti.

- Don't use multimethods merely to handle optional arguments or recursion.

When in doubt, try writing the function in both styles and pick the one that seems more readable.

Wrapping Up

Multimethods support arbitrary dispatch. Usually multimethods work based on type relationships. Sometimes these types are formal, as in Java classes. Other times they are informal and ad hoc and emerge from the properties of objects in the system.

CHAPTER 10

Java Interop

Clojure's Java support is both powerful and lean. It's powerful, in that it brings the expressiveness of Lisp syntax, plus some syntactic sugar tailored to Java. It's lean, in that it compiles to bytecode without a translation layer and can thus achieve Java-level performance in nearly every case.

Clojure embraces Java and its libraries. Idiomatic Clojure code calls Java libraries directly and doesn't try to wrap everything under the sun to look like Lisp. This surprises many new Clojure developers but is very pragmatic. Where Java isn't broken, Clojure doesn't fix it. In this chapter, you'll see how Clojure's access to Java is convenient, elegant, and fast. In addition, you'll see how to flip the script and call Clojure from Java.

Clojure's exception handling is easy to use. Better yet, explicit exception handling is rarely necessary. Clojure's exception primitives are the same as Java's. However, Clojure does not require you to deal with checked exceptions and makes it easy to clean up resources using the with-open idiom.

Clojure is *fast*, unlike many other dynamic languages on the JVM. You can use custom support—for type hints, primitives, and arrays—to cause Clojure's compiler to generate the same code that a Java compiler would generate.

Clojure is designed to let you get things done and have fun while doing it. However, an important part of getting things done is being able to use your platform to its full potential. Let's start by seeing how to extend Java interfaces and classes in Clojure.

Creating Java Objects in Clojure

When calling Java libraries or the Java standard library, you'll often need to pass in Java objects that either implement an interface or extend a particular class. Clojure provides solutions for this problem in several ways—direct use of Java types and interfaces, anonymous interface implementation with reify, and class extension with proxy.

Direct Use of Java Types

Clojure's implementation reuses Java's own concrete types like String, Character, Boolean, the numeric classes, Date, and more. Because these Clojure objects are actually Java objects, they can be passed directly to Java APIs without wrapping or modification.

Additionally, many Clojure objects implement key Java interfaces where applicable, so they play directly with existing APIs without additional effort. For example, Clojure functions implement the interfaces Runnable and Callable making them useful in many concurrency and task-oriented APIs. For example, a Thread is started with a Runnable so any Clojure function can be used:

```
(defn say-hi []
  (println "Hello from thread" (.getName (Thread/currentThread))))

(dotimes [_ 3]
  (.start (Thread. say-hi)))
```

Each of the last three lines will start a new thread, running the say-hi function, so you should see (in possibly a different order):

```
Hello from thread Thread-1
Hello from thread Thread-2
Hello from thread Thread-3
```

Additionally, the Clojure data structures implement key interfaces from the Java Collections API, such as Collection, List, Map, and Set. This means that any Java interface that takes a collection can be directly passed the collection created in Clojure without wrapping or copying the data.

For example, consider the Java library class java.util.Collections, which has helpful utility methods for Java collections. One provided method is binarySearch, which takes a sorted list and uses a binary search algorithm to determine whether the list contains an element. If the list also implements the RandomAccess interface (which Clojure vectors do), this can be accomplished in $O(\log n)$ element comparisons.

Since the Clojure collections implement the proper interfaces, they can be passed directly to this Java method:

```
(java.util.Collections/binarySearch [1 13 42 1000] 42)
-> 2
```

The binarySearch method returns the index in the collection where the element can be found.

Between Clojure's direct use of Java primitives and extensive use of Java interfaces, a lot of Java interop will simply do what you expect when you invoke a method, both in the code as well as in the underlying bytecode. There's no magic here, just Clojure adhering to good Java implementation principles.

However, you'll inevitably encounter cases where you need to invoke a method that takes an instance conforming to a Java interface where you need to provide that instance. In the next section, we'll see some options for how to do this.

Implementing Java Interfaces

When invoking a Java method takes an instance implementing a Java interface, one of the key questions is whether you need to generate that instance just for the purposes of the call or you need to make and reuse that instance in many places.

In the first case (common when creating callbacks or using event-based APIs), it's easiest to just create an anonymous instance at the point of use with reify.

For example, the java.io.File class contains a method list(FilenameFilter filter) to obtain a list of files in a directory that satisfy the filter. The FilenameFilter class has just one method, accept(File dir, String name).

Consider building a function list-files that takes a directory and a suffix and returns a sequence of all files with that suffix in the directory:

```
(import [java.io File FilenameFilter])

(defn suffix-filter [suffix]
  (reify FilenameFilter
    (accept [this dir name]
      (.endsWith name suffix))))

(defn list-files [dir suffix]
  (seq (.list (File. dir) (suffix-filter suffix))))

(list-files "." ".clj")
-> ("project.clj")
```

When we invoke the list method, we need to pass a suffix-accepting instance of FilenameFilter. Because we have a short-term need for that instance, it's best to just use reify to create an anonymous instance implementing that interface.

The suffix-filter helper function takes care of creating the instance. The reify function takes an interface, which is followed by implementations of each method in that interface. The first argument to each method is always the anonymous instance itself, which is commonly called this (although there's nothing special about this name). Any number of interfaces can be implemented in a single call to reify. Any interface methods that are not specified will be added automatically and will throw an UnsupportedOperationException.

In other cases, you'll want to create an object with data fields and a type that implements a Java interface. Both defrecord and deftype can be used to implement interfaces inline.

For example, consider creating a Counter instance with a field n for how high to count. You could create this with reify, but you'd be unable to get or modify the data field inside the instance, and you'd have no concrete type for the instances.

Instead we could use defrecord to implement Runnable directly:

```
(defrecord Counter [n]
  Runnable
  (run [this] (println (range n))))
-> user.Counter

(def c (->Counter 5))
-> #'user/c

(.start (Thread. c))
-> (0 1 2 3 4)
```

The advantage here is that c is not just an opaque anonymous object. It has a concrete type (user.Counter), which can be used for polymorphism and a field n that can be retrieved and/or updated.

```
(:n c)
-> 5

(def c2 (assoc c :n 8))
-> #'user/c2

(.start (Thread. c2))
-> (0 1 2 3 4 5 6 7)
```

To create stateful objects, we extend this further by using fields that hold reference types like atoms.

So far we've only looked at implementing interfaces. Next we'll consider how to deal with the need to extend an actual class.

Extending Classes with Proxies

In addition to interfaces, many Java APIs provide base classes that can be used to ease the implementation of custom instances of an interface. In particular, this is common in places like Swing or XML parsers. Clojure can easily generate one-off proxies or classes on disk when needed.

A good example is parsing XML with a Simple API for XML (SAX) parser. To get ready for this example, go ahead and import the following classes. We'll need them all before we're done:

```
(import '[org.xml.sax InputSource]
        '[org.xml.sax.helpers DefaultHandler]
        '[java.io StringReader]
        '[javax.xml.parsers SAXParserFactory])
```

To use a SAX parser, you need to implement a callback mechanism. The easiest way is often to extend the DefaultHandler class. In Clojure, you can extend a class with the proxy function:

```
(proxy class-and-interfaces super-cons-args & fns)
```

As a simple example, use proxy to create a DefaultHandler that prints the details of all calls to startElement:

```
(def print-element-handler
  (proxy [DefaultHandler] []
    (startElement [uri local qname atts]
      (println (format "Saw element: %s" qname)))))
```

proxy generates an instance of a proxy class. The first argument to proxy is [DefaultHandler], a vector of the superclass and superinterfaces. The second argument, [], is a vector of arguments to the base class constructor. In this case, no arguments are needed.

After the proxy setup, comes the implementation code for zero or more proxy methods. The proxy shown earlier has one method. Its name is startElement, and it takes four arguments and prints the name of the qname argument.

Now you need a parser to pass the handler to. This requires plowing through a pile of Java factory methods and constructors. For a simple exploration at the REPL, you can create a function that parses XML in a string:

```
(defn demo-sax-parse [source handler]
  (.. SAXParserFactory newInstance newSAXParser
      (parse (InputSource. (StringReader. source)) handler)))
```

Now the parse is easy:

```
(demo-sax-parse "<foo>
  <bar>Body of bar</bar>
  </foo>" print-element-handler)
  | Saw element: foo
  | Saw element: bar
```

The previous example demonstrates the mechanics of creating a Clojure proxy to deal with Java's XML interfaces. You can take a similar approach to implementing your own custom Java interfaces. But if all you're doing is XML processing, the clojure.data.xml library already has terrific XML support and can work with any SAX-compatible Java parser.

For one-off tasks, such as XML and thread callbacks, Clojure's proxies are quick and easy to use. If you need a longer-lived class, you can generate an entirely new class from Clojure using gen-class, which is an advanced topic that won't be discussed here.

Now that we've seen how to invoke Java APIs from Clojure, let's turn things around and consider how to invoke Clojure from Java.

Calling Clojure From Java

While using Java APIs from Clojure is common due to Clojure's embrace of the host platform, there are times when you'll need to invoke Clojure directly from Java. For these cases, Clojure provides a Java API that can be used to directly access Clojure namespaces, vars, and functions.

The main entry point for the Clojure Java API is the clojure.java.api.Clojure class, which provides a few static methods for reading data, finding vars, and invoking unctions. With this handful of tools, you can invoke almost any aspect of Clojure.

For example, in a Java program, you can find the + function by using the var method of the Clojure class, which takes the namespace and name of a var and returns its value (in this case a function). All Clojure function instances implement the clojure.lang.IFn interface, which can be invoked with arguments:

```
IFn plus = Clojure.var("clojure.core", "+");
System.out.println(plus.invoke(1, 2, 3));
```

Note that the Java interfaces for Clojure functions generally take Object and return Object.

The Clojure class also provides a read method that can be used to read literal data into Clojure data structures:

```
Object vector = Clojure.read("[1 2 3]");
```

By default, the Clojure Java API requires clojure.core, and thus all core functions are available without needing to load them. When you need to load another namespace, you can do so using require through the var interface to load namespaces just like you would at the REPL:

```
IFn require = Clojure.var("clojure.core", "require");
require.invoke(Clojure.read("clojure.set"));
```

That covers the basics of using the Clojure Java API. As you can see, the tools provided cover just the basics of reading, function lookup, and invocation, but that's enough to handle the majority of Clojure usage. Next we'll look at how to handle catching and throwing exceptions in our Clojure code.

Exception Handling

In Java code, exception handling crops up for three reasons:

- Wrapping checked exceptions (see *Checked Exceptions,* on page 231 if you're unfamiliar with checked exceptions)

- Using a finally block to clean up nonmemory resources, such as file and network handles

- Responding to the problem: ignoring the exception, retrying the operation, converting the exception to a nonexceptional result, and so on

Checked Exceptions

Java's checked exceptions must be explicitly caught or rethrown from every method where they can occur in Java. This seemed like a good idea at first: checked exceptions could use the type system to rigorously document error handling, with compiler enforcement. Most Java programmers now consider checked exceptions a failed experiment, because their costs in code bloat and maintainability outweigh their advantages. For more on the history of checked exceptions, see Rod Waldhoff's article[a] and the accompanying links.

---

a.   http://tinyurl.com/checked-exceptions-mistake

In Clojure, things are similar but simpler. The try and throw special forms give you all the capabilities of Java's try, catch, finally, and throw. But you shouldn't have to use them very often, because Clojure doesn't require you to deal with checked exceptions, and there are helpful macros like with-open to encapsulate resource cleanup.

Let's see what this looks like in practice.

Keeping Exception Handling Simple

Java programs often wrap checked exceptions at abstraction boundaries. A good example is Apache Ant, which tends to wrap low-level exceptions (such as I/O exceptions) with an Ant-level build exception:

```
try {
  newManifest = new Manifest(r);
} catch (IOException e) {
  throw new BuildException(...);
}
```

In Clojure, you're not forced to deal with checked exceptions. You don't have to catch them or declare that you throw them. So the previous code would translate to the following:

```
(Manifest. r)
```

The absence of exception wrappers makes idiomatic Clojure code easier to read, write, and maintain than idiomatic Java. That said, nothing prevents you from explicitly catching, wrapping, and rethrowing exceptions in Clojure. It simply is not required. You *should* catch exceptions when you plan to respond to them in a meaningful way, and in the next exception, we'll see how Clojure handles this in its data-centric way.

Rethrowing with ex-info

In Java it's common to create many custom exception subclasses corresponding to all manner of contingencies. Often these are built in deeply nested exception hierarchies. In practice, the majority of these exception classes add little value beyond their specific class name, which can be caught and handled.

In Clojure, we instead have a single custom exception class provided with the language (IExceptionInfo), which carries a map of data where you can place any information that's necessary or useful to handle the error.

For example, a common use for custom exceptions is inside the code that serves a web request. Various error conditions might result in different HTTP status codes. Rather than have dozens of exceptions, we can simply throw a custom exception with a map of data, including the status code that should be returned:

```
(defn load-resource
  [path]
  (try
    (if (forbidden? path)
      (throw (ex-info "Forbidden resource"
                      {:status 403, :resource path}))
      (slurp path))
```

```
(catch FileNotFoundException e
  (throw (ex-info "Missing resource"
                  {:status 404, :resource path})))
      (catch IOException e
  (throw (ex-info "Server error"
                  {:status 500, :resource path}))))))
```

The load-resource function first checks to see whether the resource is forbidden. If so, we throw a 403. Otherwise, we try to read and return the resource. We also handle two different types of errors—the case where something is missing and an unknown IO failure. In all of these cases, we use the ex-info function to create a custom exception instance with a message and the map of data.

Higher up the call stack, some other code can catch this exception (with type IExceptionInfo) and retrieve the map of data using ex-data. This handler or middleware could then construct the proper HTTP response message to return.

When using external resources, it's important to properly close and dispose of those resources. Often in Java this can become a tangle of exception handling code. In the next section, we'll look at some options Clojure provides for easier cleanup.

Cleaning Up Resources

Garbage collection will clean up resources in memory. If you use resources that live outside of garbage-collected memory, such as file handles, you need to make sure that you clean them up, even in the event of an exception. In Java, this is normally handled in a finally block.

If the resource you need to free follows the convention of having a close method, you can use Clojure's with-open macro:

```
(with-open [name init-form] & body)
```

Internally, with-open creates a try block, sets name to the result of init-form, and then runs the forms in body. Most important, with-open always closes the object bound to name in a finally block. A good example of with-open is the spit function in clojure.string:

```
(clojure.core/spit file content)
```

spit simply writes a string to file. Try it:

```
(spit "hello.out" "hello, world")
-> nil
```

You should now find a file at hello.out with the contents hello, world.

The implementation of spit is simple:

```
; from clojure.core
(defn spit
  "Opposite of slurp.  Opens f with writer, writes content, then
  closes f. Options passed to clojure.java.io/writer."
  {:added "1.2"}
  [f content & options]
  (with-open [^java.io.Writer w (apply jio/writer f options)]
    (.write w (str content))))
```

spit creates a PrintWriter on f, which can be just about anything that is writable: a file, a URL, a URI, or any of Java's various writers or output streams. It then prints content to the writer. Finally, with-open guarantees that the writer is closed at the end of spit.

If you need to do something other than close in a finally block, the Clojure try form looks like this:

```
(try expr* catch-clause* finally-clause?)
; catch-clause -> (catch classname name expr*)
; finally-clause -> (finally expr*)
```

You can use it as follows:

```
(try
  (throw (Exception. "something failed")))
(finally
  (println "we get to clean up")))
| we get to clean up
-> java.lang.Exception: something failed
```

The previous fragment also demonstrates Clojure's throw form, which simply throws whatever exception is passed to it.

Responding to an Exception

The most interesting case is when an exception handler attempts to respond to the problem in a catch block. As a simple example, write a function to test whether a particular class is available at runtime:

src/examples/interop.clj
```
; not caller-friendly
(defn class-available? [class-name]
  (Class/forName class-name))
```

This approach is not very caller-friendly. The caller just wants a yes/no answer but instead gets an exception:

```
(class-available? "borg.util.Assimilate")
-> java.lang.ClassNotFoundException: borg.util.Assimilate
```

A friendlier approach uses a catch block to return false:

src/examples/interop.clj

```
(defn class-available? [class-name]
  (try
   (Class/forName class-name) true
   (catch ClassNotFoundException _ false)))
```

The caller experience is much better now:

```
(class-available? "borg.util.Assimilate")
-> false

(class-available? "java.lang.String")
-> true
```

Clojure gives you everything you need to throw and catch exceptions and to cleanly release resources. At the same time, Clojure keeps exceptions in their place. They're important but not so important that your mainline code is dominated by the exceptional.

Optimizing for Performance

In Clojure, it's idiomatic to call Java using the techniques described in *Calling Java*, on page 39. The resulting code will be fast enough for 90 percent of scenarios. When you need to, though, you can make localized changes to boost performance. These changes will not change how outside callers invoke your code, so you're free to make your code work and then make it fast.

One of the most common ways to make Java interop faster is by adding type hints to remove reflective calls. We'll look at that first, and then we'll consider how to use Java primitives and arrays as a way to optimize memory use and numeric calculation performance.

Adding Type Hints

Clojure supports adding type hints to function parameters, let bindings, variable names, and expressions. These type hints serve two purposes:

- Optimizing critical performance paths
- Documenting the required type

For example, consider the following function, which returns information about a Java class:

```
(defn describe-class [c]
  {:name (.getName c)
   :final (java.lang.reflect.Modifier/isFinal (.getModifiers c))})
```

You can ask Clojure how much type information it can infer, by setting the special variable *warn-on-reflection* to true:

```
(set! *warn-on-reflection* true)
-> true
```

The exclamation point on the end of set! is an idiomatic indication that set! changes mutable state. set! is described in detail in *Working with Java Callback APIs*, on page 155. With *warn-on-reflection* set to true, compiling describe-class will produce the following warnings:

```
Reflection warning, line: 87
- reference to field getName can't be resolved.

Reflection warning, line: 88
- reference to field getModifiers can't be resolved.
```

These warnings indicate that Clojure has no way of knowing the type of c. You can provide a type hint to fix this, using the metadata syntax ^Class:

```
(defn describe-class [^Class c]
  {:name (.getName c)
   :final (java.lang.reflect.Modifier/isFinal (.getModifiers c))})
```

With the type hint in place, the reflection warnings will disappear. The compiled Clojure code will be exactly the same as compiled Java code. Further, attempts to call describe-class with something other than a Class will fail with a ClassCastException:

```
(describe-class StringBuffer)
-> {:name "java.lang.StringBuffer", :final true}

(describe-class "foo")
| IllegalArgumentException No matching field found: getName
| for class java.lang.String
```

When you provide a type hint, Clojure will insert an appropriate class cast to avoid making slow, reflective calls to Java methods. But if your function doesn't actually call any Java methods on a hinted object, then Clojure will not insert a cast. Consider this wants-a-string function:

```
(defn wants-a-string [^String s] (println s))
-> #'user/wants-a-string
```

You might expect that wants-a-string would complain about nonstring arguments. In fact, it'll be perfectly happy:

```
(wants-a-string "foo")
| foo
```

```
(wants-a-string 0)
| 0
```

Clojure can tell that wants-a-string never actually uses its argument as a string (println will happily try to print any kind of argument). Since no string methods need to be called, Clojure doesn't attempt to cast s to a string.

When you need speed, type hints will let Clojure code compile down to the same code Java will produce. But you won't need type hints that often. Make your code work first, and then worry about making it fast.

Integer Math

Clojure provides three different sets of operations for integer types:

- The default operators
- The promoting operators
- The unchecked operators

The following table gives a sampling of these operator types.

Default	Promoting	Unchecked
+	+'	unchecked-add
-	-'	unchecked-subtract
*	*'	unchecked-multiply
inc	inc'	unchecked-inc
dec	dec'	unchecked-dec

The unchecked operators correspond exactly with primitive math in Java. They are fast but dangerous, in that they can overflow silently and give incorrect answers. In Clojure, the unchecked operators should be used only in the rare situation that overflow is the desired behavior (like hashing) or when performance is paramount, and you're certain overflow is impossible or irrelevant.

```
(unchecked-add 9223372036854775807 1)
-> -9223372036854775808
```

The default operators use Java primitives where possible for performance but always make overflow checks and throw an exception.

```
(+ 9223372036854775807 1)
-> ArithmeticException integer overflow
```

The promoting operators automatically promote from primitives to big numbers on overflow. This makes it possible to handle an arbitrary range but at significant performance cost. Because primitives and big numbers share no common base type, math with the promoting operators precludes the use of primitives as return types.

```
(+' 9223372036854775807 1)
-> 9223372036854775808N
```

Clojure relies on Java's BigDecimal class for arbitrary-precision decimal numbers. See the online documentation[1] for details. BigDecimals provide arbitrary precision but at a price: BigDecimal math is significantly slower than Java's floating-point primitives.

Clojure has its own BigInt class to handle BigInteger conversions. Clojure's BigInt has some performance improvements over using Java's BigInteger directly. It also wraps some of the rough edges of BigInteger. In particular, it properly implements hashCode. This makes equality take precedence over representation, which you'll see in almost every abstraction in the language.

Under the hood, Clojure uses Java's BigInteger. The performance difference comes in how BigInt treats its values. A BigInt consists of a Long part and a BigInteger part. When the value passed into a BigInt is small enough to be treated as a Long, it is. When numerical operations are performed on BigInts, if their result is small enough to be treated as a Long, it is. This gives the user the ability to add the overflow hint (N) without paying the BigInteger cost until it's absolutely necessary.

Using Primitives for Performance

In the previous sections, function parameters carry no type information. Clojure simply does the right thing. Depending on your perspective, this is either a strength or a weakness. It's a strength, because your code is clean and simple. But it's also a weakness, because a reader of the code can't be certain of datatypes, and because doing the right thing carries some performance over-head. Consider a function that calculates the sum of the numbers from 1 to n:

```
; performance demo only, don't write code like this
(defn sum-to [n]
  (loop [i 1 sum 0]
    (if (<= i n)
      (recur (inc i) (+ i sum))
      sum)))
```

You can verify that this function works with a small input value:

```
(sum-to 10)
=>  55
```

---

1. http://docs.oracle.com/javase/8/docs/api/java/math/BigDecimal.html

Let's see how sum-to performs. To time an operation, you can use the time function. When benchmarking, you'll tend to want to take several measurements so that you can eliminate startup overhead plus any outliers; therefore, you can call time from inside a dotimes macro:

```
(dotimes bindings & body)
```

dotimes will execute its body repeatedly, with the name bound to integers from zero to n-1. Using dotimes, you can collect five timings of sum-to as follows:

```
(dotimes [_ 5] (time (sum-to 100000)))
|   "Elapsed time: 0.397831 msecs"
|   "Elapsed time: 0.420645 msecs"
|   "Elapsed time: 0.363732 msecs"
|   "Elapsed time: 0.365856 msecs"
-> "Elapsed time: 0.368997 msecs"
```

Benchmark Timings

Don't worry if you see much different timings for this on your own machine, in particular, in the first few timings. The JVM has extensive abilities to compile and recompile code based on repeated use. Triggering this behavior often takes tens of thousands of invocations, which makes benchmarking these operations tricky. Try running each example a few times to make sure the times you see are representative.

You might also see an occasional spike where one timing is much higher than the ones before and after it. This is usually due to the JVM doing extra work, either in recompilation or more commonly, garbage collection.

To speed things up, you can hint the argument and return type as long. Clojure's type inference will flow this hint to all the internal operations and function calls inside the function.

```
(defn integer-sum-to ^long [^long n]
  (loop [i 1 sum 0]
    (if (<= i n)
      (recur (inc i) (+ i sum))
      sum)))
```

The integer-sum-to is indeed faster:

```
(dotimes [_ 5] (time (integer-sum-to 100000)))
|   "Elapsed time: 0.152525 msecs"
|   "Elapsed time: 0.112546 msecs"
|   "Elapsed time: 0.112313 msecs"
|   "Elapsed time: 0.112196 msecs"
-> "Elapsed time: 0.112155 msecs"
```

Clojure's primitive math is still correct, in that it will check for overflow and throw an exception. Is that as fast as things can get? Java programmers have access to super-fast busted math: arithmetic operations that have the maximum possible performance but can silently overflow and corrupt data.

Clojure provides access to Java's arithmetic semantics through the unchecked family of functions. Maybe you can get an even faster function by using the unchecked version of +, unchecked-add:

```
(defn unchecked-sum-to ^long [^long n]
  (loop [i 1 sum 0]
    (if (<= i n)
      (recur (inc i) (unchecked-add i sum))
      sum)))
```

The unchecked-sum-to is not significantly faster:

```
(dotimes [_ 5] (time (unchecked-sum-to 100000)))
|   "Elapsed time: 0.112321 msecs"
|   "Elapsed time: 0.075186 msecs"
|   "Elapsed time: 0.075046 msecs"
|   "Elapsed time: 0.075116 msecs"
-> "Elapsed time: 0.093338 msecs"
```

Orders of magnitude are important! Primitive hinting can make certain operations significantly faster. However, switching to Java's unchecked semantics is generally a losing proposition. You get a trivial performance gain on average, with the possibility of data corruption tomorrow.

Clojure provides these operations for the relatively rare cases where they're needed (like hash computations) and for cases where you need to interoperate with other libraries that expect this behavior. Additionally, there are some performance-sensitive cases where you're willing to give up safety for maximum performance.

Prefer accuracy first and then optimize for speed only where necessary. integer-sum-to will throw an exception on overflow. This is bad, but the problem is easily detected:

```
(integer-sum-to 10000000000)
-> java.lang.ArithmeticException: integer overflow
```

unchecked-sum-to will fail silently on overflow. In a program setting, it can quietly but catastrophically corrupt data:

```
(unchecked-sum-to 10000000000)
-> -5340232216128654848 ; WRONG!!
```

Given the competing concerns of correctness and performance, you should normally prefer simple, undecorated code such as the original sum-to. If profiling identifies a bottleneck, you can force Clojure to use a primitive type in just the places that need it.

The sum-to example is deliberately simple to demonstrate the various options for integer math in Clojure. In a real Clojure program, it would be more expressive to implement sum-to using reduce. Summing a sequence is the same as summing the first two items, adding that result to the next item, and so on. That is exactly the loop that (reduce + ...) provides. With reduce, you can rewrite sum-to as a one-liner:

```
(defn better-sum-to [n]
  (reduce + (range 1 (inc n))))
```

The example also demonstrates an even more general point: pick the right algorithm to begin with. The sum of numbers from 1 to n can be calculated directly as follows.

```
(defn best-sum-to [n]
  (/ (* n (inc n)) 2))
```

Even without performance hints, this is faster than implementations based on repeated addition:

```
(dotimes [_ 5] (time (best-sum-to 100000)))
|   "Elapsed time: 0.043821 msecs"
|   "Elapsed time: 0.004646 msecs"
|   "Elapsed time: 0.003991 msecs"
|   "Elapsed time: 0.004111 msecs"
-> "Elapsed time: 0.003898 msecs"
```

Performance is a tricky subject. Don't write ugly code in search of speed. Start by choosing appropriate algorithms and getting your code to work correctly. If you have performance issues, profile to identify the problems. Then, introduce only as much complexity as you need to solve those problems.

Using Java Arrays

Clojure's collections supplant the Java collections for most purposes. Clojure's collections are concurrency safe, have good performance characteristics, and implement the appropriate Java collection interfaces. So you should generally prefer Clojure's own collections when you're working in Clojure and even pass them back into Java when convenient.

If you do choose to use the Java collections, nothing in Clojure will stop you. From Clojure's perspective, the Java collections are classes like any other, and all the various Java interop forms will work. But the Java collections are designed for lock-based concurrency. They will not provide the concurrency guarantees that Clojure collections do and won't work well with Clojure's software transactional memory.

One place where you'll need to deal with Java collections is the special case of Java arrays. In Java, arrays have their own syntax and their own bytecode instructions. Java arrays don't implement any Java interface. Clojure collections cannot masquerade as arrays. (Java collections can't either!) The Java platform makes arrays a special case in every way, so Clojure does, too.

Clojure provides make-array to create Java arrays:

```
(make-array class length)
(make-array class dim & more-dims)
```

make-array takes a class and a variable number of array dimensions. For a one-dimensional array of strings, you might say this:

```
(make-array String 5)
-> #object["[Ljava.lang.String;" 0x6a129a7d "[Ljava.lang.String;@6a129a7d"]
```

The odd output is courtesy of Java's implementation of toString() for arrays: [Ljava.lang.String; is the JVM specification's encoding for "one-dimensional array of strings." That's not very useful at the REPL, so you can use Clojure's seq to wrap any Java array as a Clojure sequence so that the REPL can print the individual array entries:

```
(seq (make-array String 5))
-> (nil nil nil nil nil)
```

Clojure also includes a family of functions with names such as int-array for creating arrays of Java primitives. You can issue the following command at the REPL to review the documentation for these and other array functions:

```
(find-doc "-array")
```

Clojure provides a set of low-level operations on Java arrays, including aset, aget, and alength:

```
(aset java-array index value)
(aset java-array index-dim1 index-dim2 ... value)
(aget java-array index)
(aget java-array index-dim1 index-dim2 ...)
(alength java-array)
```

Use make-array to create an array and then experiment with using aset, aget, and alength to work with the array:

```
(defn painstakingly-create-array []
  (let [arr (make-array String 5)]
    (aset arr 0 "Painstaking")
    (aset arr 1 "to")
    (aset arr2 "fill")
    (aset arr 3" in")
    (aset arr 4 "arrays")
    arr))
(aget (paintakingly-create-array) 0)
-> "Painstaking"

(alength (painstakingly-create-array))
-> 5
```

Most of the time, you'll find it simpler to use higher-level functions such as to-array, which creates an array directly from any collection:

```
(to-array sequence)
```

to-array always creates an Object array:

```
(to-array ["Easier" "array" "creation"])
-> (to-array ["Easier" "array" "creation"])
```

to-array is also useful for calling Java methods that take a variable argument list, such as String/format:

```
; example. prefer clojure.core/format (String/format "Training Week: %s Mileage: %d"
(String/format "Training Week: %s Mileage: %d"
               (to-array [2 26]))
-> "Training Week: 2 Mileage: 26"
```

to-array's cousin into-array can create an array with a more specific type than Object.

```
(into-array type? seq)
```

You can pass an explicit type as an optional first argument to into-array:

```
(into-array String ["Easier", "array", "creation"])
-> #object["[Ljava.lang.String;" 0x21072f13 "[Ljava.lang.String;@21072f13"]
```

If you omit the type argument, into-array will guess the type based on the first item in the sequence:

```
(into-array ["Easier" "array" "creation"])
-> #object["[Ljava.lang.String;" 0x88821c2 "[Ljava.lang.String;@88821c2"]
```

As you can see, the array contains Strings, not Objects. If you want to transform every element of a Java array without converting to a Clojure sequence, you can use amap:

```
(amap a idx ret expr)
```

amap creates a clone of the array a, binding that clone to the name you specify in ret. It then executes expr once for each element in a, with idx bound to the index of the element. Finally, amap returns the cloned array. You could use amap to uppercase every string in an array of strings:

```
(def strings (into-array ["some" "strings" "here"]))
-> #'user/strings

(seq (amap strings idx _ (.toUpperCase (aget strings idx))))
-> ("SOME" "STRINGS" "HERE")
```

The ret parameter is set to _ to indicate that it's not needed in the map expression, and the wrapping seq is simply for convenience in printing the result at the REPL. Similar to amap is areduce:

```
(areduce a idx ret init expr)
```

Where amap produces a new array, areduce produces anything you want. The ret is initially set to init and later set to the return value of each subsequent invocation of expr. areduce is normally used to write functions that "tally up" a collection in some way. For example, the following call finds the length of the longest string in the strings array:

```
(areduce strings idx ret 0 (max ret (.length (aget strings idx))))
-> 7
```

amap and areduce are special-purpose macros for interoperating with Java arrays.

A Real-World Example

While it's great to talk about the different interop cases and learn how to eke out some additional performance using Java's primitive forms, you still need to have some practical, hands-on knowledge. In this example, we will build an application to test the availability of websites. The goal here is to check to see whether the website returns an HTTP 200 OK response. If anything other than our expected response is received, the website should be marked as unavailable.

Again, we'll use the clj build tool. Refer to *Clojure Coding Quick Start*, on page 9 if you don't have clj installed already. Let's start by creating a directory to hold our project and switch to it:

```
mkdir pinger
cd pinger
```

You can start a REPL for the pinger project using clj:

```
clj
```

By default, source files will be loaded from the src directory, according to the namespace of the code. We plan to work in the pinger.core namespace, so we need to create the directory structure:

```
mkdir -p src/pinger
```

First we need to write the code that connects to a URL and captures the response code. We can accomplish this by using Java's URL class. We'll create this code in src/pinger/core.clj:

```
(ns pinger.core
  (:import [java.net URL HttpURLConnection]))

(defn response-code [address]
  (let [conn ^HttpURLConnection (.openConnection (URL. address))
        code (.getResponseCode conn)]
    (when (< code 400)
      (-> conn .getInputStream .close))
    code))
```

Give it a try in the REPL:

```
(require 'pinger.core)
(in-ns 'pinger.core)

(response-code "http://google.com")
-> 200
```

Now let's create a predicate function that uses response-code and decides whether the specified URL is available. We will define available in our context as "returning an HTTP 200 response code."

```
(defn available? [address]
  (= 200 (response-code address)))

(available? "http://google.com")
-> true

(available? "http://google.com/badurl")
-> false
```

Next we need a way to start our program and have it check every so often a list of URLs that we care about and report their availability. Let's create a -main function.

```
(defn -main []
  (let [addresses ["https://google.com"
                   "https://clojure.org"
                   "http://google.com/badurl"]]
    (while true
      (doseq [address addresses]
        (println address ":" (available? address)))
      (Thread/sleep (* 1000 60)))))
```

In this example, we create a list of addresses (two good and one bad) and use a simple while loop that never exits, to obtain a never-ending program execution. It will continue to check these URLs once a minute until the program is terminated.

It's time to run our program:

```
clj -m pinger.core
https://google.com : true
https://clojure.org : true
http://google.com/badurl : false
```

You should see your program start and continue to run until you press Ctrl-C to stop it.

A while loop that's always true will continue to run until terminated, but it's not really the cleanest way to obtain the result because it doesn't allow for a clean shutdown. We can use a scheduled thread pool that will start and execute the desired command in a similar fashion as the while loop but with a much greater level of control. Create a file src/pinger/scheduler.clj and enter the following code:

```clojure
(ns pinger.scheduler
  (:import [java.util.concurrent Executors ExecutorService
                                 ScheduledExecutorService
                                 ScheduledFuture TimeUnit]))

(set! *warn-on-reflection* true)

(defn scheduled-executor
  "Create a scheduled executor."
  ^ScheduledExecutorService [threads]
  (Executors/newScheduledThreadPool threads))

(defn periodically
  "Schedule function f to run on executor e every 'delay'
   milliseconds after a delay of 'initial-delay' Returns
   a ScheduledFuture."
  ^ScheduledFuture
  [^ScheduledExecutorService e f initial-delay delay]
  (.scheduleWithFixedDelay e f initial-delay delay TimeUnit/MILLISECONDS))

(defn shutdown-executor
  "Shutdown an executor."
  [^ExecutorService e]
  (.shutdown e))
```

This namespace provides functions to create and shut down a Java ScheduledExecutorService. It also defines a function called periodically that will accept an executor, a function, an initial-delay, and a repeated delay. It will execute the function for the first time after the initial delay and then continue to execute the function with the delay specified thereafter. This will continue to run until the thread pool is shut down.

Let's update pinger.core to take advantage of the scheduling code as well as make the -main function responsible only for calling a function that starts the loop. Replace the old -main with the following functions:

```
(defn check []
  (let [addresses ["https://google.com"
                   "https://clojure.org"
                   "http://google.com/badurl"]]
    (doseq [address addresses]
      (println address ":" (available? address)))))
(def immediately 0)
(def every-minute (* 60 1000))

(defn start [e]
  "REPL helper. Start pinger on executor e."
  (scheduler/periodically e check immediately every-minute))

(defn stop [e]
  "REPL helper. Stop executor e."
  (scheduler/shutdown-executor e))

(defn -main []
  (start (scheduler/scheduled-executor 1)))
```

Make sure to update your namespace declaration to include the scheduler code:

```
(ns pinger.core
  (:require [pinger.scheduler :as scheduler])
  (:import [java.net HttpURLConnection URL]))
```

Not everything in the previous sample is necessary, but it makes for more readable code. Adding the start and stop functions makes it easy to work interactively from the REPL, which will be a huge advantage should you choose to extend this example. Give the program another try—everything should function exactly as it did before.

We could easily expand on this example by extending the check for a valid web page, checking its response time, or enhancing how sites are persisted or stored.

Wrapping Up

We just covered a good chunk of how Clojure and Java get along. We even mixed the two up in some interesting ways. In the next and final chapter we'll look at another larger example and see how Clojure's features work in combination to provide both power and expressivity.

CHAPTER 11

Building an Application

Now that you've learned the basics of the Clojure language, it's time to begin using Clojure in your own projects. But when you start to work on your own killer Clojure app, you'll quickly discover that knowledge of the language is only part of what you need to work effectively. You also need to consider questions of workflow, data structures, polymorphism, testing, and more.

As our sample application, we'll implement a version of the game Hangman where a player uncovers a word by guessing a sequence of letters. Whereas we show you all the code as we go, this chapter is not really about code. It's about how we approach solving problems in Clojure, by focusing on how to represent our problem in data, then building functional algorithms around that data.

We'll also look at how we can use specs to describe both our data and the functions used in the program, then test those functions with generative testing.

Getting Started

Before you start writing code, it's good to initialize a project directory on your file system. While there are a variety of build tools and editors for Clojure, all of them expect the root of the project directory to contain a definition of the project, to have a directory containing all of the source code, a directory containing all of the test code, and so on.

We won't need all of those—for our purposes we just need a src directory that will hold a single file of source that matches its namespace:

```
$ mkdir -p src/hangman
```

With that sorted out, create the default source file (src/hangman/core.clj) in your Clojure editor of choice. Add the namespace declaration:

```
(ns hangman.core)
```

You should also ensure that you have a REPL running in the context of this project. The exact procedure for that will vary depending your editor, so we won't provide instructions for that here. If you want a REPL at the command line, you can start one by running clj.

Now, you're ready to start working on the application.

Developing the Game Loop

There are many paths to developing successful applications with Clojure (or any language) and many ways this application could be written. However, writing any program involves starting from high-level goals and breaking the problem down into smaller problems, until it's easy to solve each subproblem with a single (usually small) function.

Our application is a game with a single player where the player guesses letters to slowly reveal a word. The goal for the player is to guess all of the letters in the word with as few guesses as possible.

When you don't know where to start, it's always useful to think about the problem and ask what inputs the code must take and what it will return. That's enough to give you the shape of a function. Then break that function down into smaller problems and repeat.

The inputs to our game are the word the player will guess and a player that can make guesses, so those will be your initial arguments. The return value will be the score the player received.

```
(defn game [word player] ...)
```

This game (and most games) centers around a repeated series of actions where the player makes a choice, the game state is updated, and the player makes another choice. This game loop gives us the overall framework for the game.

The game loop also serves as a guide for what code you need to write next. As you break the loop into steps, these help you identify both the functions that are the sub-problems and the data structures passed between the functions. Repeat this process for each function until you hit the bottom, where you'll find functions that are self-contained.

Within each iteration, the game needs to ask the player for the next guess and update the progress made on the word. If the word has been guessed, the game is complete and the game should exit with the number of guesses that were made.

In almost every use of a loop, you'll see a check for termination. If the game is complete, the loop should terminate with the final score. Otherwise, a recur should take the game back to the top of the loop, ready for the next iteration.

```
(defn game
  [word player]
  (loop [progress (new-progress word), guesses 1]
    (let [guess (next-guess player progress)
          progress' (update-progress progress word guess)]
      (if (complete? progress' word)
        guesses
        (recur progress' (inc guesses))))))
```

This code maps very closely to the textual description of the game, with a lot of missing details. There are two pieces of state carried by the loop across iterations: the progress in guessing the word and the score.

The game function invokes next-guess to obtain the next guess from a player, and we'll consider this later in the chapter when you implement the players.

The other functions we used but didn't define all relate to creating, updating, or checking the progress of the game: new-progress, update-progress, and complete?. We haven't yet defined the data structure of the word progress, but it's clearly a central part of the implementation.

At this point, it's good to create empty functions for all of the functions we invented while writing the game loop. These empty functions serve as a road map of work you still need to complete. They also allow you to successfully start loading and running the code in the REPL.

```
(defn next-guess [player progress])
(defn new-progress [])
(defn update-progress [progress word guess])
(defn complete? [progress])
```

You can't write any of the functions to create, update, or check the game progress without knowing what the progress data structure looks like, so that's where you should focus next.

Representing Progress

The word the player is guessing is a string, made up of characters. Two of the most important kinds of data structures we deal with in Clojure are maps (keyed by an index) and sequences (which rely on sequential traversal). We have a number of choices for representing the progress in the game, but choosing between an indexed or sequential view is the critical decision.

So let's think, at least at a high level, about the operations that use this data structure in the code. The update-progress function seems like the one we care about the most. Given the word and the guessed letter, you need to check whether each letter in the word matches the guess, and if so, update the progress, which keeps track of all letters guessed so far in the word.

Looking back at that description of the update operation, you need to check whether "each letter in the word" has some property. This indicates that a sequential traversal based on the original word would be a good match (considering all values). You then need to update the progress data structure in the corresponding location if there is a match.

If the progress is an indexed data structure, you need to traverse the original word and keep track of the index as you do so, to know which index to update in the progress. The Clojure sequence library includes some functions, keep-indexed and map-indexed, that help with this kind of thing.

If you instead treat the progress as a sequential data structure and update it at the same time that you traverse the original word, you can avoid tracking or using the indexes at all. When the progress is a sequential data structure where each element might need to be updated, you should strongly consider map, which transforms every element. Additionally, map is one of the only sequence functions that can traverse multiple sequences at the same time.

So let's proceed on the assumption that a sequential structure with each element corresponding to a letter in the original word is the working model. You could use some kind of flag to indicate which letters have been guessed: (false false true true false). Or you could use the actual letters and a known "blank" character: (_ _ \l \l _). (Recall that literal characters are represented with a leading \ in Clojure.) The latter representation gives you a built-in human readable representation of our progress, so it might be slightly more useful, but in truth either would work.

We've spent enough time thinking about our data structure at this point. While that took a while, it was time well spent because you can proceed with your functions with a clear sense of the needs and constraints of the data.

Start with new-progress. Given a word (a string), you need a sequence of blank characters of the same length. Here you can reach into the sequence function bag of tricks and pull out repeat, which creates a sequence of the same element of a specific length, here the count of the word:

hangman/src/hangman/core.clj
```clojure
(defn new-progress [word]
  (repeat (count word) \_))
```

Now for the update. We already established that you want to map over both the word (a string, automatically treated as a sequence of characters) and the progress (a sequence of characters, either the actual character or a blank). The map function will take two inputs—a letter from the word and the corresponding letter from the progress. It needs to output the new letter in the updated progress. You also have available from the outer function the letter that was the guess.

Putting all that together is actually pretty easy—you just need to check whether the guessed letter matches the word character, and if so, include it in the updated progress. If not, then use the original progress character to remember the progress so far.

hangman/src/hangman/core.clj
```
(defn update-progress [progress word guess]
  (map #(if (= %1 guess) guess %2) word progress))
```

Finally, checking whether the player is "done" is just a check of whether the characters in the original word match the progress. Because the word is a string, explicitly convert it to a sequence for comparison purposes.

hangman/src/hangman/core.clj
```
(defn complete? [progress word]
  (= progress (seq word)))
```

And that's the core of our game loop. Now you need a player.

Implementing Players

Your interaction with the player so far has been represented by a single function, next-guess. It's time to fill out that idea a bit more. There are many potential ways to implement either a human or computer player. Any time you determine a function is open for extension, you should strongly consider using a multimethod or protocol to make that possible.

In this case, you only have a single function, so either choice is viable. There might be a need for players to keep state (remembering what they've guessed), so protocols are a bit easier to use, by encapsulating that state in a record which extends the protocol.

So replace that function with a protocol:

hangman/src/hangman/core.clj
```
(defprotocol Player
  (next-guess [player progress]))
```

Given this protocol, consider a first player that just makes random guesses without regard to previous guesses.

To start with the random player, you'll need a pool of letters to draw from. All characters have an integer mapping, and you can leverage this, along with standard core functions like range, to build a vector of all legal letters:

hangman/src/hangman/core.clj
```
(defonce letters (mapv char (range (int \a) (inc (int \z)))))
```

You can then build a function that generates a random letter by using 'rand-nth':

hangman/src/hangman/core.clj
```
(defn rand-letter []
  (rand-nth letters))
```

And finally, you have everything you need to build your first player. Because you don't need any state for a random player, you can just use reify to create an anonymous implementation of the random player:

hangman/src/hangman/core.clj
```
(def random-player
  (reify Player
    (next-guess [_ progress] (rand-letter))))
```

Now that you have a player, you can actually run the game and see how the random player does.

```
(game random-player "hello")
-> 92
```

Not so good. Given only 26 letters in the alphabet, any score over 26 is pretty bad. If you can give your player some memory, it could at least avoid guessing the same (bad) letters over and over again.

In fact, keeping in mind that the maximum number of guesses you should need to make is 26, it's reasonable to create a player that is simply given the choices to make in order.

Memory requires state, so you'll need to use one of the stateful Clojure constructs to store that memory. Since each player will only be used in a single thread and does not require state coordination or asynchronous updating, an atom is sufficient.

The choices-player will use an atom containing the sequence of choices to make. The next-guess implementation then simply takes the first choice and updates the atom to retain the rest of the choices for the next call.

The player could be implemented by closing over the atom and using reify as you did with random-player, but instead use a record to hold the state and extend it to the protocol:

```
hangman/src/hangman/core.clj
(defrecord ChoicesPlayer [choices]
  Player
  (next-guess [_ progress]
    (let [guess (first @choices)]
      (swap! choices rest)
      guess)))

(defn choices-player [choices]
  (->ChoicesPlayer (atom choices)))
```

You can then create a shuffled-player that guesses each letter in a random order by just shuffling the letters vector:

```
hangman/src/hangman/core.clj
(defn shuffled-player []
  (choices-player (shuffle letters)))
```

Run a few games and try it:

```
(game (shuffled-player) "hello")
-> 24

(game (shuffled-player) "hello")
-> 19

(game (shuffled-player) "hello")
-> 21
```

That's certainly better than 92, but it still doesn't seem very good. You could instead implement a player that picks the letters in alphabetical order instead of shuffled order by just not shuffling:

```
hangman/src/hangman/core.clj
(defn alpha-player []
  (choices-player letters))
```

You only need to run this test once as there's no random element:

```
(game (alpha-player) "hello")
-> 15
```

That's a better score for this word, but it would be worse for others—you can actually predict the score, as it will be the index of the latest letter in the alphabet (here "o" which is 15th).

Over a wide range of words, you would expect the frequency of letters in English words[1] to be a good ordering. You can just hard-code that into a freq-player:

---

1. https://en.wikipedia.org/wiki/Letter_frequency#Relative_frequencies_of_letters_in_the_English_language

hangman/src/hangman/core.clj
```
(defn freq-player []
  (choices-player (seq "etaoinshrdlcumwfgypbvkjxqz")))
```

Give it a try:

```
(game (freq-player) "hello")
-> 11
```

Just letting the computer play isn't very fun though. Next let's add an interactive player so you can play, too.

Interactive Play

As you consider interactive play, you'll need to make a few additions to the program. Right now the game only returns the final score, but an interactive game should report progress as the game progresses. Also, right now you're choosing the word to guess, but we really need to let the program choose a random word so it's a mystery to a human player.

Let's tackle the random word first. Included in the hangman project is a file words.txt, which contains about 4000 words that you can use as a word bank. First, read those words into a data structure.

hangman/src/hangman/core.clj
```
(defn valid-letter? [c]
  (<= (int \a) (int c) (int \z)))

(defonce available-words
  (with-open [r (jio/reader "words.txt")]
    (->> (line-seq r)
         (filter #(every? valid-letter? %))
         vec)))
```

The clojure.java.io namespace (aliased here to jio) has a number of helpful functions for interacting with the Java I/O library. Java has several I/O abstractions for different purposes. For example, *streams* represent binary streams of data and *readers* and *writers* are used for reading and writing character-based data. The jio/reader function will coerce many input sources into a Java reader.

Once you have the reader, you can break it into lines with line-seq, filter to keep only those that contain valid letters (omitting those with punctuation), and finally leave the final result in a vector. This is a typical sequence processing pipeline, tied together with the ->> thread-last operator.

Note that defonce is used here. defonce is a special wrapper for def that will prevent re-execution if this namespace is reloaded. This change avoids re-reading the word file, which is expensive. This mostly helps during development.

Now that you have a vector of valid words, you can easily pick a random one with rand-nth:

hangman/src/hangman/core.clj
```
(defn rand-word []
  (rand-nth available-words))
```

Try it out:

```
(repeatedly 5 rand-word)
-> ("sophisticated" "humor" "proclaim" "threshold" "obtain")
```

Next, let's revisit our game function and add some printing to reveal the game progress. It's common to add optional keyword arguments to the end of an invocation, so define a new :verbose option. Clojure supports destructuring the varargs sequential arguments as if they were a map for this purpose. It's also good practice to declare defaults using the :or destructuring syntax.

Within the game loop, add a call to report progress when the verbose flag is set:

hangman/src/hangman/core.clj
```
(defn game
  [word player & {:keys [verbose] :or {verbose false}}]
  (when verbose
    (println "You are guessing a word with" (count word) "letters"))
  (loop [progress (new-progress word), guesses 1]
    (let [guess (next-guess player progress)
          progress' (update-progress progress word guess)]
      (when verbose (report progress guess progress'))
      (if (complete? progress' word)
        guesses
        (recur progress' (inc guesses))))))
```

Calling out to a function here keeps the reporting out of the main loop and makes the core loop code easier to read. The progress reporting looks like this:

hangman/src/hangman/core.clj
```
(defn report [begin-progress guess end-progress]
  (println)
  (println "You guessed:" guess)
  (if (= begin-progress end-progress)
    (if (some #{guess} end-progress)
      (println "Sorry, you already guessed:" guess)
      (println "Sorry, the word does not contain:" guess))
    (println "The letter" guess "is in the word!"))
  (println "Progress so far:" (apply str end-progress)))
```

And finally, you need to create the interactive player, which will accept guesses interactively from the player:

```
hangman/src/hangman/core.clj
(def interactive-player
  (reify Player
    (next-guess [_ progress] (take-guess))))
```

Like the random-player, no state is being used here, so you can just define a single interactive-player to use that does nothing more than defer to a function take-guess that interacts with the console.

Clojure provides access to the stdin input stream via the *in* dynamic variable, which will be an instance of java.io.Reader. Here's the full code:

```
hangman/src/hangman/core.clj
(defn take-guess []
  (println)
  (print "Enter a letter: ")
  (flush)
  (let [input (.readLine *in*)
        line (str/trim input)]
    (cond
      (str/blank? line) (recur)
      (valid-letter? (first line)) (first line)
      :else (do
              (println "That is not a valid letter!")
              (recur)))))
```

Start by printing the instructions to the user using print, which will not print a newline character at the end but will instead wait for the user's response. Next, call flush to force the buffered output stream to print so the user will see it. Then you're ready to read the user's input from the input stream—just call readLine via Java interop.

Once the user hits enter, you can consider their response. If the line is blank, you can recur back to the top of the function (remember that functions serve as implicit loop targets) to try again. If the response starts with a valid letter, return that. And if the letter is invalid, notify the user and try again. Now you can put all this together and play a game yourself.

```
(game (rand-word) interactive-player :verbose true)

You are guessing a word with 4 letters

Enter a letter: a
The player guessed: a
The letter a is in the word!
Progress so far: _a__

Enter a letter: e
The player guessed: e
The letter e is in the word!
Progress so far: ea__
```

```
Enter a letter: c
The player guessed: c
Sorry, the word does not contain: c
Progress so far: ea__

Enter a letter: s
The player guessed: s
The letter s is in the word!
Progress so far: eas_

Enter a letter: t
The player guessed: t
Sorry, the word does not contain: t
Progress so far: eas_

Enter a letter: y
The player guessed: y
The letter y is in the word!
Progress so far: easy
-> 6
```

Seems like the interactive player works. Next let's consider how we can use specs to document and test the program.

Documenting and Testing Your Game

You have a working game at this point, but you also need to consider the poor developer who's going to pick this up six months from now (particularly if it's you). You worked hard to pick a good data structure and implement your functions, but you need to communicate those data structures for future use.

If you write some specs, you can describe the key data structures, annotate the functions, and even generate some automated tests that check whether everything works (especially when you start making changes at some future date).

When you started working on the implementation earlier, we quickly honed in on the progress data structure and the trio of internal functions (new-progress, update-progress, and complete?) that dealt with creating, updating, and checking that data structure. Because that data structure is critical to the internals of the game, it's also a good place to start writing specs.

The signature for new-progress takes a word and returns the initial progress value. Our spec defines the structure of the arguments and return value of that function.

```
(s/fdef hangman.core/new-progress
  :args (s/cat :word ::word)
  :ret ::progress)
```

You haven't defined a ::word or ::progress spec yet, but that's ok—these show us what you need to do next.

Words are made up of letters, and you've already made some definitions in our code for letters that you can use. This is a common case when writing specs—often the implementation and the specs use the same predicates and talk in the same "language", which is why specs feel so expressive.

hangman/src/hangman/specs.clj
```
(s/def ::letter (set letters))
```

A ::letter spec is the set of valid letters, which you already defined in the random player. We also could have used the predicate valid-letter?; however, we want to have our specs act as generators as well. The valid-letter? predicate doesn't have an automatically created generator, whereas these are provided for sets.

Now you can create a spec for a word, which is just a string that consists of at least one valid letter:

```
(s/def ::word
  (s/and string?
         #(pos? (count %))
         #(every? valid-letter? (seq %))))
```

Clojure spec will attempt to create an automatic generator from this spec, but it uses a wide range of characters, certainly more than our narrow ::letter spec will allow. The automatic generator will produce strings of this broader character set, then filter to just strings of the allowed characters, which requires much more work than seems necessary (and it may not work at all). Instead, you should supply your own generator, tailored to our character set.

The s/with-gen macro wraps a spec and attaches a custom generator. In this case, we want to generate a collection of one or more valid letters, then create a string from those letters. In clojure.spec.gen.alpha, the fmap function takes a source generator and applies an arbitrary function to each sample, defining a new generator:

hangman/src/hangman/specs.clj
```
(s/def ::word
  (s/with-gen
    (s/and string?
           #(pos? (count %))
           #(every? valid-letter? (seq %)))
    #(gen/fmap
       (fn [letters] (apply str letters))
       (s/gen (s/coll-of ::letter :min-count 1)))))
```

You can test it out directly at the REPL:

```
(gen/sample (s/gen ::word))
-> ("hilridqg"
    "ipllomgodmzhh"
    "xbsllzg"
    "etdjwdtvquuswpox"
    "adrgrhntbuzewbdvfa"
        ... )
```

Those look appropriately word-like for our purposes. You now have a spec
for words, so let's think about the ::progress spec. We decided that progress
would be represented by a sequence of either letters or _ to indicate an
unguessed character. Since we added an additional character, we'll need a
new spec ::progress-letter that expands ::letter to include _. The ::progress spec is
then a collection of at least one of that expanded letter set:

hangman/src/hangman/specs.clj
```
(s/def ::progress-letter
  (conj (set letters) \_))

(s/def ::progress
  (s/coll-of ::progress-letter :min-count 1))
```

That's enough specs to start testing new-progress. You can use stest/check for that
and summarize what happened with summarize-results:

```
(stest/summarize-results (stest/check 'hangman.core/new-progress))
{:sym hangman.core/new-progress}
-> {:total 1, :check-passed 1}
```

You tested one function and it passed. However, you aren't really testing as
much as you could in this function. If you look again at the args (the word)
and the return value (the progress value), there's another constraint—both
values should be the same length. You can encode this in the :fn spec of the
new-progress spec, which takes a map of the conformed :args and :ret spec values.
Constraints that include both the args and the ret value are always recorded
in the :fn spec.

hangman/src/hangman/specs.clj
```
(defn- letters-left
  [progress]
  (->> progress (keep #{\_}) count))

(s/fdef hangman.core/new-progress
  :args (s/cat :word ::word)
  :ret ::progress
  :fn (fn [{:keys [args ret]}]
        (= (count (:word args)) (count ret) (letters-left ret))))
```

First, create a helper function letters-left to compute the number of unguessed
letters in a progress data structure. You can then check that the number of

letters in the input word, the number of letters in the progress, and the number of unguessed letters are all the same. Rerunning the test reveals no unseen problems, but it's good to have the extra constraint for future changes.

Next, you can handle the update-progress function using specs you've already defined for ::progress, ::word, and ::letter. Again, you can add a useful :fn constraint to verify that the number of letters left unguessed is less than or equal to the number unguessed at the beginning.

hangman/src/hangman/specs.clj
```
(s/fdef hangman.core/update-progress
  :args (s/cat :progress ::progress :word ::word :guess ::letter)
  :ret ::progress
  :fn (fn [{:keys [args ret]}]
        (>= (-> args :progress letters-left)
          (-> ret letters-left))))
```

And finally, the spec for complete? is straightforward:

hangman/src/hangman/specs.clj
```
(s/fdef hangman.core/complete?
  :args (s/cat :progress ::progress :word ::word)
  :ret boolean?)
```

Now that you've described the progress functions, you can turn to the main game function itself. The game function takes a word, a player, an optional verbose tag and returns a score.

We've not yet considered how to spec a player, but you can just check the protocol in a predicate. In the ::player spec, we want the generator to work and produce a player, so let's just have it choose a random one of the players you've defined:

hangman/src/hangman/specs.clj
```
(defn player? [p]
  (satisfies? Player p))

(s/def ::player
  (s/with-gen player?
    #(s/gen #{random-player
              shuffled-player
              alpha-player
              freq-player})))
```

While you could spec the verbose flag and score in-line with the game spec, pulling these out as independent specs creates better, more concrete names, which are potentially reusable. For the verbose flag, you want your tests to be quiet, so the generator is hard-coded to always return false.

```
hangman/src/hangman/specs.clj
(s/def ::verbose (s/with-gen boolean? #(s/gen false?)))
(s/def ::score pos-int?)

(s/fdef hangman.core/game
  :args (s/cat :word ::word
               :player ::player
               :opts (s/keys* :opt-un [::verbose]))
  :ret ::score)
```

If you test this out by running check, you'll see that everything looks good. check runs 1000 games with a random player and word. It's also useful to verify all of the function specs you have while running these tests. You can do that by instrumenting all of the specs before running check:

```
(stest/instrument (stest/enumerate-namespace 'hangman.core))
=> [hangman.core/update-progress hangman.core/new-progress
    hangman.core/game hangman.core/complete?]
```

Any time you run stest/instrument, it's good to verify that the return value states all of the instrumented functions you expect to see as a test of reasonability.

If you rerun the check, you still see no issues, but now all of the arg specs are being verified as well, giving you greater confidence in the correctness of the code. You can then do a final check that runs check on all spec'ed functions we defined:

```
(-> 'hangman.core
    stest/enumerate-namespace
        stest/check
        stest/summarize-results)
{:sym hangman.core/update-progress}
{:sym hangman.core/new-progress}
{:sym hangman.core/game}
{:sym hangman.core/complete?}
-> {:total 4, :check-passed 4}
```

You could go further with testing some of the details of the individual players, but this should give you a taste for testing with spec.

Farewell

Congratulations. You have come a long way in a short time. You have learned the many ideas that combine to make Clojure great: Lisp, Java, functional programming, and explicit concurrency. And in this chapter, you saw one (of a great many) possible workflows for developing a full application in Clojure.

We've only scratched the surface of Clojure's great potential, and we hope you'll take the next step and become an active part of the Clojure community.

Bibliography

[Goe06]   Brian Goetz. *Java Concurrency in Practice*. Addison-Wesley, Boston, MA, 2006.

[Hof99]   Douglas R. Hofstadter. *Gödel, Escher, Bach: An Eternal Golden Braid*. Basic Books, New York, NY, 20th Anniv, 1999.

Index

Thank you!

How did you enjoy this book? Please let us know. Take a moment and email us at support@pragprog.com with your feedback. Tell us your story and you could win free ebooks. Please use the subject line "Book Feedback."

Ready for your next great Pragmatic Bookshelf book? Come on over to https://pragprog.com and use the coupon code BUYANOTHER2017 to save 30% on your next ebook.

Void where prohibited, restricted, or otherwise unwelcome. Do not use ebooks near water. If rash persists, see a doctor. Doesn't apply to *The Pragmatic Programmer* ebook because it's older than the Pragmatic Bookshelf itself. Side effects may include increased knowledge and skill, increased marketability, and deep satisfaction. Increase dosage regularly.

And thank you for your continued support,

Andy Hunt, Publisher

More Clojure

For more on Clojure, check out these titles.

Clojure Applied

Think in the Clojure way! Once you're familiar with Clojure, take the next step with extended lessons on the best practices and most critical decisions you'll need to make while developing. Learn how to model your domain with data, transform it with pure functions, manage state, spread your work across cores, and structure apps with components. Discover how to use Clojure in the real world, and unlock the speed and power of this beautiful language on the Java Virtual Machine.

Ben Vandgrift and Alex Miller
(238 pages) ISBN: 9781680500745. $38
https://pragprog.com/book/vmclojeco

Mastering Clojure Macros

Level up your skills by taking advantage of Clojure's powerful macro system. Macros make hard things possible and normal things easy. They can be tricky to use, and this book will help you deftly navigate the terrain. You'll discover how to write straightforward code that avoids duplication and clarifies your intentions. You'll learn how and why to write macros. You'll learn to recognize situations when using a macro would (and wouldn't!) be helpful. And you'll use macros to remove unnecessary code and build new language features.

Colin Jones
(120 pages) ISBN: 9781941222225. $17
https://pragprog.com/book/cjclojure

Long Live the Command Line!

Use tmux and Vim for incredible mouse-free productivity.

tmux 2

Your mouse is slowing you down. The time you spend context switching between your editor and your consoles eats away at your productivity. Take control of your environment with tmux, a terminal multiplexer that you can tailor to your workflow. With this updated second edition for tmux 2.3, you'll customize, script, and leverage tmux's unique abilities to craft a productive terminal environment that lets you keep your fingers on your keyboard's home row.

Brian P. Hogan
(102 pages) ISBN: 9781680502213. $21.95
https://pragprog.com/book/bhtmux2

Modern Vim

Turn Vim into a full-blown development environment using Vim 8's new features and this sequel to the beloved bestseller *Practical Vim*. Integrate your editor with tools for building, testing, linting, indexing, and searching your codebase. Discover the future of Vim with Neovim: a fork of Vim that includes a built-in terminal emulator that will transform your workflow. Whether you choose to switch to Neovim or stick with Vim 8, you'll be a better developer.

Drew Neil
(190 pages) ISBN: 9781680502626. $39.95
https://pragprog.com/book/modvim

Exercises and Teams

From exercises to make you a better programmer to techniques for creating better teams, we've got you covered.

Exercises for Programmers

When you write software, you need to be at the top of your game. Great programmers practice to keep their skills sharp. Get sharp and stay sharp with more than fifty practice exercises rooted in real-world scenarios. If you're a new programmer, these challenges will help you learn what you need to break into the field, and if you're a seasoned pro, you can use these exercises to learn that hot new language for your next gig.

Brian P. Hogan
(118 pages) ISBN: 9781680501223. $24
https://pragprog.com/book/bhwb

Creating Great Teams

People are happiest and most productive if they can choose what they work on and who they work with. Self-selecting teams give people that choice. Build well-designed and efficient teams to get the most out of your organization, with step-by-step instructions on how to set up teams quickly and efficiently. You'll create a process that works for you, whether you need to form teams from scratch, improve the design of existing teams, or are on the verge of a big team re-shuffle.

Sandy Mamoli and David Mole
(102 pages) ISBN: 9781680501285. $17
https://pragprog.com/book/mmteams

The Joy of Mazes and Math

Rediscover the joy and fascinating weirdness of mazes and pure mathematics.

Mazes for Programmers

A book on mazes? Seriously?

Yes!

Not because you spend your day creating mazes, or because you particularly like solving mazes.

But because it's fun. Remember when programming used to be fun? This book takes you back to those days when you were starting to program, and you wanted to make your code do things, draw things, and solve puzzles. It's fun because it lets you explore and grow your code, and reminds you how it feels to just think.

Sometimes it feels like you live your life in a maze of twisty little passages, all alike. Now you can code your way out.

Jamis Buck
(286 pages) ISBN: 9781680500554. $38
https://pragprog.com/book/jbmaze

Good Math

Mathematics is beautiful—and it can be fun and exciting as well as practical. *Good Math* is your guide to some of the most intriguing topics from two thousand years of mathematics: from Egyptian fractions to Turing machines; from the real meaning of numbers to proof trees, group symmetry, and mechanical computation. If you've ever wondered what lay beyond the proofs you struggled to complete in high school geometry, or what limits the capabilities of the computer on your desk, this is the book for you.

Mark C. Chu-Carroll
(282 pages) ISBN: 9781937785338. $34
https://pragprog.com/book/mcmath

The Pragmatic Bookshelf

The Pragmatic Bookshelf features books written by developers for developers. The titles continue the well-known Pragmatic Programmer style and continue to garner awards and rave reviews. As development gets more and more difficult, the Pragmatic Programmers will be there with more titles and products to help you stay on top of your game.

Visit Us Online

This Book's Home Page
https://pragprog.com/book/shcloj3
Source code from this book, errata, and other resources. Come give us feedback, too!

Register for Updates
https://pragprog.com/updates
Be notified when updates and new books become available.

Join the Community
https://pragprog.com/community
Read our weblogs, join our online discussions, participate in our mailing list, interact with our wiki, and benefit from the experience of other Pragmatic Programmers.

New and Noteworthy
https://pragprog.com/news
Check out the latest pragmatic developments, new titles and other offerings.

Save on the eBook

Save on the eBook versions of this title. Owning the paper version of this book entitles you to purchase the electronic versions at a terrific discount.

PDFs are great for carrying around on your laptop—they are hyperlinked, have color, and are fully searchable. Most titles are also available for the iPhone and iPod touch, Amazon Kindle, and other popular e-book readers.

Buy now at *https://pragprog.com/coupon*

Contact Us

Online Orders: *https://pragprog.com/catalog*
Customer Service: *support@pragprog.com*
International Rights: *translations@pragprog.com*
Academic Use: *academic@pragprog.com*
Write for Us: *http://write-for-us.pragprog.com*
Or Call: +1 800-699-7764

Milton Keynes UK
Ingram Content Group UK Ltd.
UKHW010918130924
448262UK00004BA/9